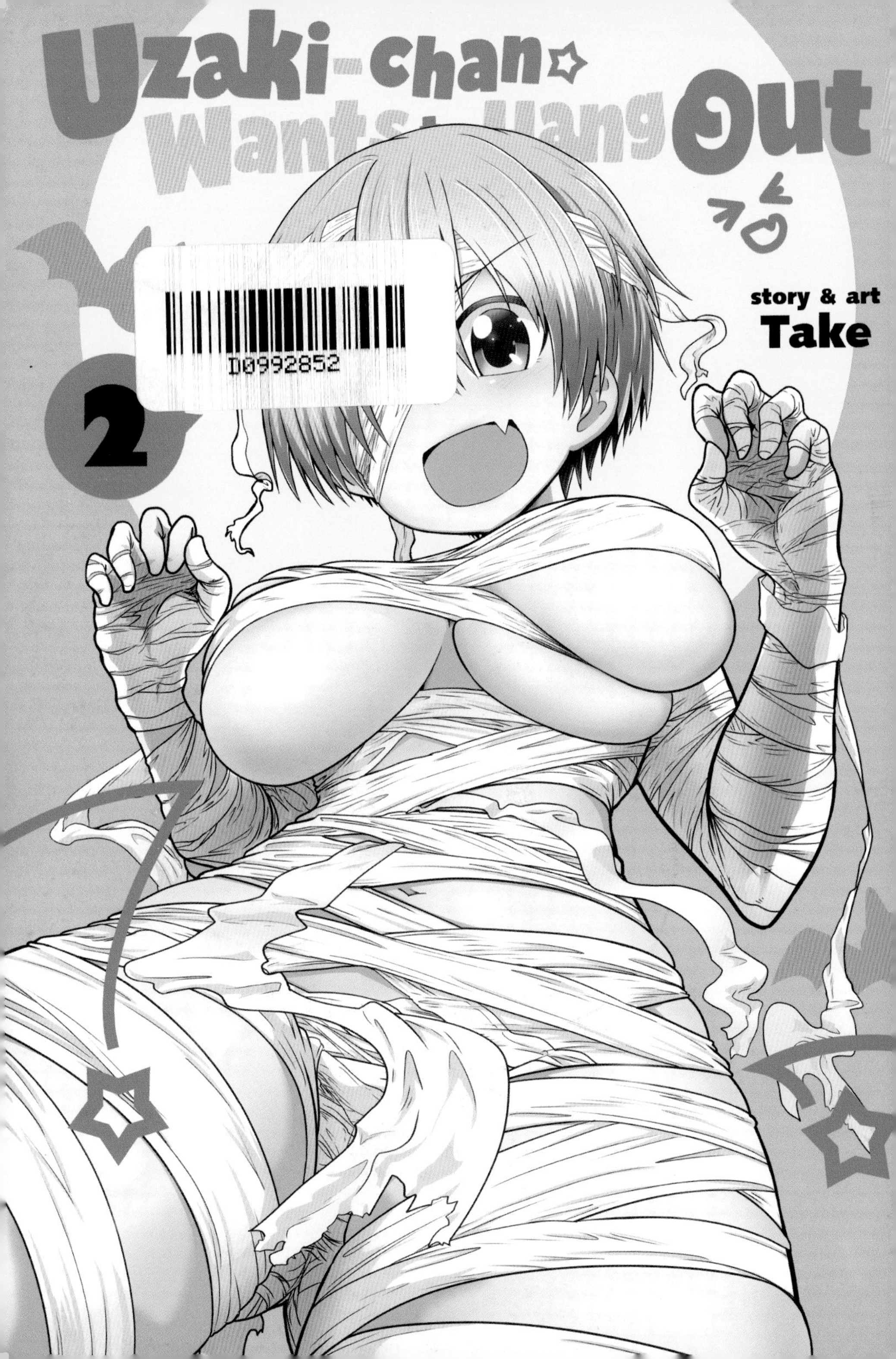
Uzaki-chan
Wants t Hang Out
2
story & art
Take

# CONTENTS

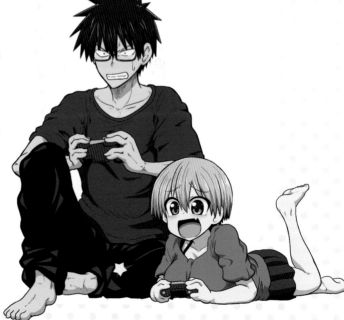

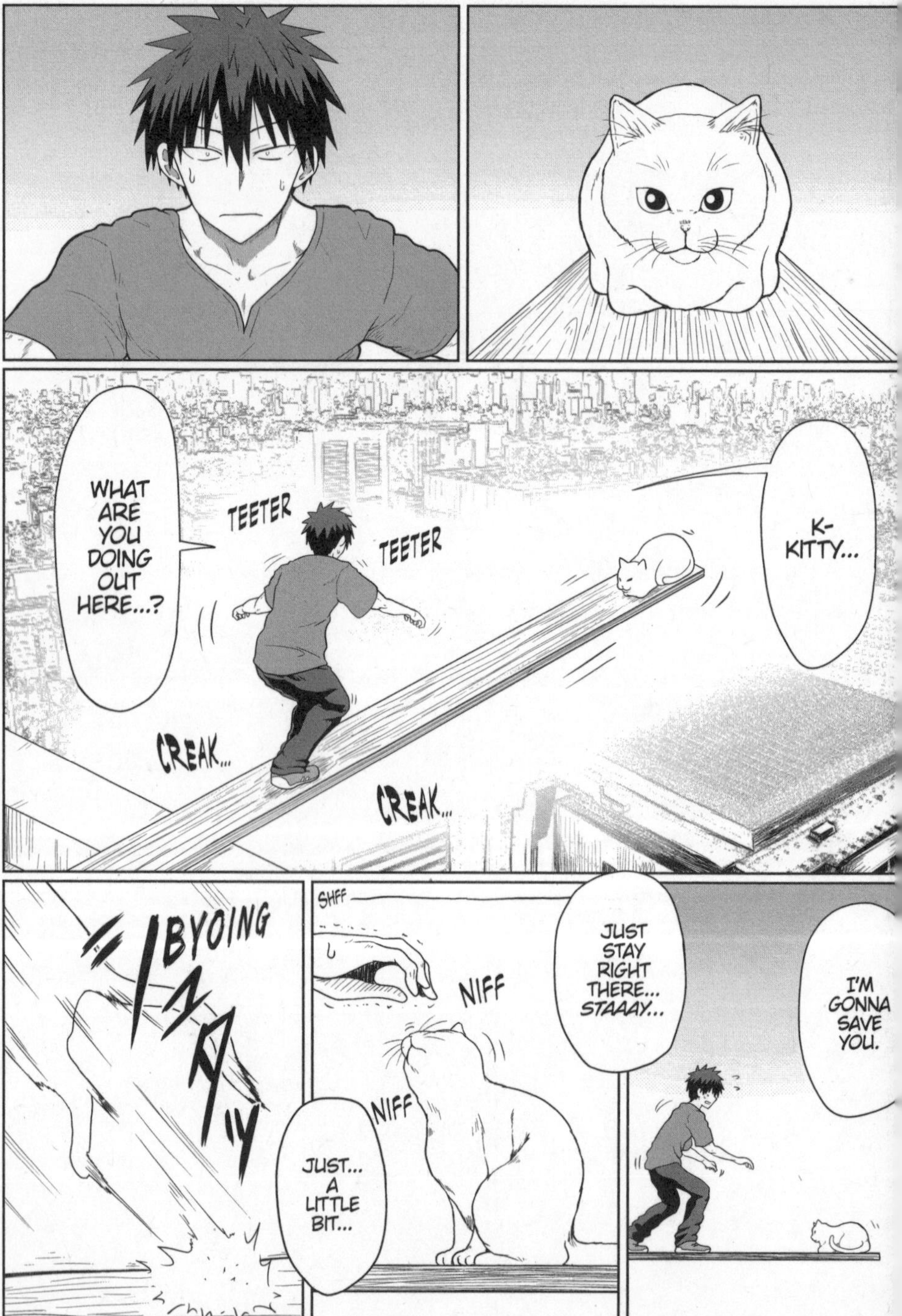
K-KITTY...
TEETER
TEETER
WHAT ARE YOU DOING OUT HERE...?
CREAK...
CREAK...
I'M GONNA SAVE YOU.
JUST STAY RIGHT THERE... STAAAY...
SHFF
NIFF
NIFF
JUST... A LITTLE BIT...
BYOING

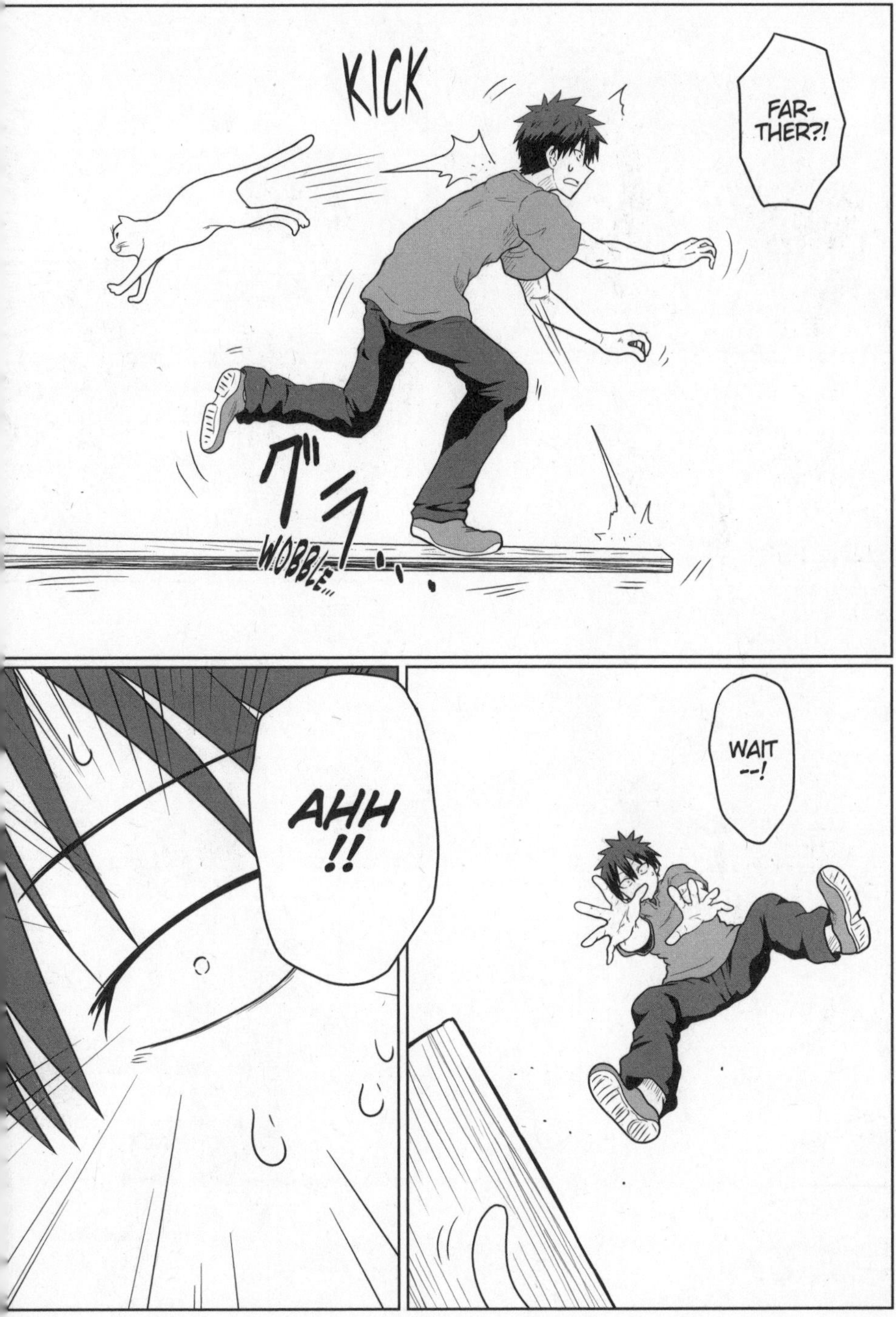
FAR-THER?!
KICK
グラ
WOBBLE...
WAIT --!
AHH !!

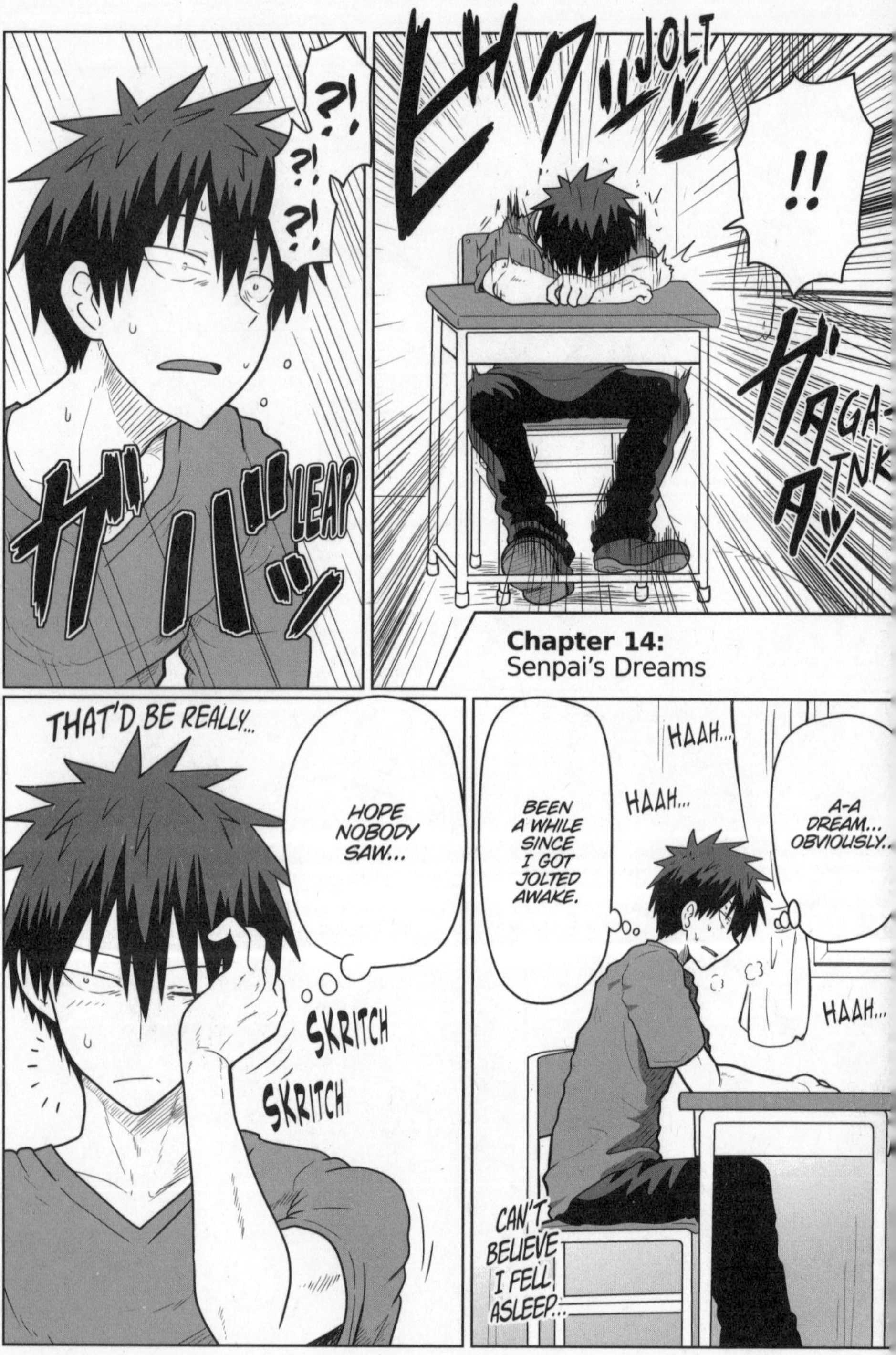
JOLT
!!
GA-TNK
?!
?!
?!
LEAP
Chapter 14:
Senpai's Dreams
HAAH...
HAAH...
HAAH...
A-A DREAM... OBVIOUSLY...
BEEN A WHILE SINCE I GOT JOLTED AWAKE.
CAN'T BELIEVE I FELL ASLEEP...
HOPE NOBODY SAW...
THAT'D BE REALLY...
SKRITCH
SKRITCH

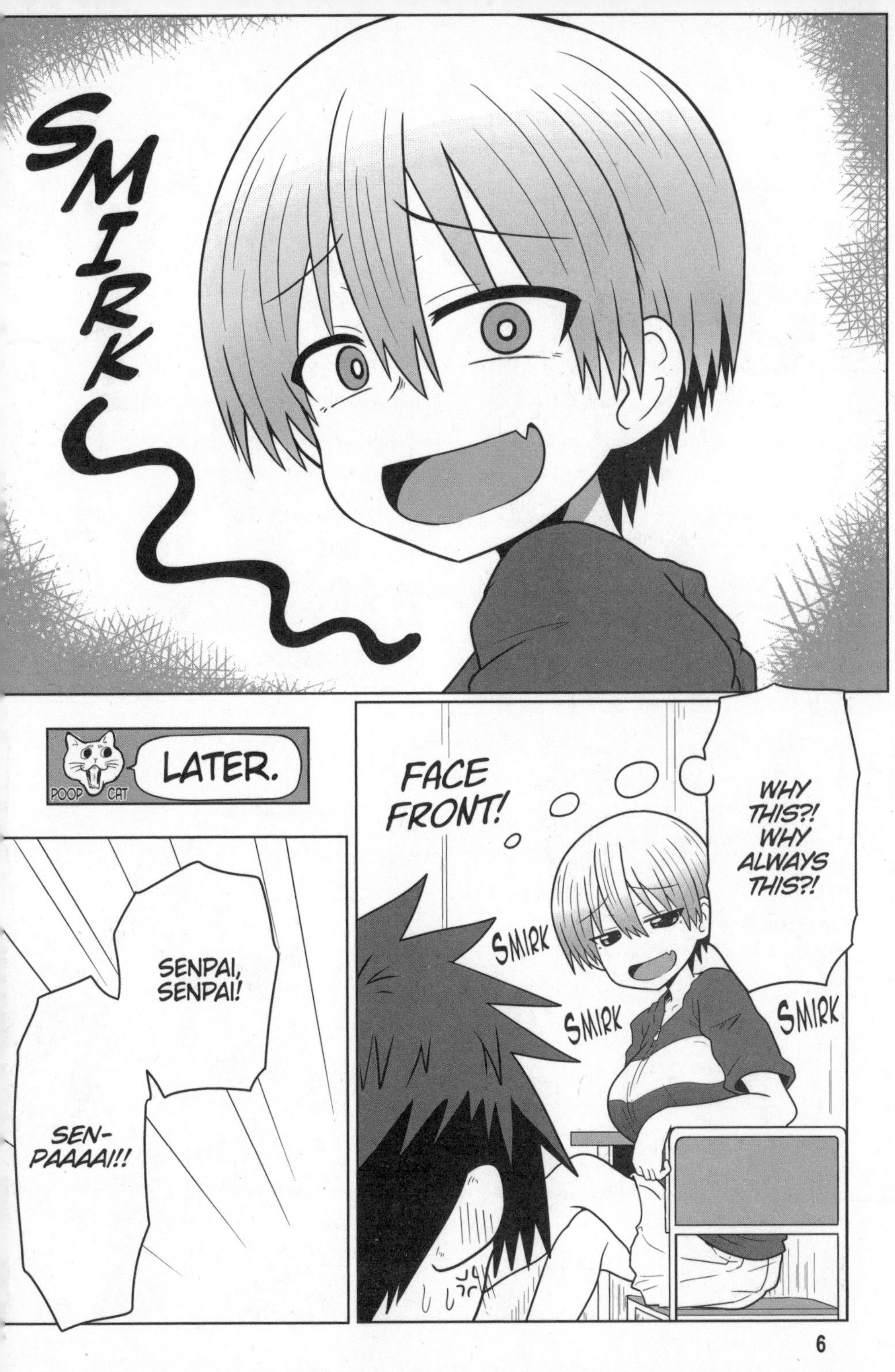
SMIRK
WHY THIS?! WHY ALWAYS THIS?!
FACE FRONT!
SMIRK
SMIRK
SMIRK
POOP CAT
LATER.
SENPAI, SENPAI!
SEN-PAAAAI!!

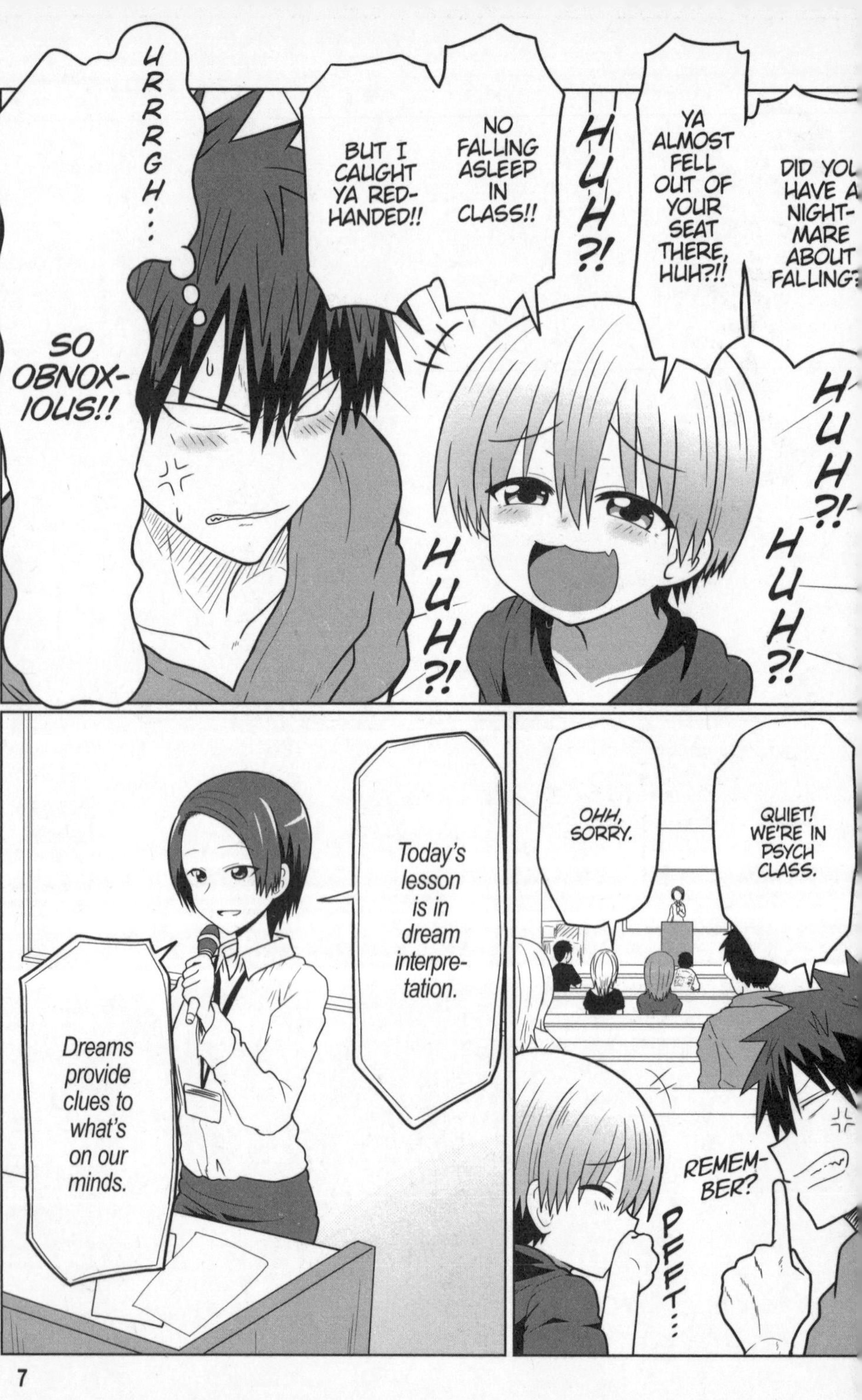
DID YOU HAVE A NIGHT-MARE ABOUT FALLING?!
YA ALMOST FELL OUT OF YOUR SEAT THERE, HUH?!!
HUH?!
NO FALLING ASLEEP IN CLASS!!
BUT I CAUGHT YA RED-HANDED!!
URRRGH...
HUH?! HUH?!
HUH?!
SO OBNOX-IOUS!!
QUIET! WE'RE IN PSYCH CLASS.
OHH, SORRY.
REMEM-BER?
PFFT...
Today's lesson is in dream interpre-tation.
Dreams provide clues to what's on our minds.

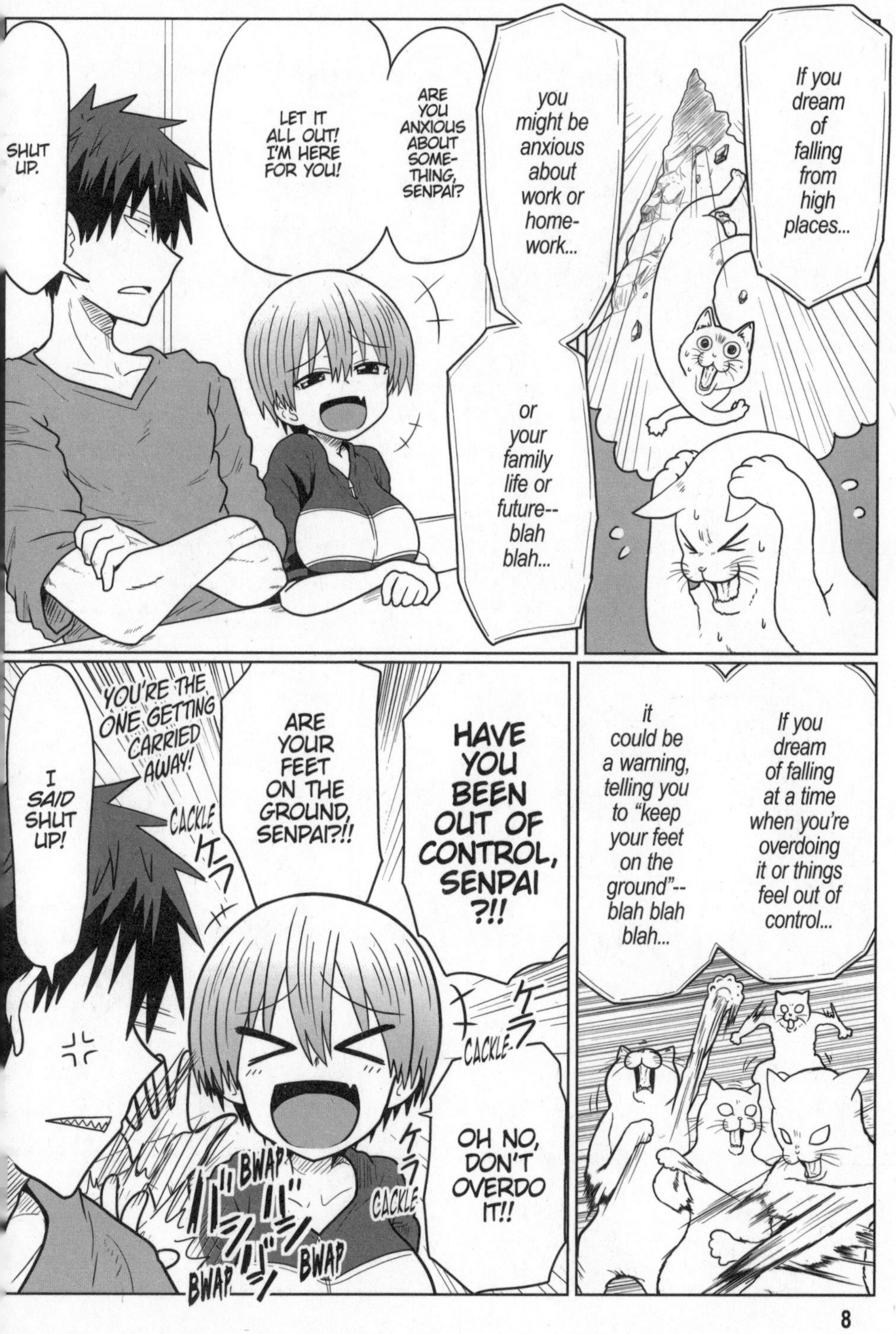
If you dream of falling from high places...
you might be anxious about work or home-work...
or your family life or future--blah blah...
ARE YOU ANXIOUS ABOUT SOME-THING, SENPAI?
LET IT ALL OUT! I'M HERE FOR YOU!
SHUT UP.
If you dream of falling at a time when you're overdoing it or things feel out of control...
it could be a warning, telling you to "keep your feet on the ground"--blah blah blah...
HAVE YOU BEEN OUT OF CONTROL, SENPAI?!!
ARE YOUR FEET ON THE GROUND, SENPAI?!!
YOU'RE THE ONE GETTING CARRIED AWAY!
I SAID SHUT UP!
CACKLE
CACKLE
CACKLE
OH NO, DON'T OVERDO IT!!
BWAP
BWAP
BWAP

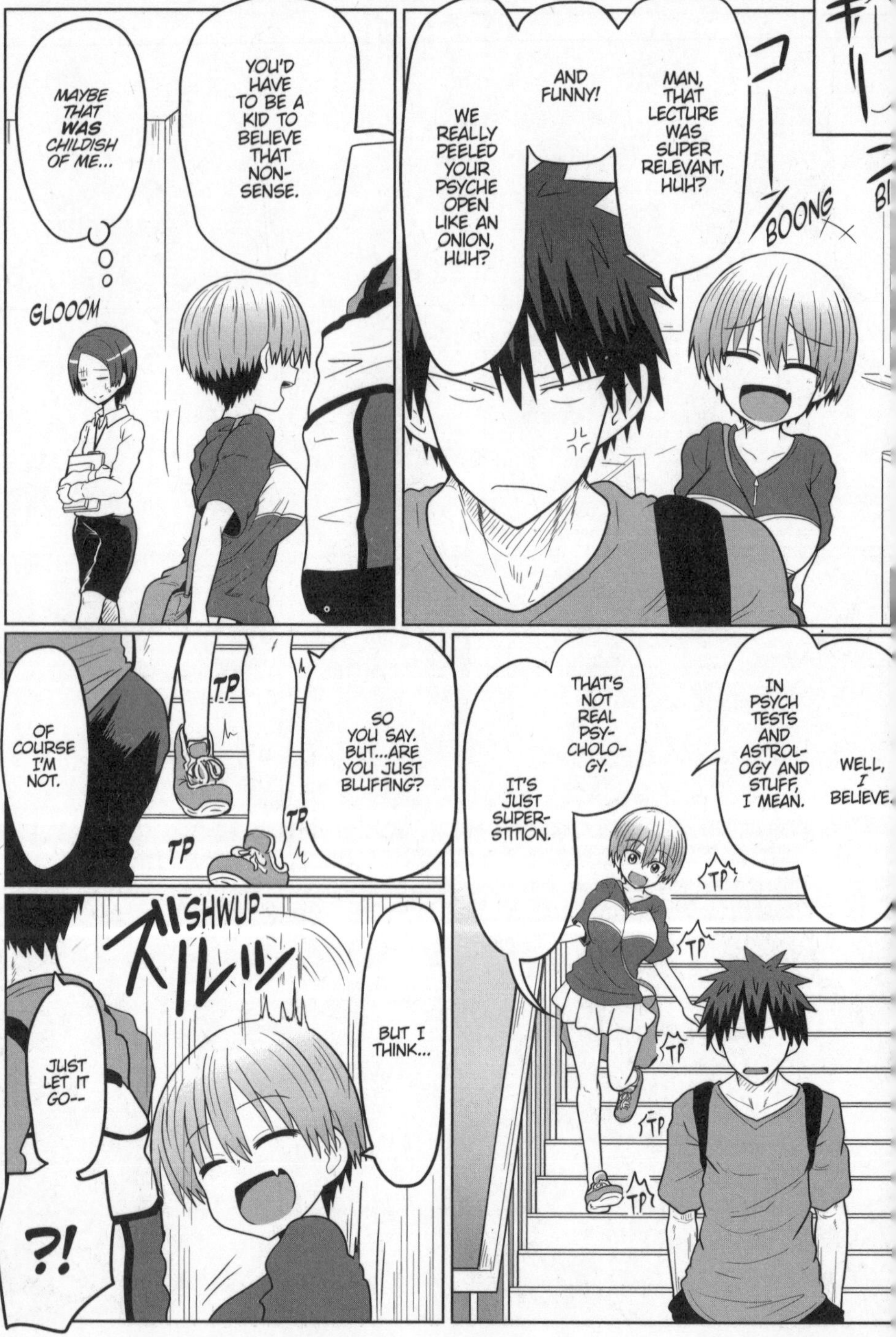
BOONG
MAN, THAT LECTURE WAS SUPER RELEVANT, HUH?
AND FUNNY!
WE REALLY PEELED YOUR PSYCHE OPEN LIKE AN ONION, HUH?
YOU'D HAVE TO BE A KID TO BELIEVE THAT NON-SENSE.
MAYBE THAT WAS CHILDISH OF ME...
GLOOOM
WELL, I BELIEVE.
IN PSYCH TESTS AND ASTROLOGY AND STUFF, I MEAN.
THAT'S NOT REAL PSY-CHOLO-GY.
IT'S JUST SUPER-STITION.
TP
TP
TP
TP
SO YOU SAY. BUT...ARE YOU JUST BLUFFING?
TP
TP
TP
OF COURSE I'M NOT.
SHWUP
BUT I THINK...
JUST LET IT GO--
?!

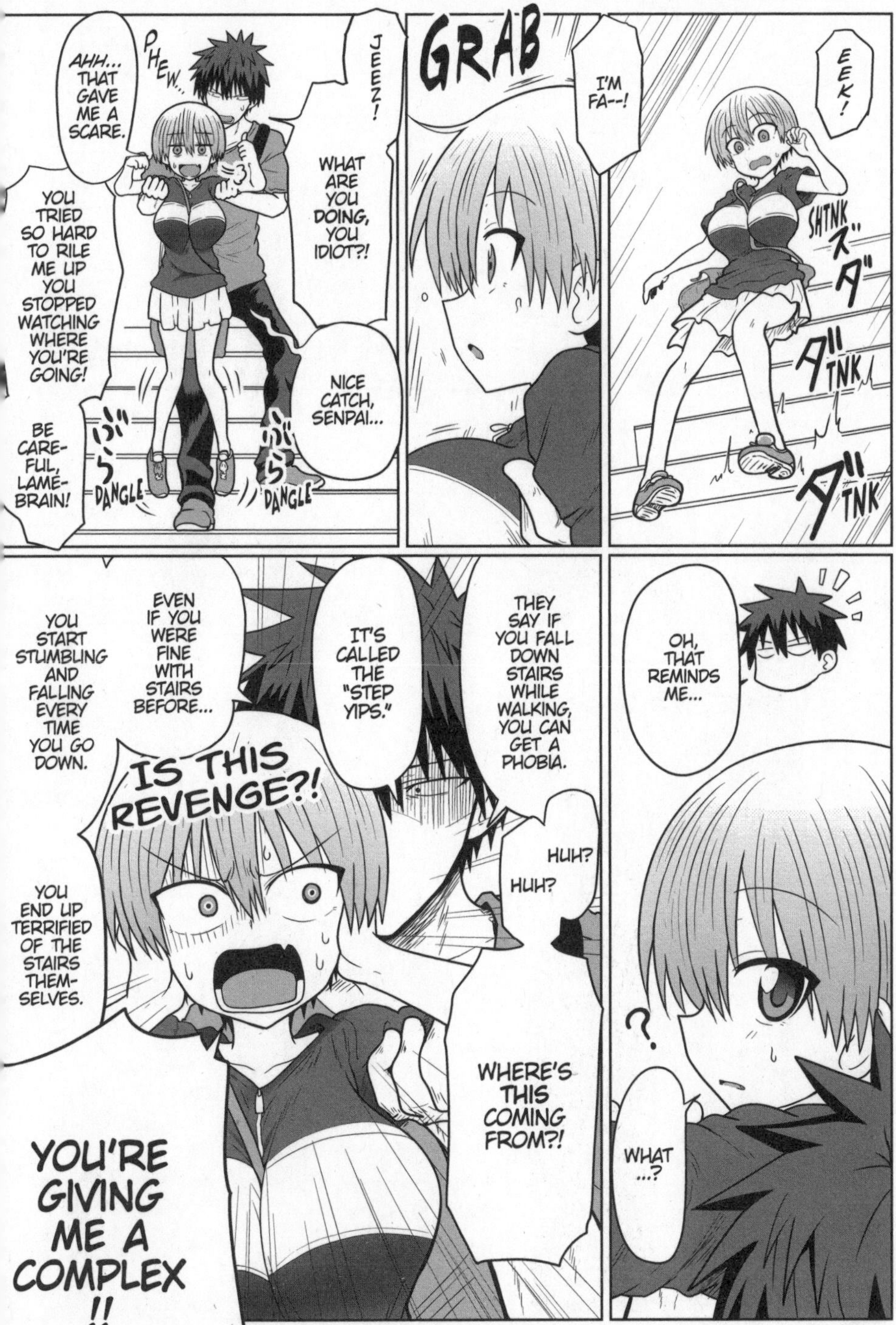
EEK!
SHTNK ズダ
ダ TNK
ダ TNK
GRAB
I'M FA--!
JEEZ!
WHAT ARE YOU DOING, YOU IDIOT?!
PHEW...
AHH... THAT GAVE ME A SCARE.
NICE CATCH, SENPAI...
YOU TRIED SO HARD TO RILE ME UP YOU STOPPED WATCHING WHERE YOU'RE GOING!
ぶら DANGLE
ぶら DANGLE
BE CARE-FUL, LAME-BRAIN!
OH, THAT REMINDS ME...
WHAT ...?
THEY SAY IF YOU FALL DOWN STAIRS WHILE WALKING, YOU CAN GET A PHOBIA.
IT'S CALLED THE "STEP YIPS."
EVEN IF YOU WERE FINE WITH STAIRS BEFORE...
YOU START STUMBLING AND FALLING EVERY TIME YOU GO DOWN.
HUH?
HUH?
IS THIS REVENGE?!
YOU END UP TERRIFIED OF THE STAIRS THEM-SELVES.
WHERE'S THIS COMING FROM?!
YOU'RE GIVING ME A COMPLEX!!

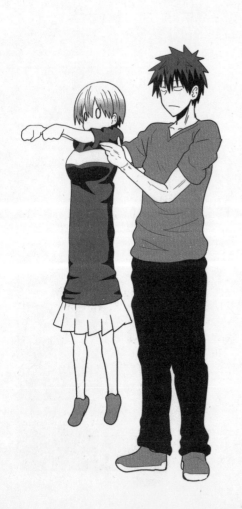

Uzaki-
chan ☆
Wants
to Hang
Out!

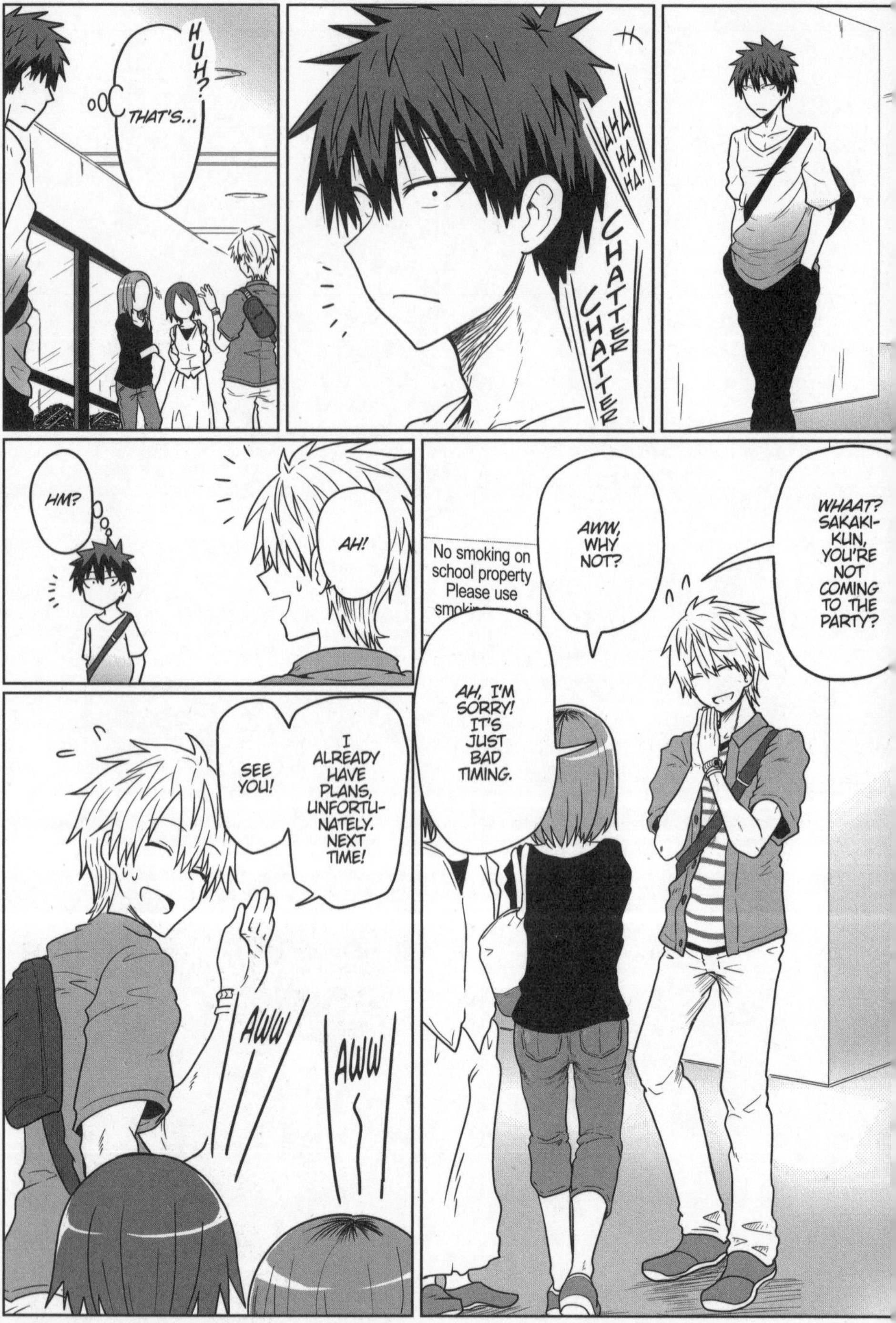
AHAHAHA!
CHATTER CHATTER
HUH?
THAT'S...
WHAAT? SAKAKI-KUN, YOU'RE NOT COMING TO THE PARTY?
AWW, WHY NOT?
No smoking on school property Please use
AH, I'M SORRY! IT'S JUST BAD TIMING.
AH!
HM?
I ALREADY HAVE PLANS, UNFORTUNATELY. NEXT TIME!
SEE YOU!
AWW
AWW

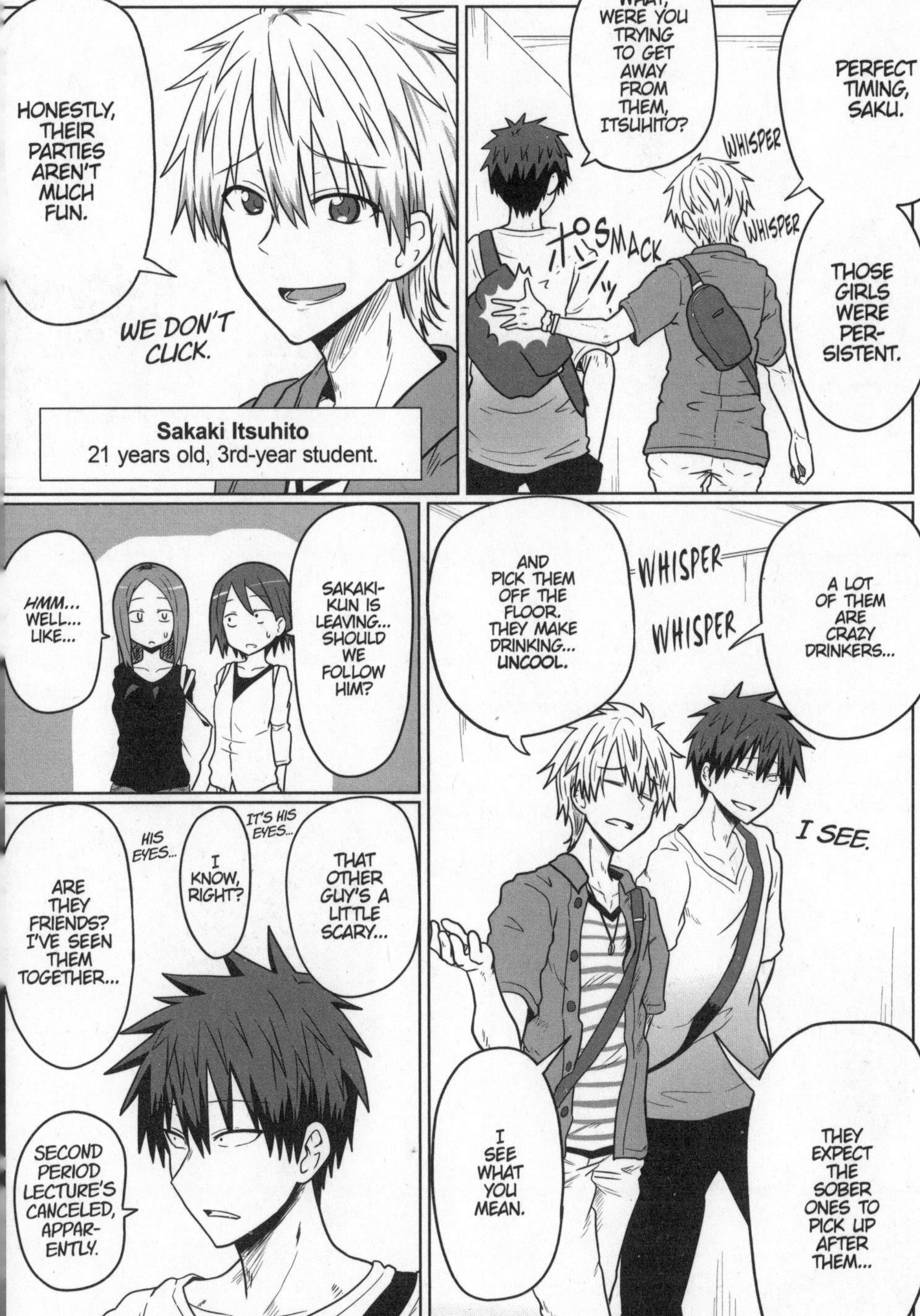
PERFECT TIMING, SAKU.
WHAT, WERE YOU TRYING TO GET AWAY FROM THEM, ITSUHITO?
WHISPER
WHISPER
SMACK
THOSE GIRLS WERE PER-SISTENT.
HONESTLY, THEIR PARTIES AREN'T MUCH FUN.
WE DON'T CLICK.
Sakaki Itsuhito
21 years old, 3rd-year student.
A LOT OF THEM ARE CRAZY DRINKERS...
WHISPER
WHISPER
AND PICK THEM OFF THE FLOOR. THEY MAKE DRINKING... UNCOOL.
I SEE.
THEY EXPECT THE SOBER ONES TO PICK UP AFTER THEM...
I SEE WHAT YOU MEAN.
SAKAKI-KUN IS LEAVING... SHOULD WE FOLLOW HIM?
HMM... WELL... LIKE...
THAT OTHER GUY'S A LITTLE SCARY...
IT'S HIS EYES...
I KNOW, RIGHT?
HIS EYES...
ARE THEY FRIENDS? I'VE SEEN THEM TOGETHER...
SECOND PERIOD LECTURE'S CANCELED, APPAR-ENTLY.

## Chapter 15: The Kouhai and Senpai's Friend

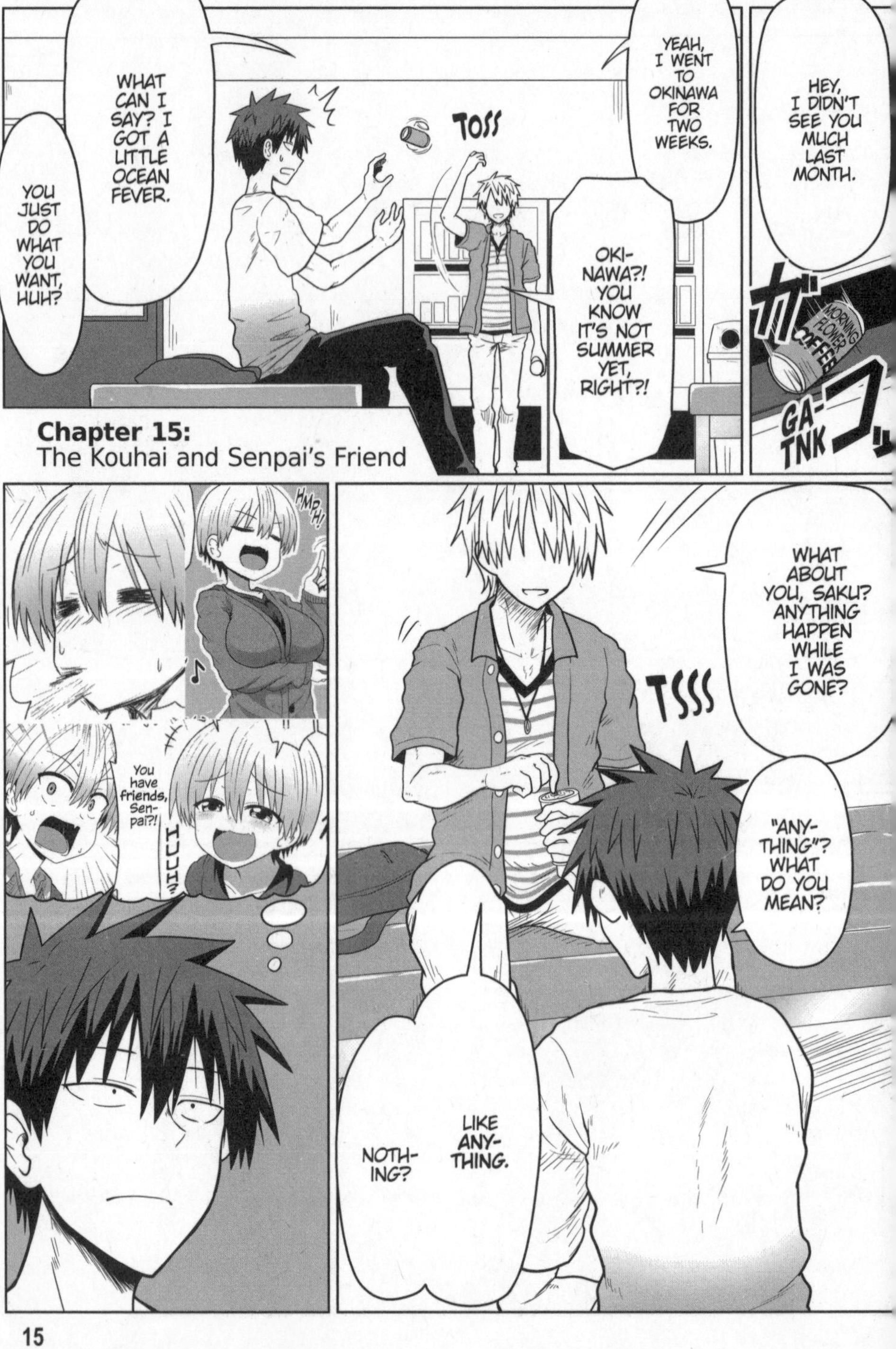

HEY, I DIDN'T SEE YOU MUCH LAST MONTH.
MORNING FLOWER COFFEE
GA-TNK
YEAH, I WENT TO OKINAWA FOR TWO WEEKS.
TOSS
OKI-NAWA?! YOU KNOW IT'S NOT SUMMER YET, RIGHT?!
WHAT CAN I SAY? I GOT A LITTLE OCEAN FEVER.
YOU JUST DO WHAT YOU WANT, HUH?
WHAT ABOUT YOU, SAKU? ANYTHING HAPPEN WHILE I WAS GONE?
TSSS
"ANY-THING"? WHAT DO YOU MEAN?
LIKE ANY-THING.
NOTH-ING?
HMPH!
You have friends, Sen-pai?!
HUUH?

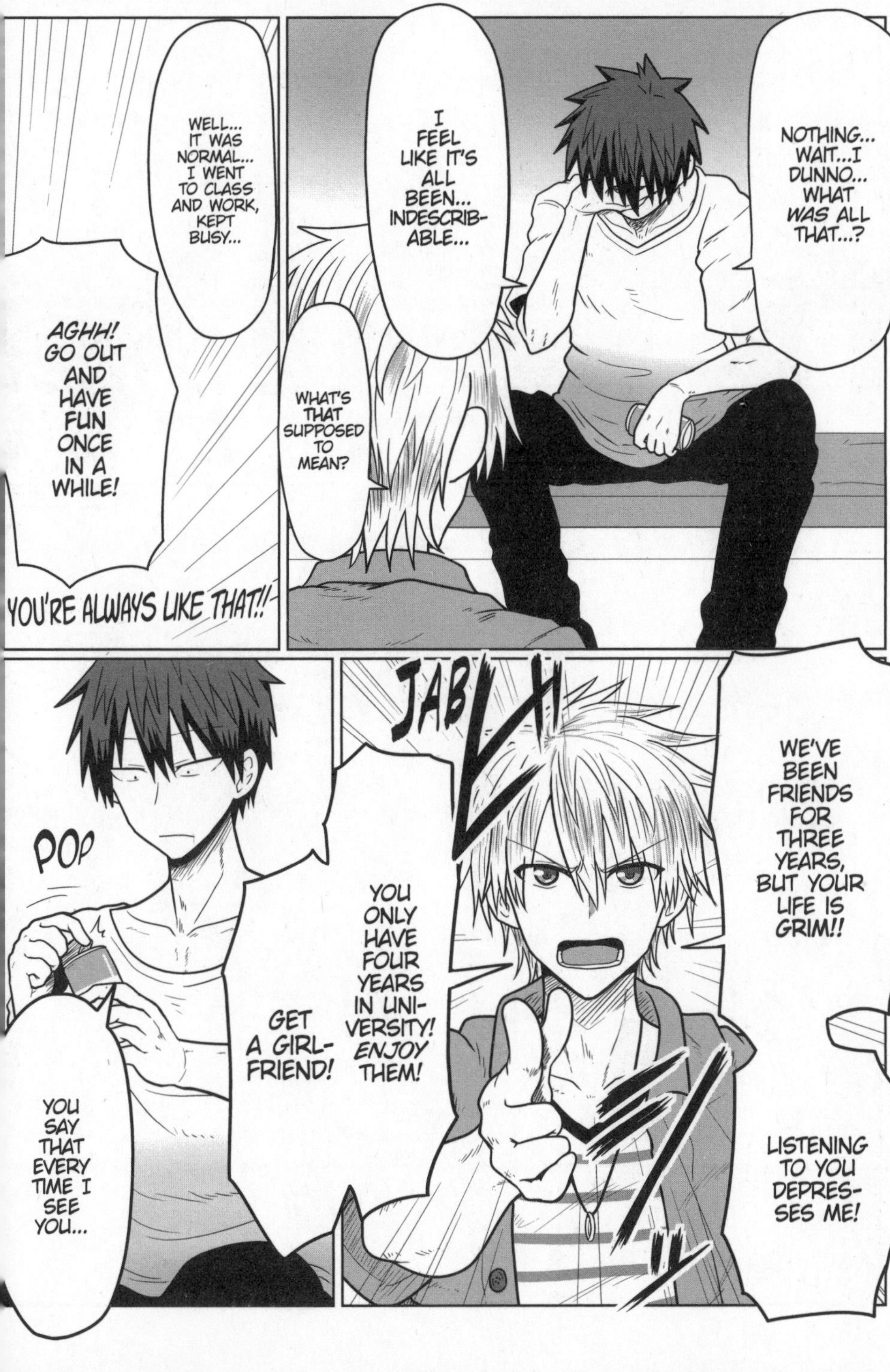
NOTHING... WAIT...I DUNNO... WHAT *WAS* ALL THAT...?
I FEEL LIKE IT'S ALL BEEN... INDESCRIBABLE...
WHAT'S THAT SUPPOSED TO MEAN?
WELL... IT WAS NORMAL... I WENT TO CLASS AND WORK, KEPT BUSY...
*AGHH!* GO OUT AND HAVE FUN ONCE IN A WHILE!
YOU'RE ALWAYS LIKE THAT!!
WE'VE BEEN FRIENDS FOR THREE YEARS, BUT YOUR LIFE IS GRIM!!
JAB
YOU ONLY HAVE FOUR YEARS IN UNIVERSITY! *ENJOY* THEM!
GET A GIRLFRIEND!
LISTENING TO YOU DEPRESSES ME!
POP
YOU SAY THAT EVERY TIME I SEE YOU...

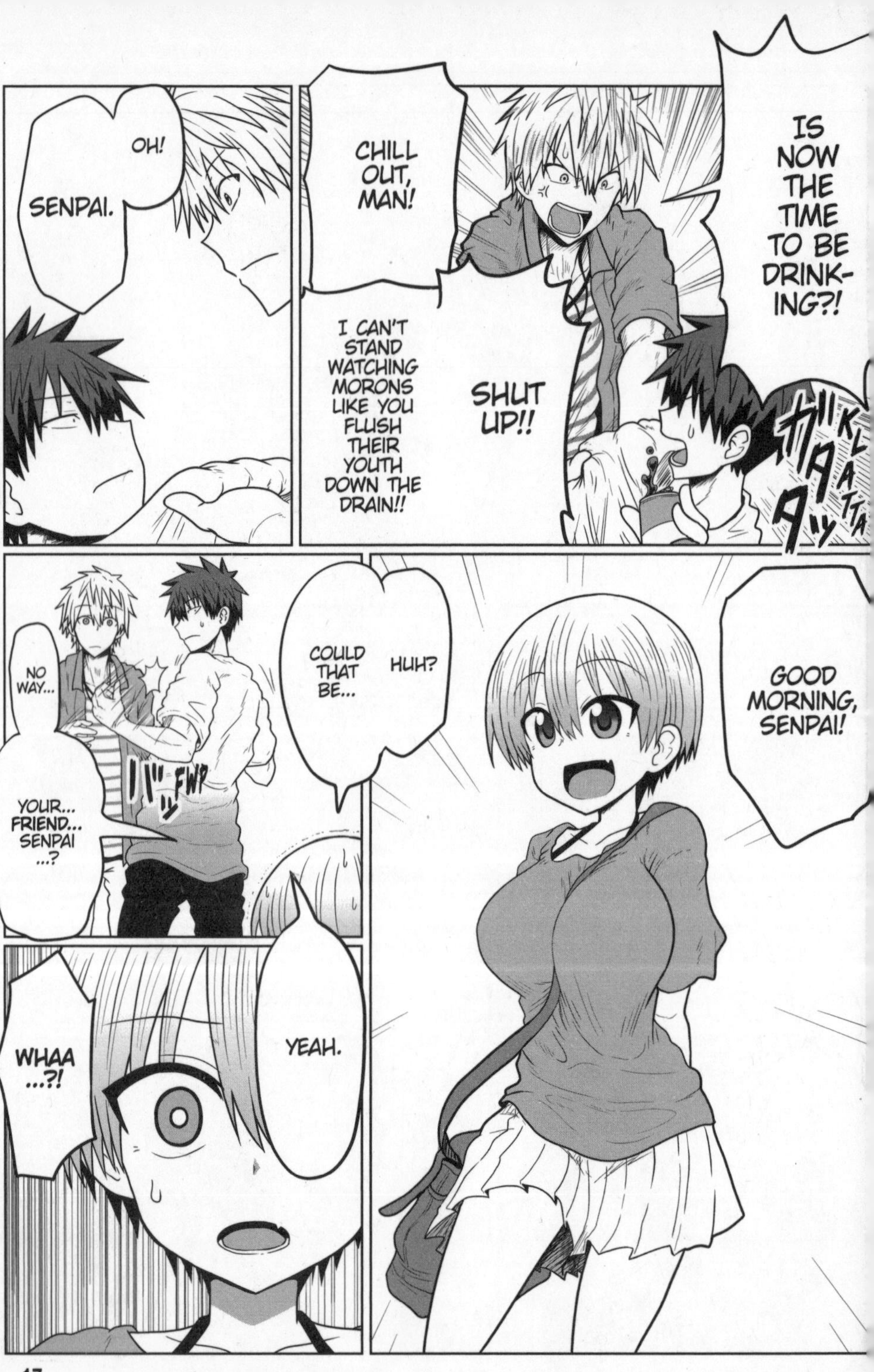
IS NOW THE TIME TO BE DRINKING?!
KLATTA
CHILL OUT, MAN!
SHUT UP!!
I CAN'T STAND WATCHING MORONS LIKE YOU FLUSH THEIR YOUTH DOWN THE DRAIN!!
OH!
SENPAI.
GOOD MORNING, SENPAI!
HUH?
COULD THAT BE...
NO WAY...
FWP
YOUR... FRIEND... SENPAI ...?
YEAH.
WHAA ...?!

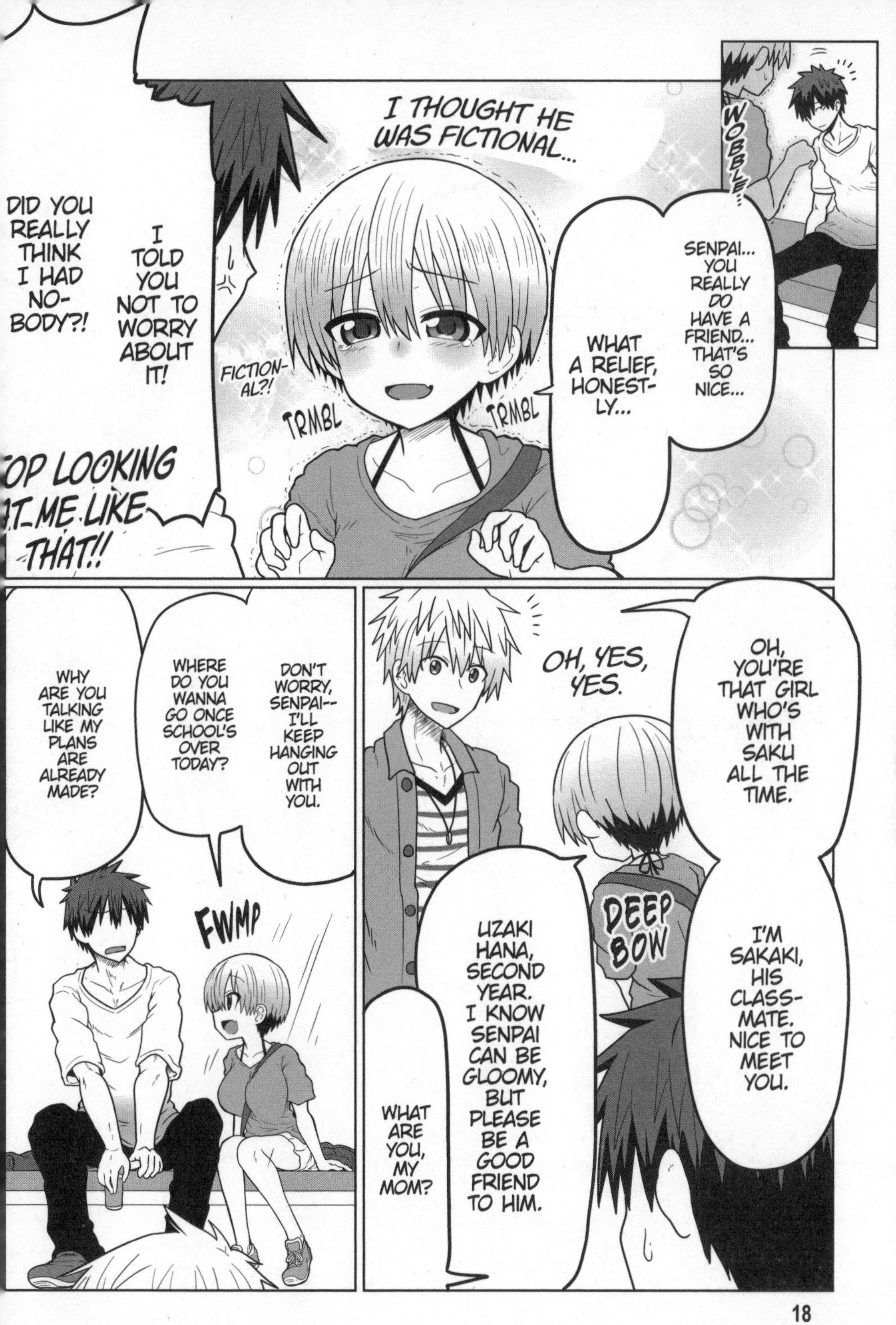
WOBBLE...
I THOUGHT HE WAS FICTIONAL...
SENPAI... YOU REALLY DO HAVE A FRIEND... THAT'S SO NICE...
WHAT A RELIEF, HONESTLY...
TRMBL
TRMBL
FICTIONAL?!
I TOLD YOU NOT TO WORRY ABOUT IT!
DID YOU REALLY THINK I HAD NOBODY?!
OP LOOKING
T ME LIKE
THAT!!
OH, YOU'RE THAT GIRL WHO'S WITH SAKU ALL THE TIME.
OH, YES, YES.
I'M SAKAKI, HIS CLASSMATE. NICE TO MEET YOU.
DEEP BOW
UZAKI HANA, SECOND YEAR. I KNOW SENPAI CAN BE GLOOMY, BUT PLEASE BE A GOOD FRIEND TO HIM.
WHAT ARE YOU, MY MOM?
DON'T WORRY, SENPAI-- I'LL KEEP HANGING OUT WITH YOU.
WHERE DO YOU WANNA GO ONCE SCHOOL'S OVER TODAY?
WHY ARE YOU TALKING LIKE MY PLANS ARE ALREADY MADE?
FWMP

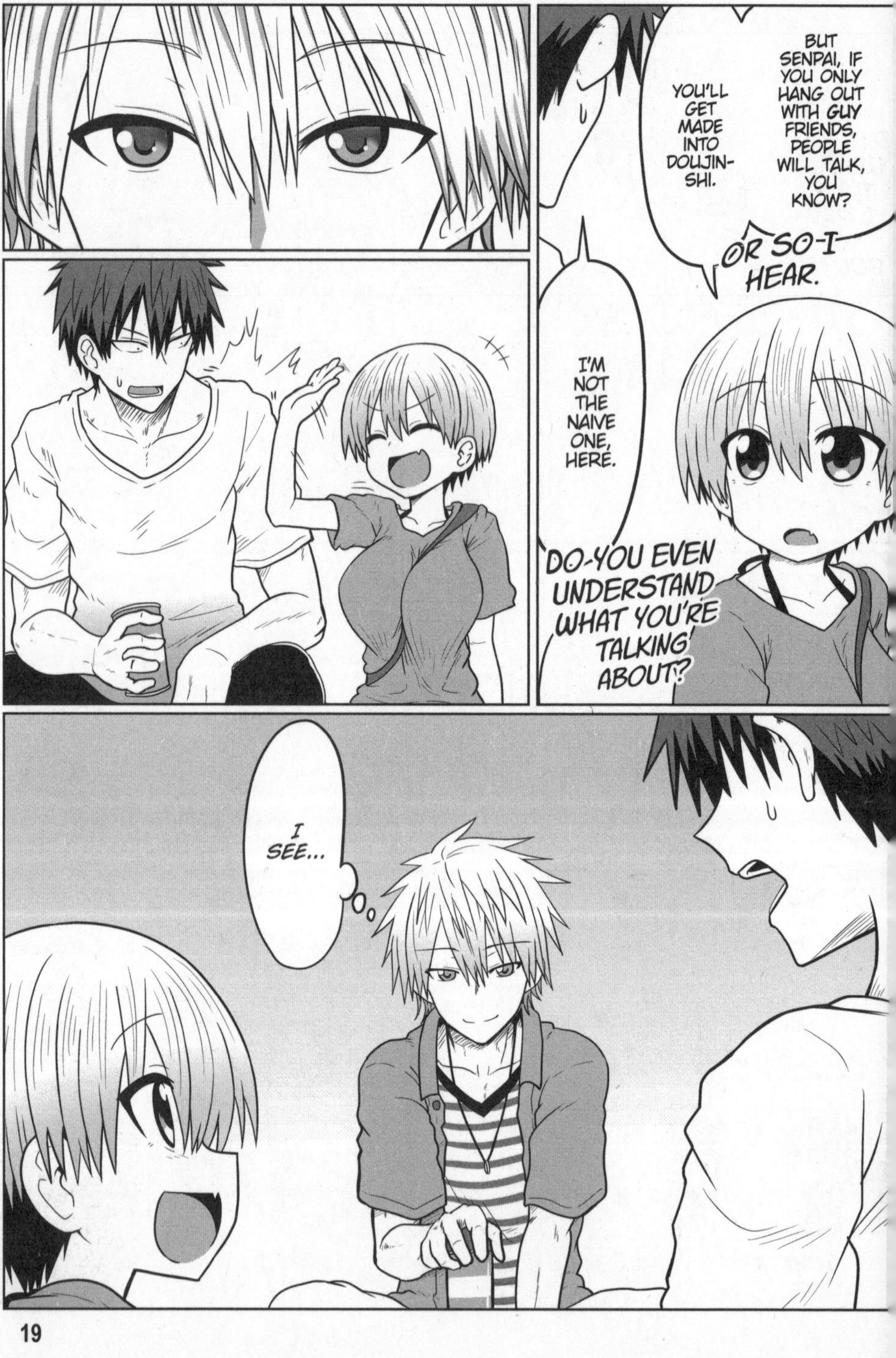
BUT SENPAI, IF YOU ONLY HANG OUT WITH GUY FRIENDS, PEOPLE WILL TALK, YOU KNOW?
YOU'LL GET MADE INTO DOUJIN-SHI.
OR SO I HEAR.
I'M NOT THE NAIVE ONE, HERE.
DO YOU EVEN UNDERSTAND WHAT YOU'RE TALKING ABOUT?
I SEE...

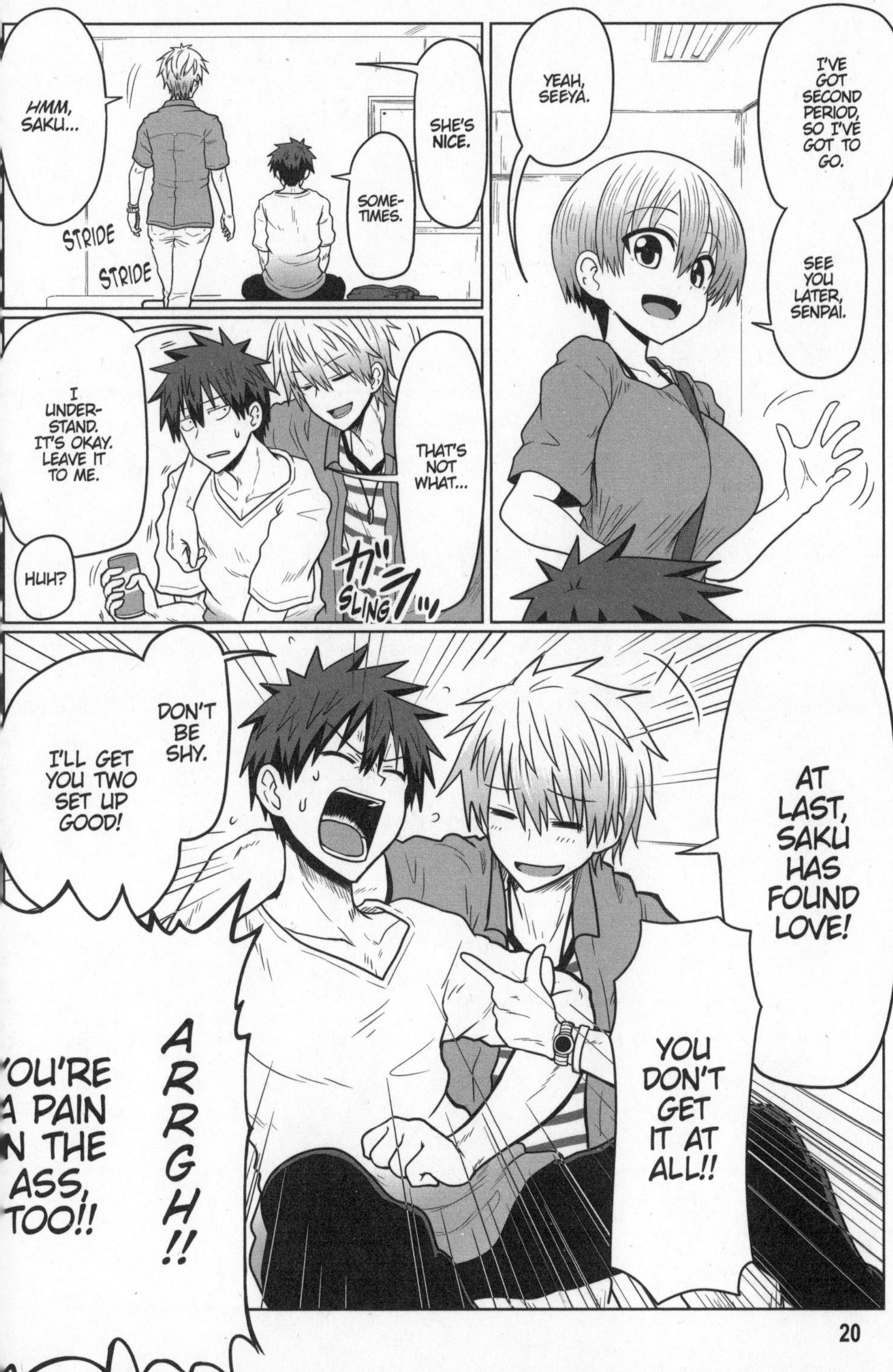
I'VE GOT SECOND PERIOD, SO I'VE GOT TO GO.
SEE YOU LATER, SENPAI.
YEAH, SEEYA.
SHE'S NICE.
SOMETIMES.
HMM, SAKU...
STRIDE
STRIDE
THAT'S NOT WHAT...
ガラッ
SLING
I UNDER-STAND. IT'S OKAY. LEAVE IT TO ME.
HUH?
AT LAST, SAKU HAS FOUND LOVE!
DON'T BE SHY.
I'LL GET YOU TWO SET UP GOOD!
YOU DON'T GET IT AT ALL!!
ARRGH!!
OU'RE A PAIN N THE ASS, TOO!!

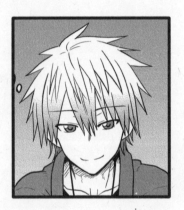

The new character, Sakaki-kun.

I'd feel bad if people thought Senpai
was actually a loner for real at school,
so I stuck Sakaki-san in.

His **face** is nice, but his personality...
not so much.

Uzaki-chan☆ Wants to Hang Out!

## Chapter 16:
The Squabbling Gardeners

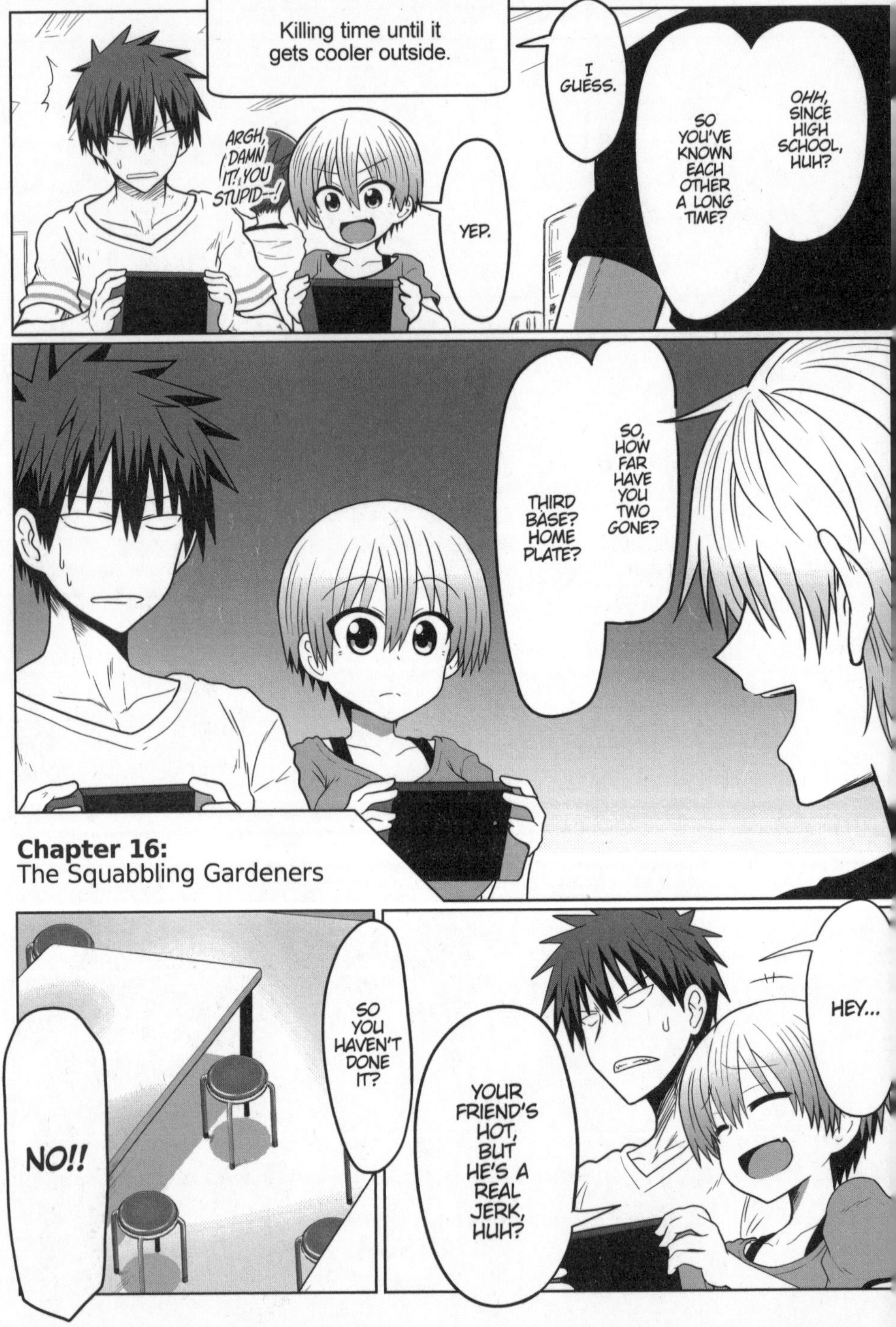

OHH, SINCE HIGH SCHOOL, HUH?
SO YOU'VE KNOWN EACH OTHER A LONG TIME?
I GUESS.
Killing time until it gets cooler outside.
YEP.
ARGH, DAMN IT! YOU STUPID--!
SO, HOW FAR HAVE YOU TWO GONE?
THIRD BASE? HOME PLATE?
HEY...
YOUR FRIEND'S HOT, BUT HE'S A REAL JERK, HUH?
SO YOU HAVEN'T DONE IT?
NO!!

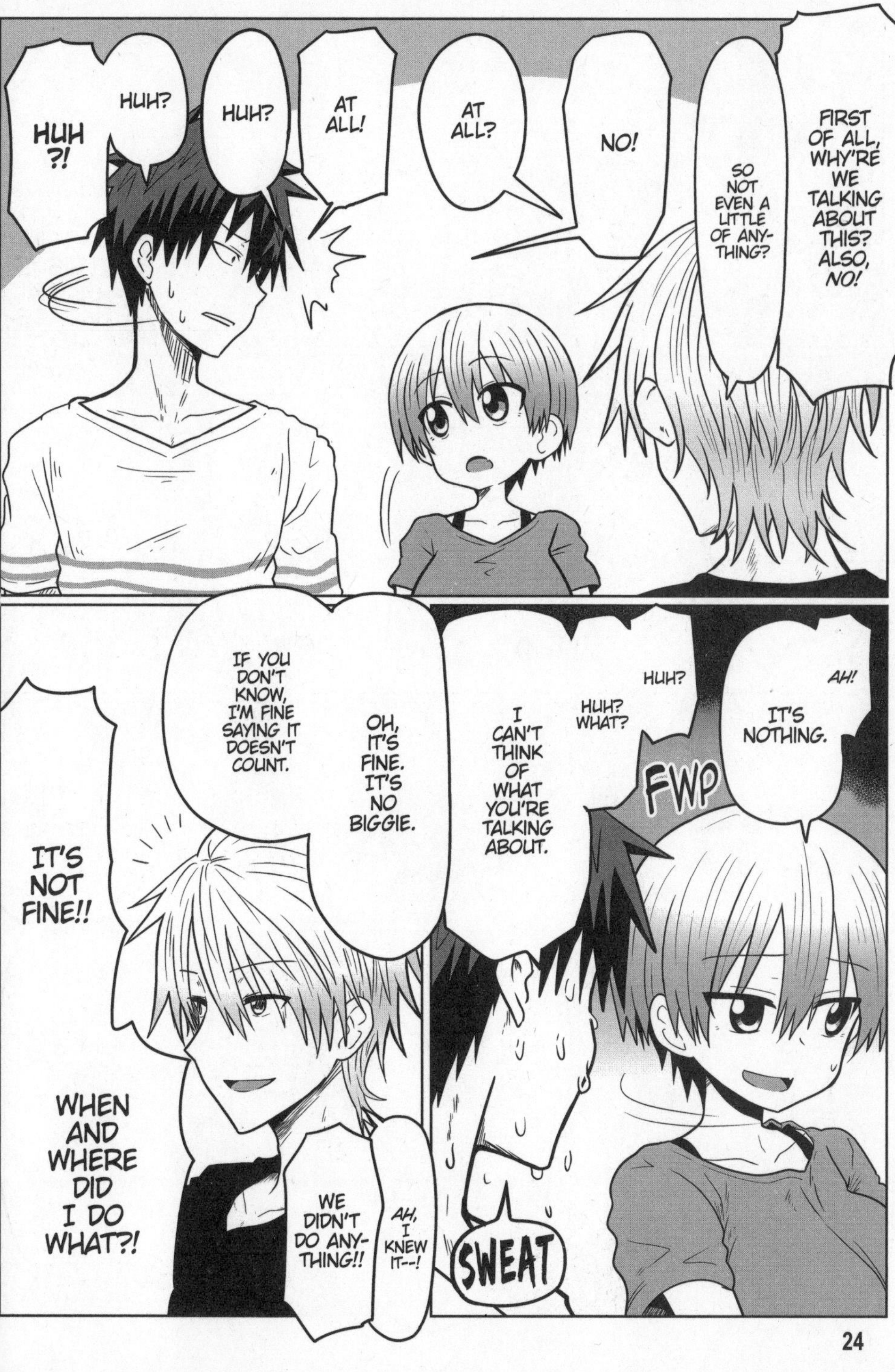
FIRST OF ALL, WHY'RE WE TALKING ABOUT THIS? ALSO, NO!
SO NOT EVEN A LITTLE OF ANY-THING?
NO!
AT ALL?
AT ALL!
HUH?
HUH?
HUH ?!
AH!
IT'S NOTHING.
FWP
HUH? WHAT?
HUH?
I CAN'T THINK OF WHAT YOU'RE TALKING ABOUT.
SWEAT
AH, I KNEW IT--!
WE DIDN'T DO ANY-THING!!
OH, IT'S FINE. IT'S NO BIGGIE.
IF YOU DON'T KNOW, I'M FINE SAYING IT DOESN'T COUNT.
IT'S NOT FINE!!
WHEN AND WHERE DID I DO WHAT?!

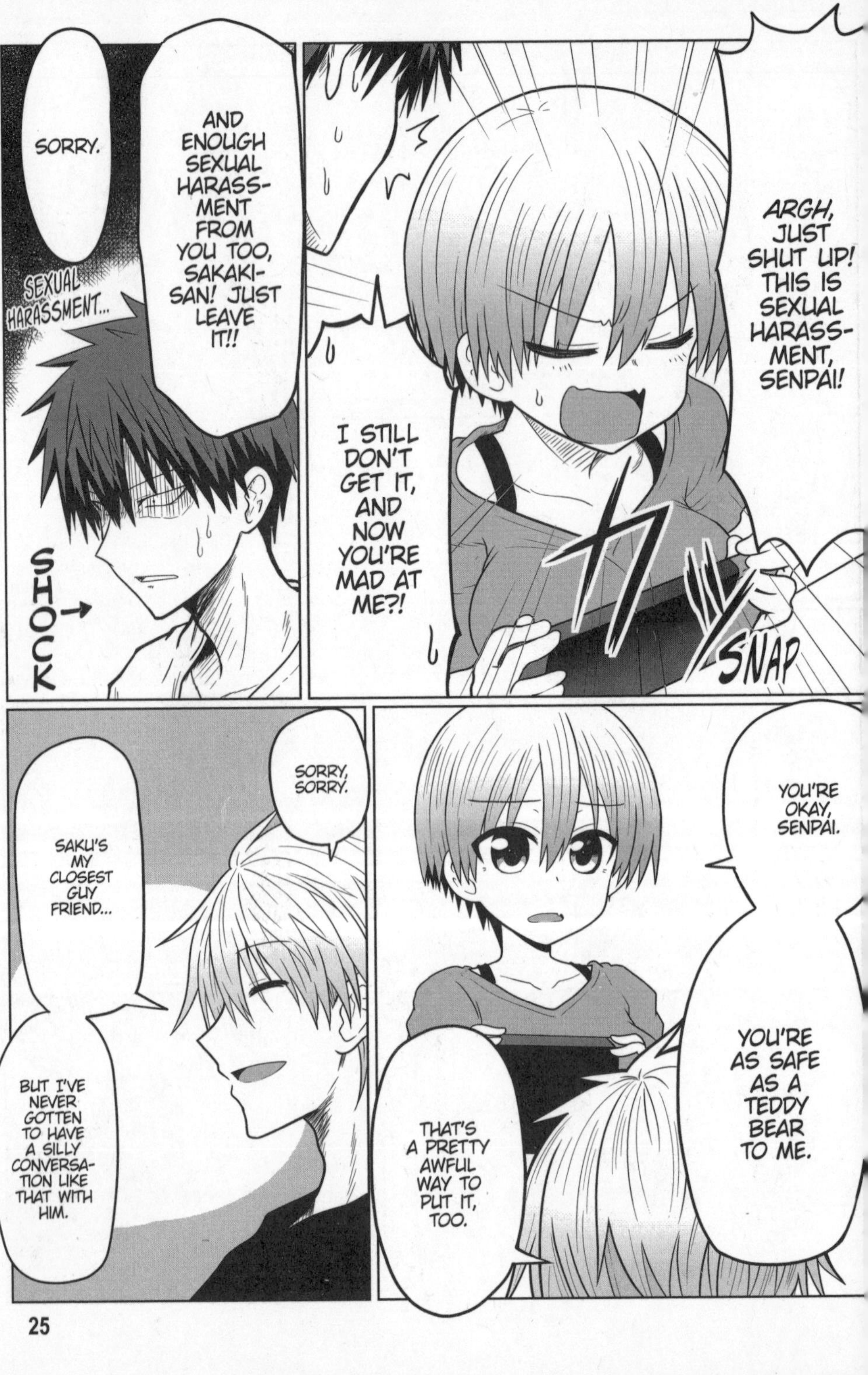
ARGH, JUST SHUT UP! THIS IS SEXUAL HARASSMENT, SENPAI!
SNAP
I STILL DON'T GET IT, AND NOW YOU'RE MAD AT ME?!
AND ENOUGH SEXUAL HARASSMENT FROM YOU TOO, SAKAKI-SAN! JUST LEAVE IT!!
SORRY.
SEXUAL HARASSMENT...
SHOCK
YOU'RE OKAY, SENPAI.
YOU'RE AS SAFE AS A TEDDY BEAR TO ME.
THAT'S A PRETTY AWFUL WAY TO PUT IT, TOO.
SORRY, SORRY.
SAKU'S MY CLOSEST GUY FRIEND...
BUT I'VE NEVER GOTTEN TO HAVE A SILLY CONVERSATION LIKE THAT WITH HIM.

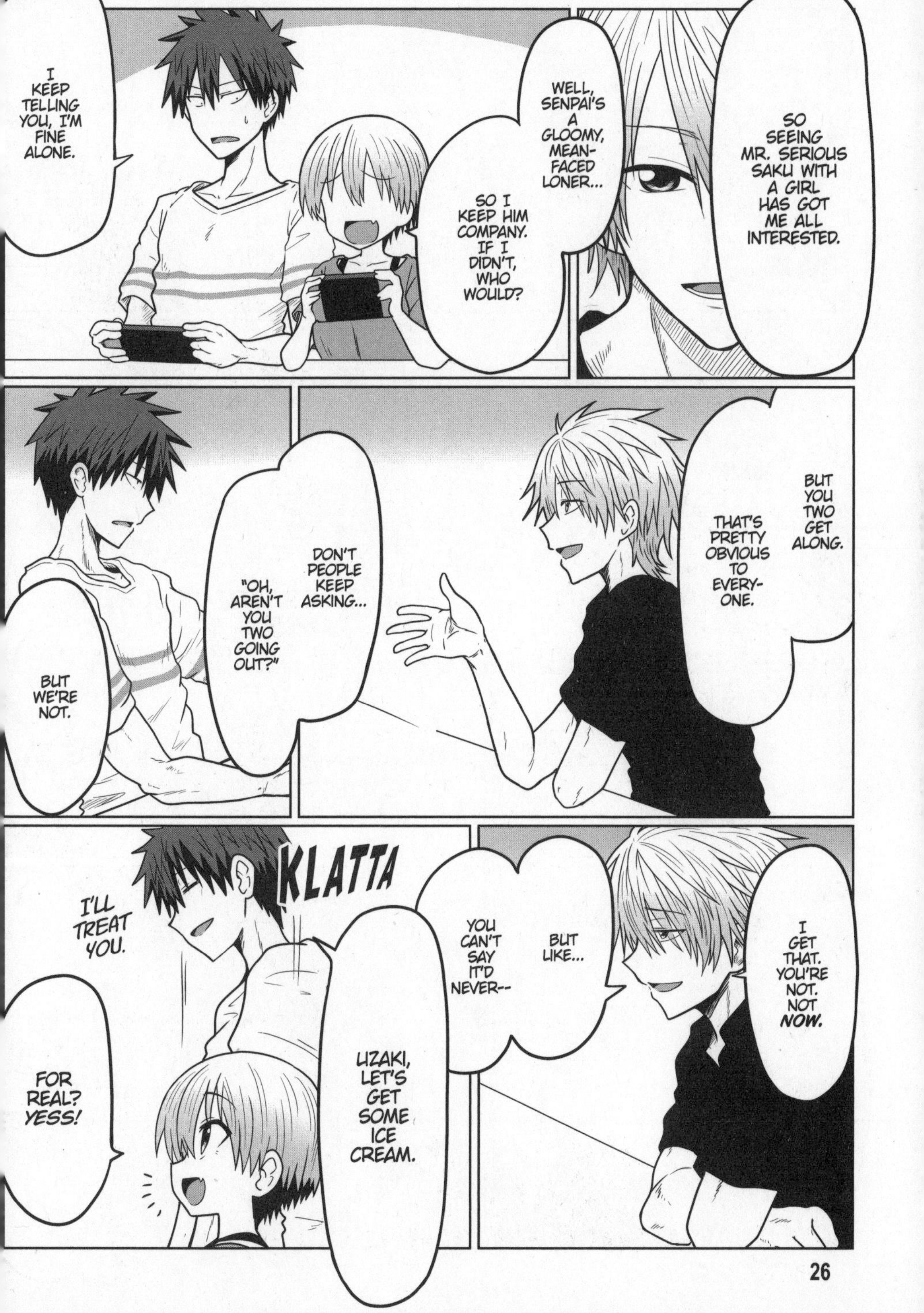
SO SEEING MR. SERIOUS SAKU WITH A GIRL HAS GOT ME ALL INTERESTED.
WELL, SENPAI'S A GLOOMY, MEAN-FACED LONER...
SO I KEEP HIM COMPANY. IF I DIDN'T, WHO WOULD?
I KEEP TELLING YOU, I'M FINE ALONE.
BUT YOU TWO GET ALONG.
THAT'S PRETTY OBVIOUS TO EVERYONE.
DON'T PEOPLE KEEP ASKING...
"OH, AREN'T YOU TWO GOING OUT?"
BUT WE'RE NOT.
I GET THAT. YOU'RE NOT. NOT *NOW*.
BUT LIKE...
YOU CAN'T SAY IT'D NEVER--
KLATTA
UZAKI, LET'S GET SOME ICE CREAM.
I'LL TREAT YOU.
FOR REAL? *YESS!*

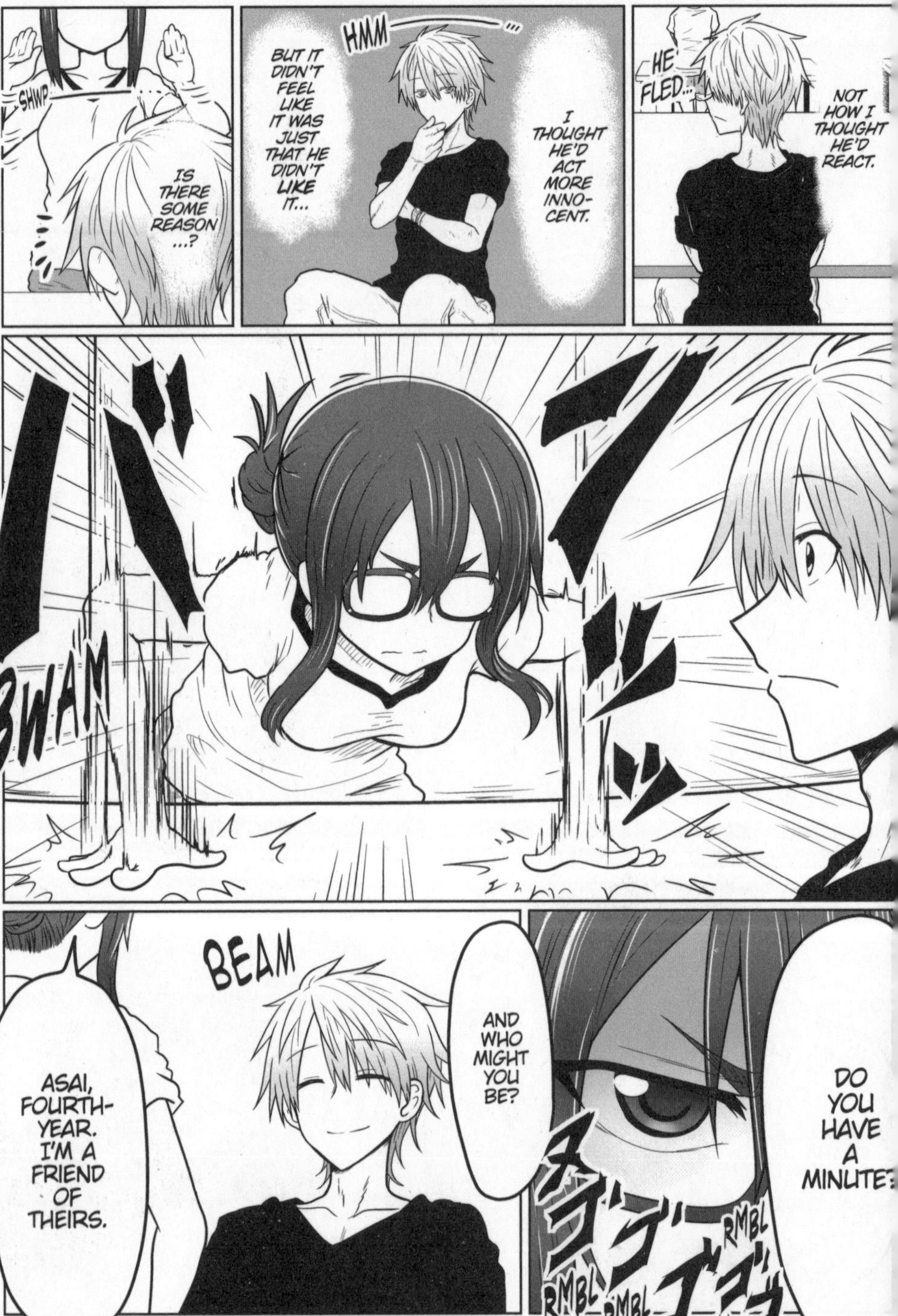
HE FLED...
NOT HOW I THOUGHT HE'D REACT.
HMM———...
I THOUGHT HE'D ACT MORE INNO-CENT.
BUT IT DIDN'T FEEL LIKE IT WAS JUST THAT HE DIDN'T LIKE IT...
SHWP
IS THERE SOME REASON ...?
BWAM
DO YOU HAVE A MINUTE?
AND WHO MIGHT YOU BE?
RMBL RMBL RMBL RMBL RMBL
BEAM
ASAI, FOURTH-YEAR. I'M A FRIEND OF THEIRS.

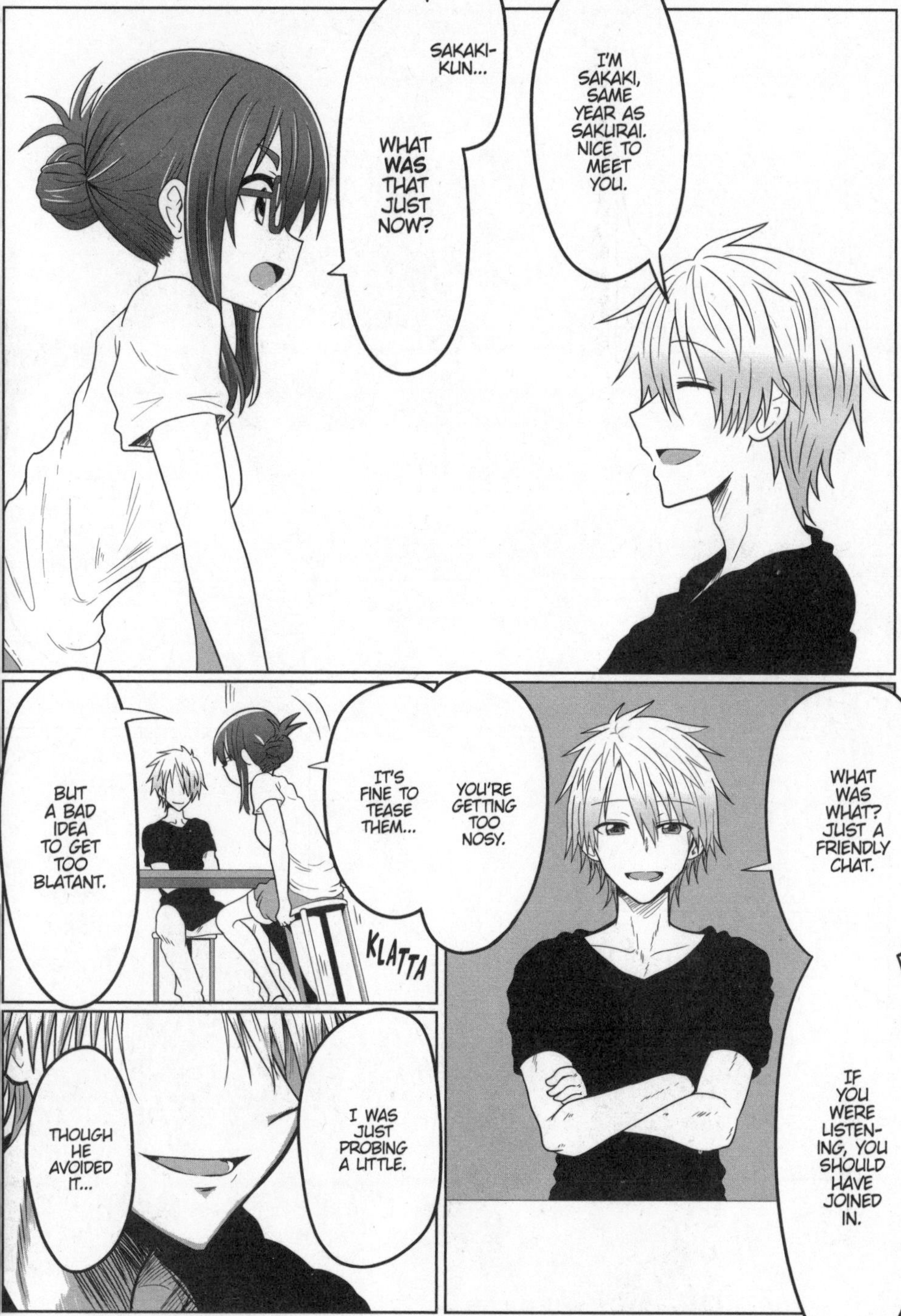
I'M SAKAKI, SAME YEAR AS SAKURAI. NICE TO MEET YOU.
SAKAKI-KUN...
WHAT WAS THAT JUST NOW?
WHAT WAS WHAT? JUST A FRIENDLY CHAT.
IF YOU WERE LISTENING, YOU SHOULD HAVE JOINED IN.
YOU'RE GETTING TOO NOSY.
IT'S FINE TO TEASE THEM...
BUT A BAD IDEA TO GET TOO BLATANT.
KLATTA
I WAS JUST PROBING A LITTLE.
THOUGH HE AVOIDED IT...

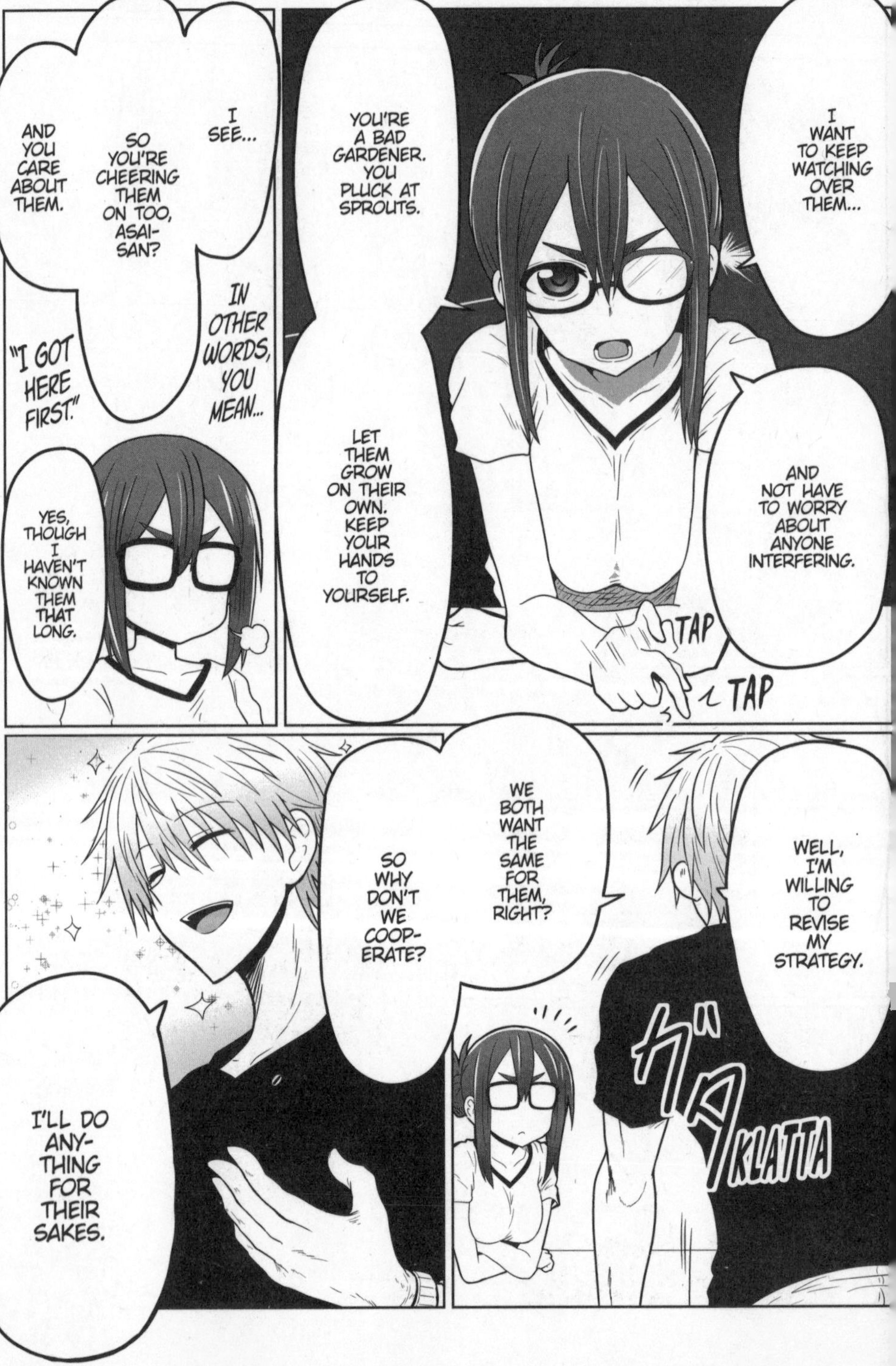
I WANT TO KEEP WATCHING OVER THEM...
AND NOT HAVE TO WORRY ABOUT ANYONE INTERFERING.
TAP
TAP
YOU'RE A BAD GARDENER. YOU PLUCK AT SPROUTS.
LET THEM GROW ON THEIR OWN. KEEP YOUR HANDS TO YOURSELF.
I SEE...
SO YOU'RE CHEERING THEM ON TOO, ASAI-SAN?
AND YOU CARE ABOUT THEM.
IN OTHER WORDS, YOU MEAN...
"I GOT HERE FIRST."
YES, THOUGH I HAVEN'T KNOWN THEM THAT LONG.
WELL, I'M WILLING TO REVISE MY STRATEGY.
KLATTA
WE BOTH WANT THE SAME FOR THEM, RIGHT?
SO WHY DON'T WE COOPERATE?
I'LL DO ANYTHING FOR THEIR SAKES.

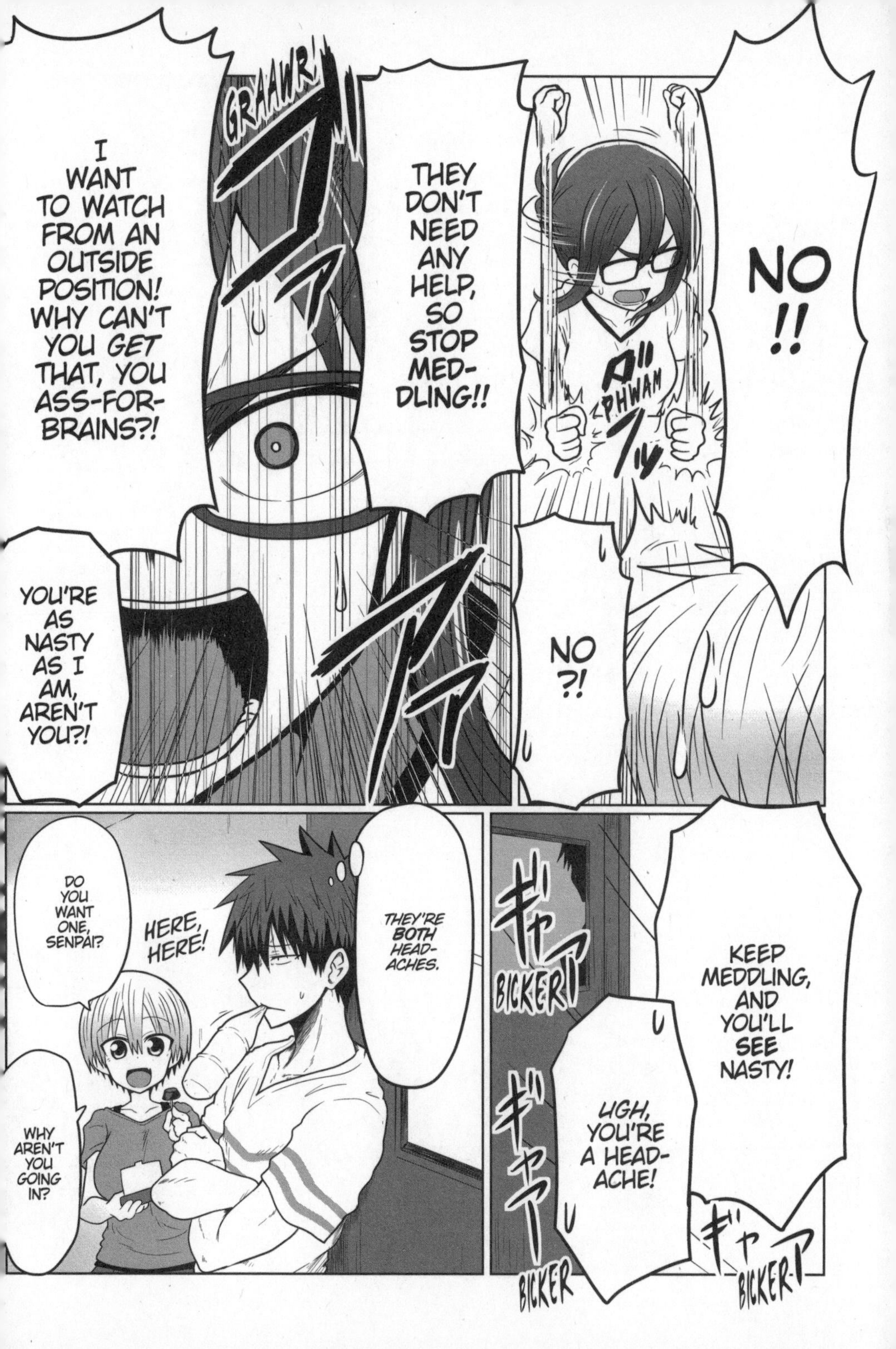
NO!!
PHWAM
THEY DON'T NEED ANY HELP, SO STOP MEDDLING!!
GRAAWR
I WANT TO WATCH FROM AN OUTSIDE POSITION! WHY CAN'T YOU GET THAT, YOU ASS-FOR-BRAINS?!
NO?!
YOU'RE AS NASTY AS I AM, AREN'T YOU?!
KEEP MEDDLING, AND YOU'LL SEE NASTY!
BICKER
UGH, YOU'RE A HEAD-ACHE!
BICKER
BICKER
THEY'RE BOTH HEAD-ACHES.
HERE, HERE!
DO YOU WANT ONE, SENPAI?
WHY AREN'T YOU GOING IN?

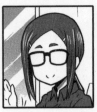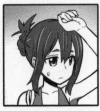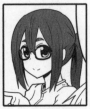

When I draw Asai, I play around with her hairstyle and leaving her glasses on or off.

**Uzaki-chan☆ Wants to Hang Out!**

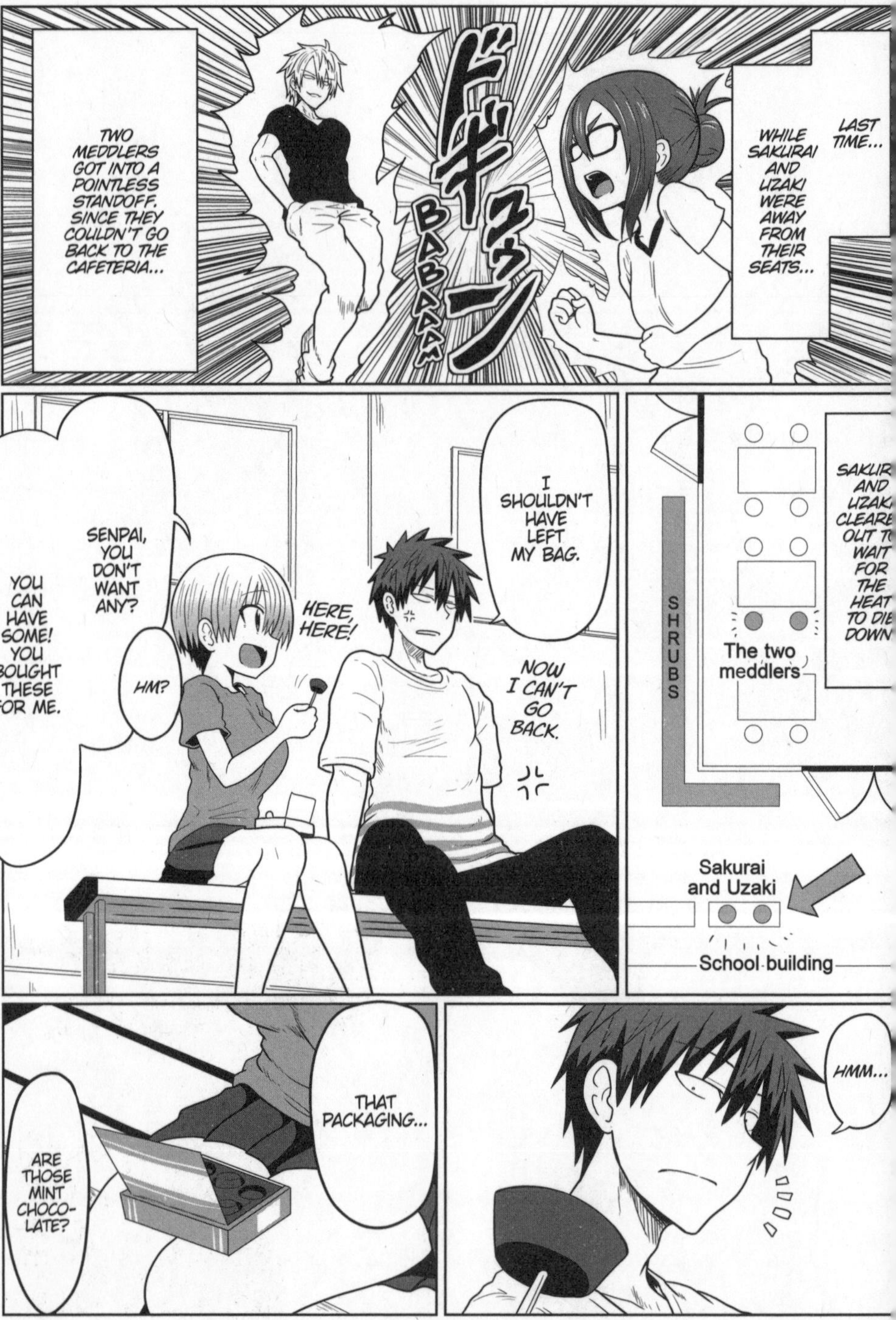
LAST TIME... WHILE SAKURAI AND UZAKI WERE AWAY FROM THEIR SEATS...
ドギューン
BABAAAM
TWO MEDDLERS GOT INTO A POINTLESS STANDOFF. SINCE THEY COULDN'T GO BACK TO THE CAFETERIA...
SAKUR AND UZAK CLEARE OUT T WAIT FOR THE HEAT TO DIE DOWN
SHRUBS
The two meddlers
Sakurai and Uzaki
School building
I SHOULDN'T HAVE LEFT MY BAG.
NOW I CAN'T GO BACK.
HERE, HERE!
SENPAI, YOU DON'T WANT ANY?
HM?
YOU CAN HAVE SOME! YOU BOUGHT THESE FOR ME.
HMM...
THAT PACKAGING...
ARE THOSE MINT CHOCO-LATE?

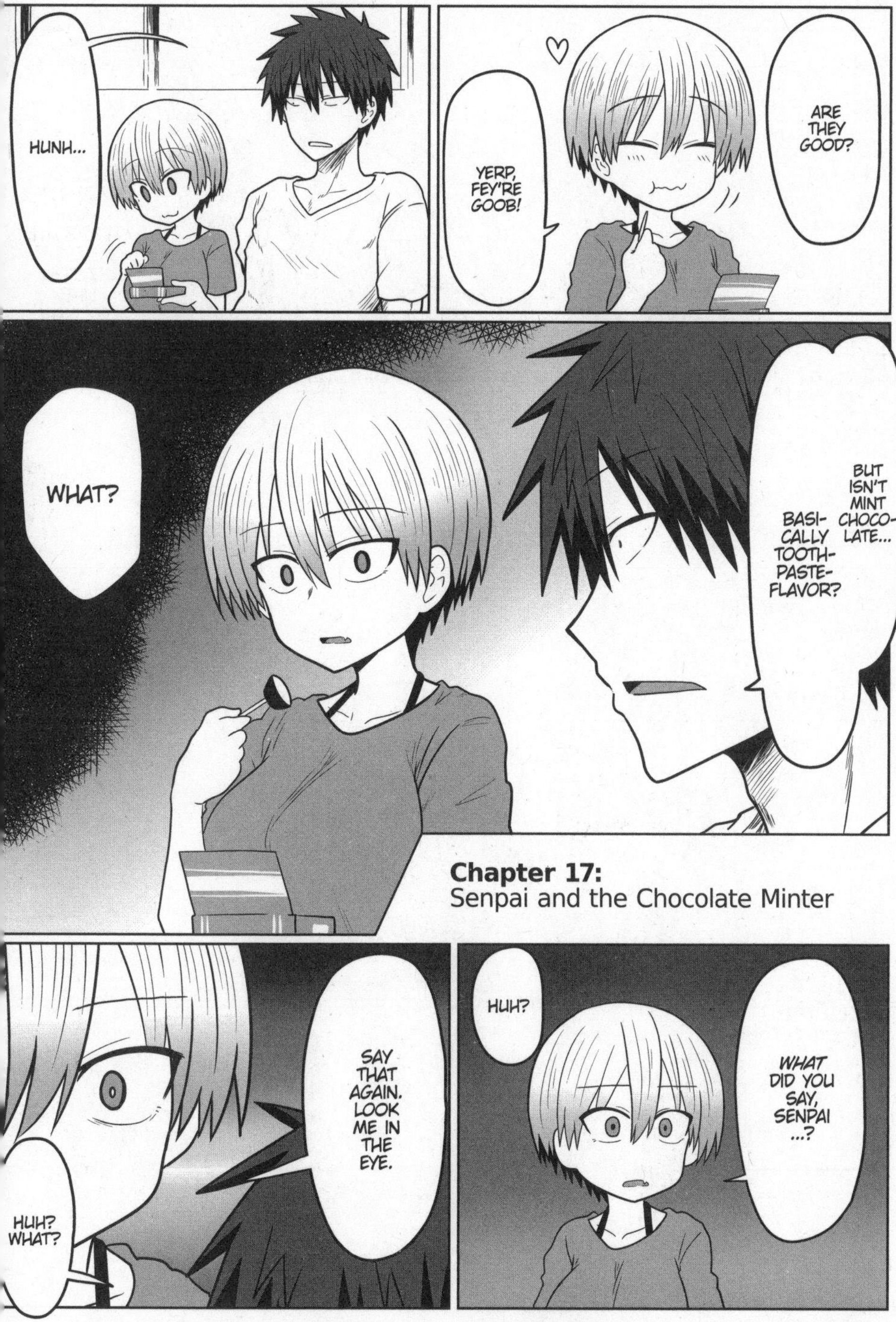
ARE THEY GOOD?
YERP, FEY'RE GOOB!
HUNH...
BUT ISN'T MINT CHOCOLATE... BASICALLY TOOTHPASTE-FLAVOR?
WHAT?
WHAT DID YOU SAY, SENPAI ...?
HUH?
SAY THAT AGAIN. LOOK ME IN THE EYE.
HUH? WHAT?

## Chapter 17:
Senpai and the Chocolate Minter

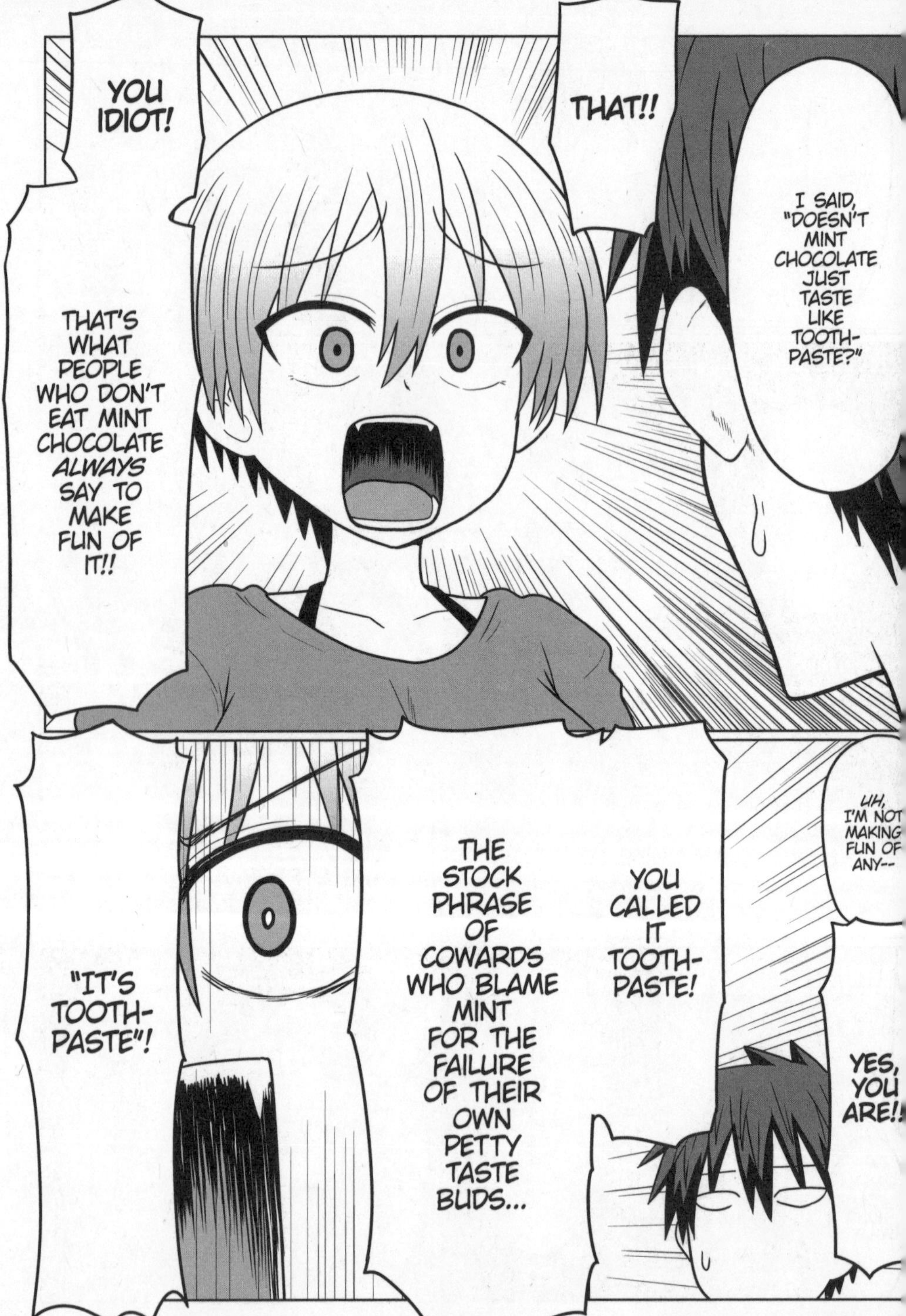
I SAID, "DOESN'T MINT CHOCOLATE JUST TASTE LIKE TOOTH-PASTE?"
THAT!!
YOU IDIOT!
THAT'S WHAT PEOPLE WHO DON'T EAT MINT CHOCOLATE *ALWAYS* SAY TO MAKE FUN OF IT!!
UH, I'M NOT MAKING FUN OF ANY--
YES, YOU ARE!!
YOU CALLED IT TOOTH-PASTE!
THE STOCK PHRASE OF COWARDS WHO BLAME MINT FOR THE FAILURE OF THEIR OWN PETTY TASTE BUDS...
"IT'S TOOTH-PASTE"!

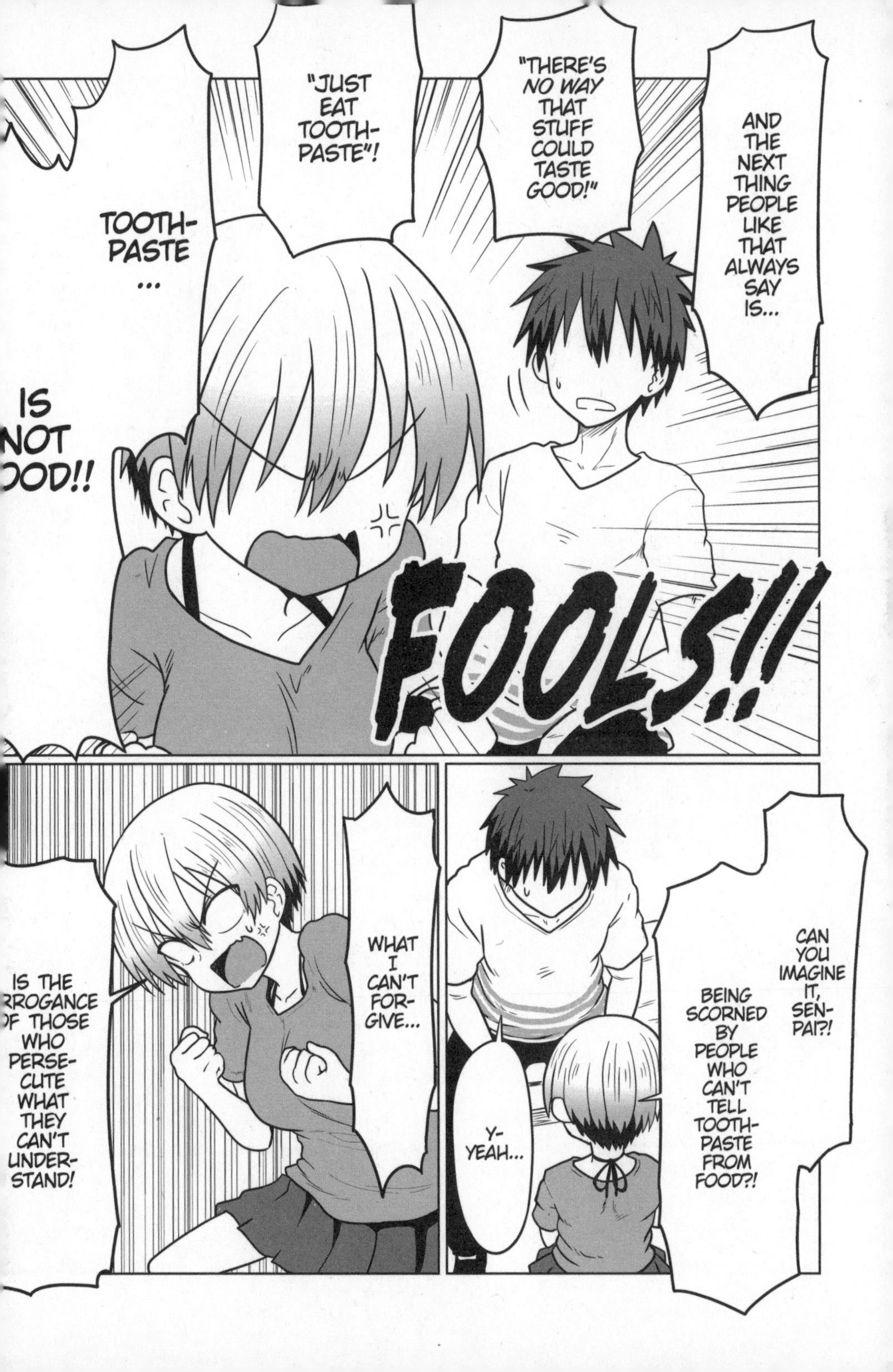
AND THE NEXT THING PEOPLE LIKE THAT ALWAYS SAY IS...
"THERE'S NO WAY THAT STUFF COULD TASTE GOOD!"
"JUST EAT TOOTH-PASTE"!
TOOTH-PASTE ...
IS NOT OOD!!
FOOLS!!
CAN YOU IMAGINE IT, SEN-PAI?!
BEING SCORNED BY PEOPLE WHO CAN'T TELL TOOTH-PASTE FROM FOOD?!
Y-YEAH...
WHAT I CAN'T FOR-GIVE...
IS THE RROGANCE F THOSE WHO PERSE-CUTE WHAT THEY CAN'T UNDER-STAND!

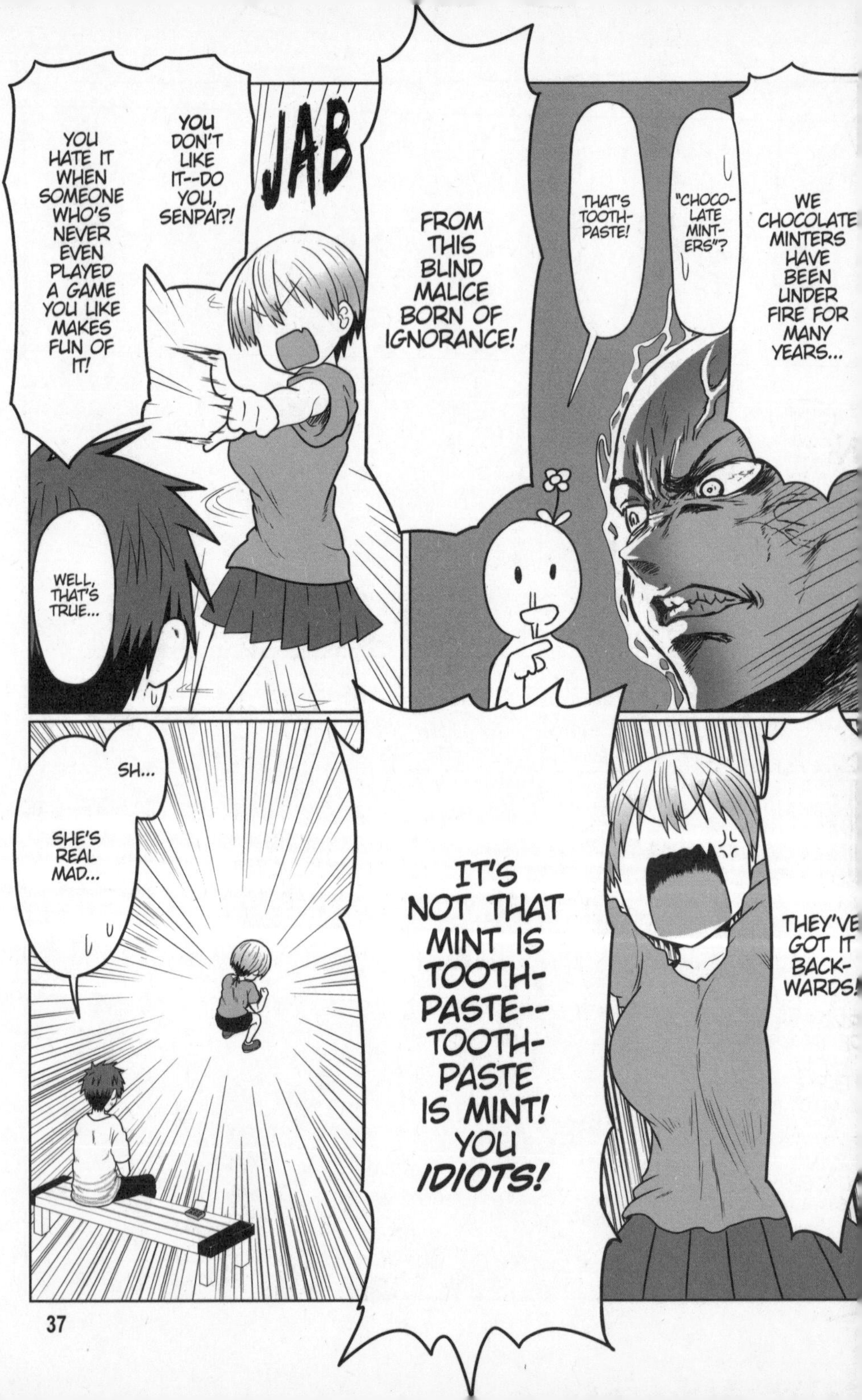
WE CHOCOLATE MINTERS HAVE BEEN UNDER FIRE FOR MANY YEARS...
"CHOCOLATE MINTERS"?
THAT'S TOOTHPASTE!
FROM THIS BLIND MALICE BORN OF IGNORANCE!
JAB
YOU DON'T LIKE IT--DO YOU, SENPAI?!
YOU HATE IT WHEN SOMEONE WHO'S NEVER EVEN PLAYED A GAME YOU LIKE MAKES FUN OF IT!
WELL, THAT'S TRUE...
THEY'VE GOT IT BACKWARDS!
IT'S NOT THAT MINT IS TOOTHPASTE--TOOTHPASTE IS MINT! YOU *IDIOTS!*
SH...
SHE'S REAL MAD...

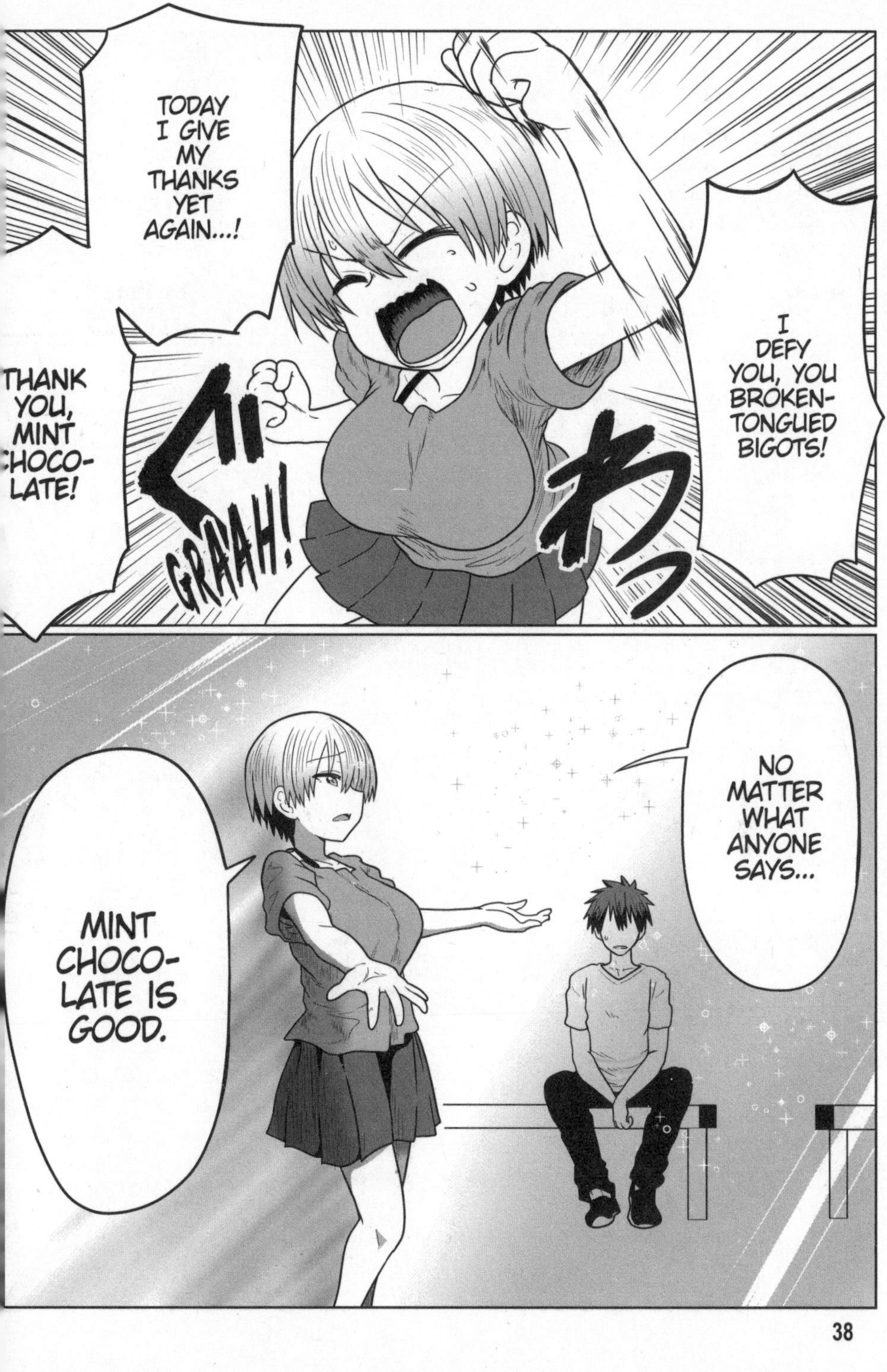
I DEFY YOU, YOU BROKEN-TONGUED BIGOTS!
わっ
GRAAH!
TODAY I GIVE MY THANKS YET AGAIN...!
THANK YOU, MINT CHOCO-LATE!
NO MATTER WHAT ANYONE SAYS...
MINT CHOCO-LATE IS GOOD.

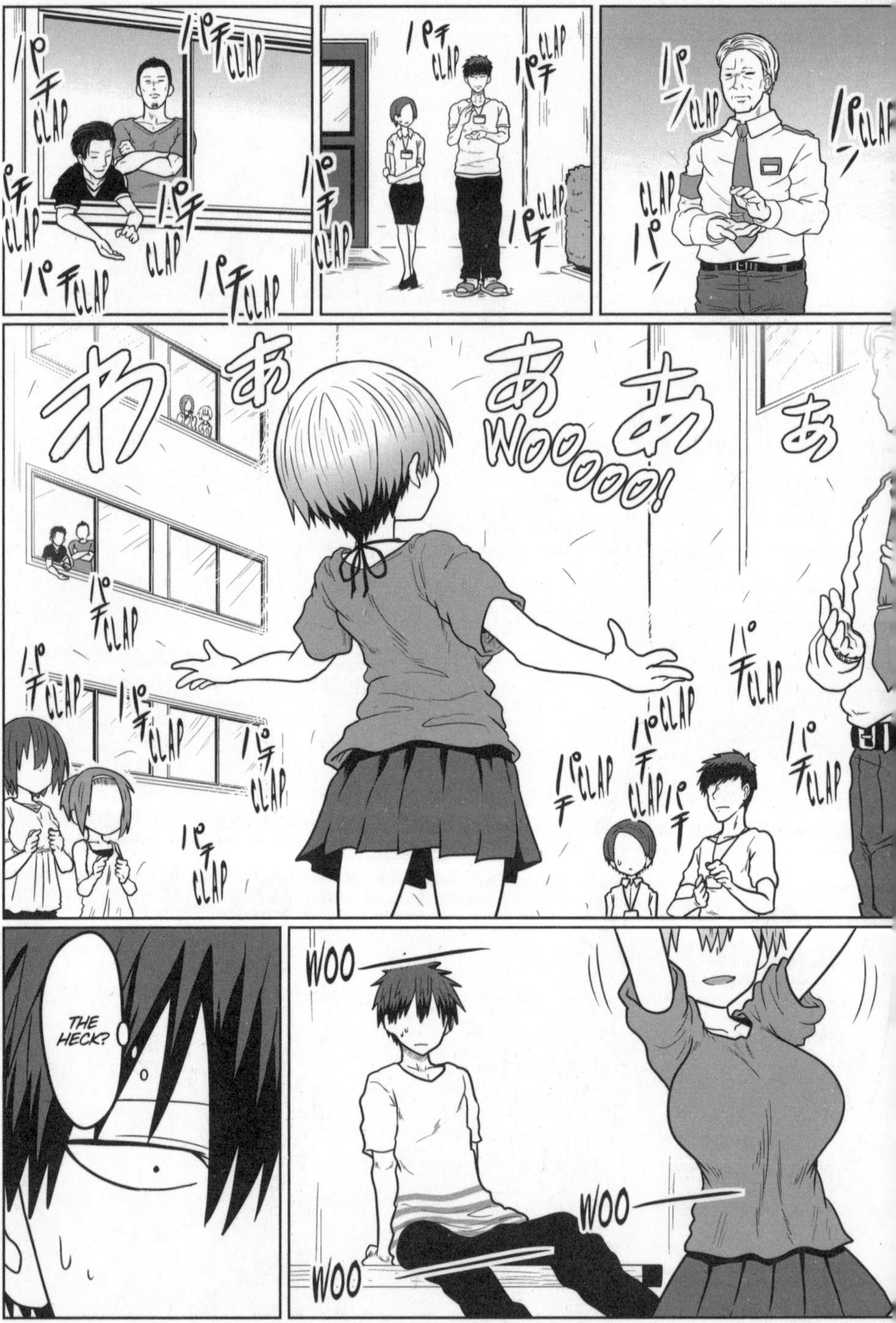
パン CLAP
パン CLAP
CLAP パン
パチ CLAP
パチ CLAP
パチ CLAP
パチ CLAP
パチ CLAP
パチ CLAP
パチ CLAP
パチ CLAP
パチ CLAP
パチ CLAP
わああああ
WOOOOOO!
パチ CLAP
パチ CLAP
パチ CLAP
パチ CLAP
パチ CLAP
パチ CLAP
パチ CLAP
パチ CLAP
パチ CLAP
パチ CLAP
WOO
WOO
WOO
THE HECK?

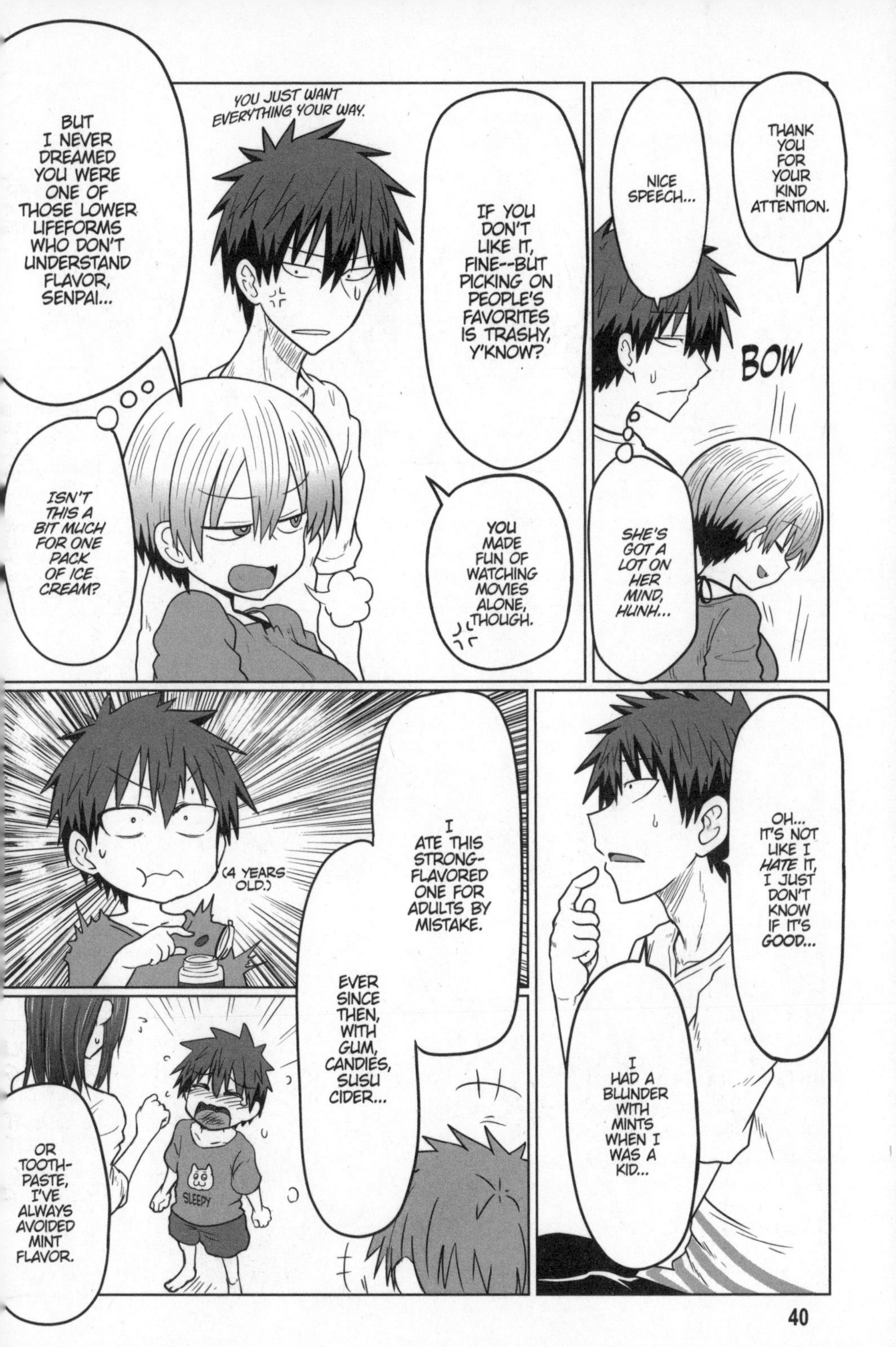
THANK YOU FOR YOUR KIND ATTENTION.
NICE SPEECH...
BOW
SHE'S GOT A LOT ON HER MIND, HUNH...
IF YOU DON'T LIKE IT, FINE--BUT PICKING ON PEOPLE'S FAVORITES IS TRASHY, Y'KNOW?
YOU JUST WANT EVERYTHING YOUR WAY.
YOU MADE FUN OF WATCHING MOVIES ALONE, THOUGH.
BUT I NEVER DREAMED YOU WERE ONE OF THOSE LOWER LIFEFORMS WHO DON'T UNDERSTAND FLAVOR, SENPAI...
ISN'T THIS A BIT MUCH FOR ONE PACK OF ICE CREAM?
OH... IT'S NOT LIKE I *HATE* IT, I JUST DON'T KNOW IF IT'S GOOD...
I HAD A BLUNDER WITH MINTS WHEN I WAS A KID...
I ATE THIS STRONG-FLAVORED ONE FOR ADULTS BY MISTAKE.
(4 YEARS OLD.)
EVER SINCE THEN, WITH GUM, CANDIES, SUSU CIDER...
SLEEPY
OR TOOTH-PASTE, I'VE ALWAYS AVOIDED MINT FLAVOR.

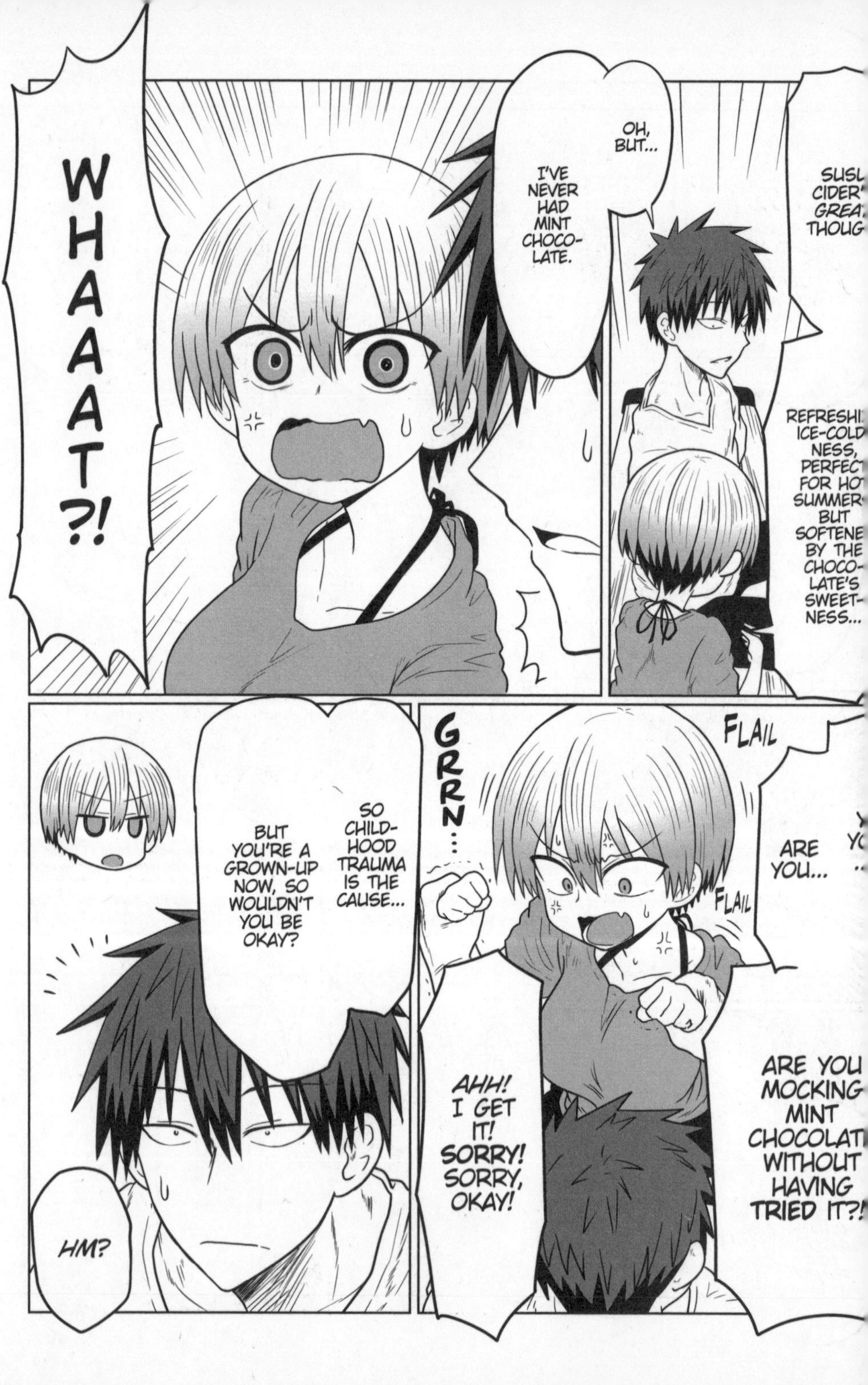
SUSL CIDER' GREAT THOUG
REFRESHI ICE-COLD NESS, PERFECT FOR HO SUMMER BUT SOFTENE BY THE CHOCO-LATE'S SWEET-NESS...
OH, BUT... I'VE NEVER HAD MINT CHOCO-LATE.
WHAAAT?!
FLAIL
ARE YOU...
FLAIL
GRRN...
ARE YOU MOCKING MINT CHOCOLAT WITHOUT HAVING TRIED IT?!
AHH! I GET IT! SORRY! SORRY, OKAY!
SO CHILD-HOOD TRAUMA IS THE CAUSE...
BUT YOU'RE A GROWN-UP NOW, SO WOULDN'T YOU BE OKAY?
HM?

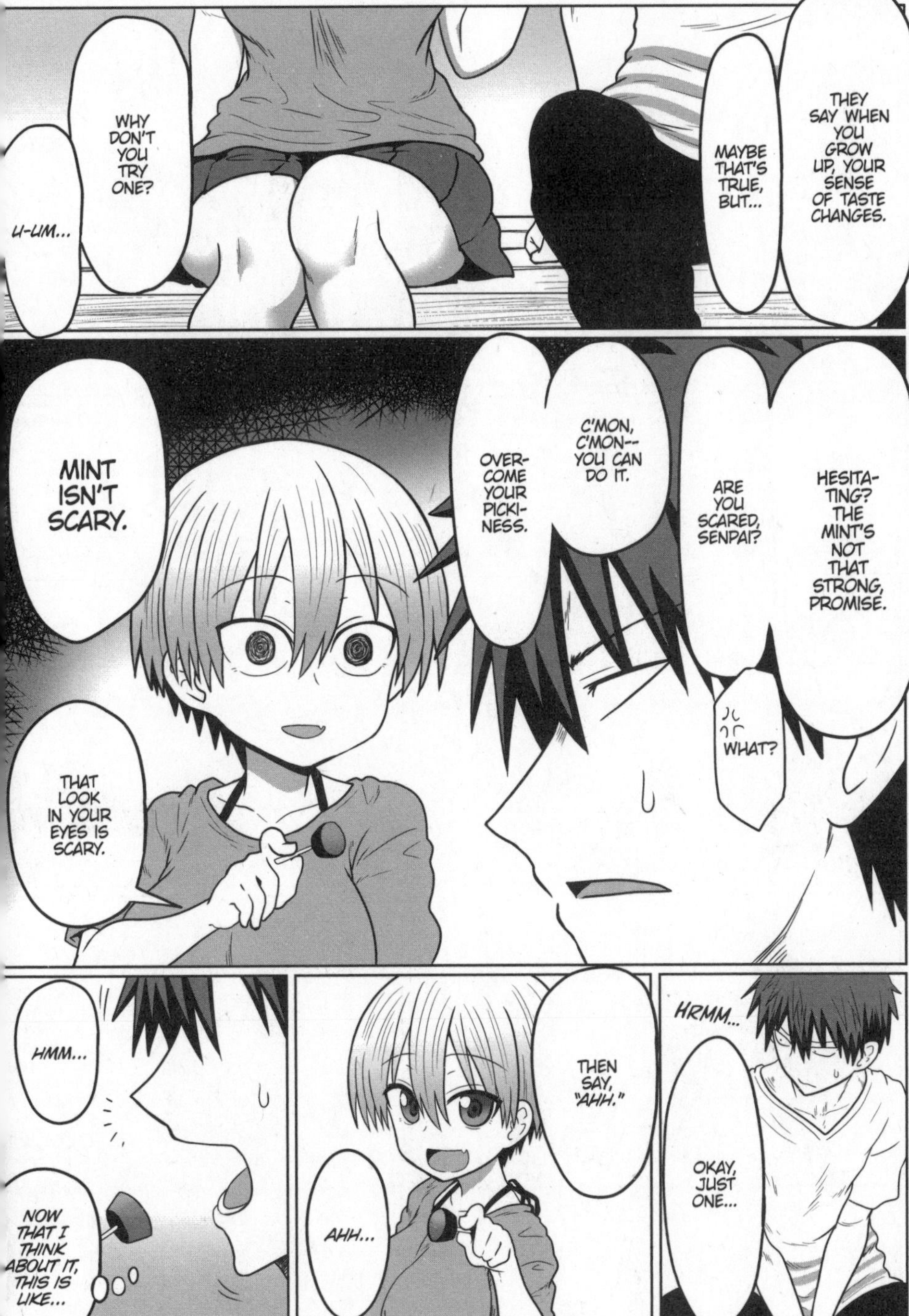
THEY SAY WHEN YOU GROW UP, YOUR SENSE OF TASTE CHANGES.
MAYBE THAT'S TRUE, BUT...
WHY DON'T YOU TRY ONE?
U-UM...
HESITA-TING? THE MINT'S NOT THAT STRONG, PROMISE.
ARE YOU SCARED, SENPAI?
C'MON, C'MON-- YOU CAN DO IT.
OVER-COME YOUR PICKI-NESS.
WHAT?
MINT ISN'T SCARY.
THAT LOOK IN YOUR EYES IS SCARY.
HRMM...
OKAY, JUST ONE...
THEN SAY, "AHH."
AHH...
HMM...
NOW THAT I THINK ABOUT IT, THIS IS LIKE...

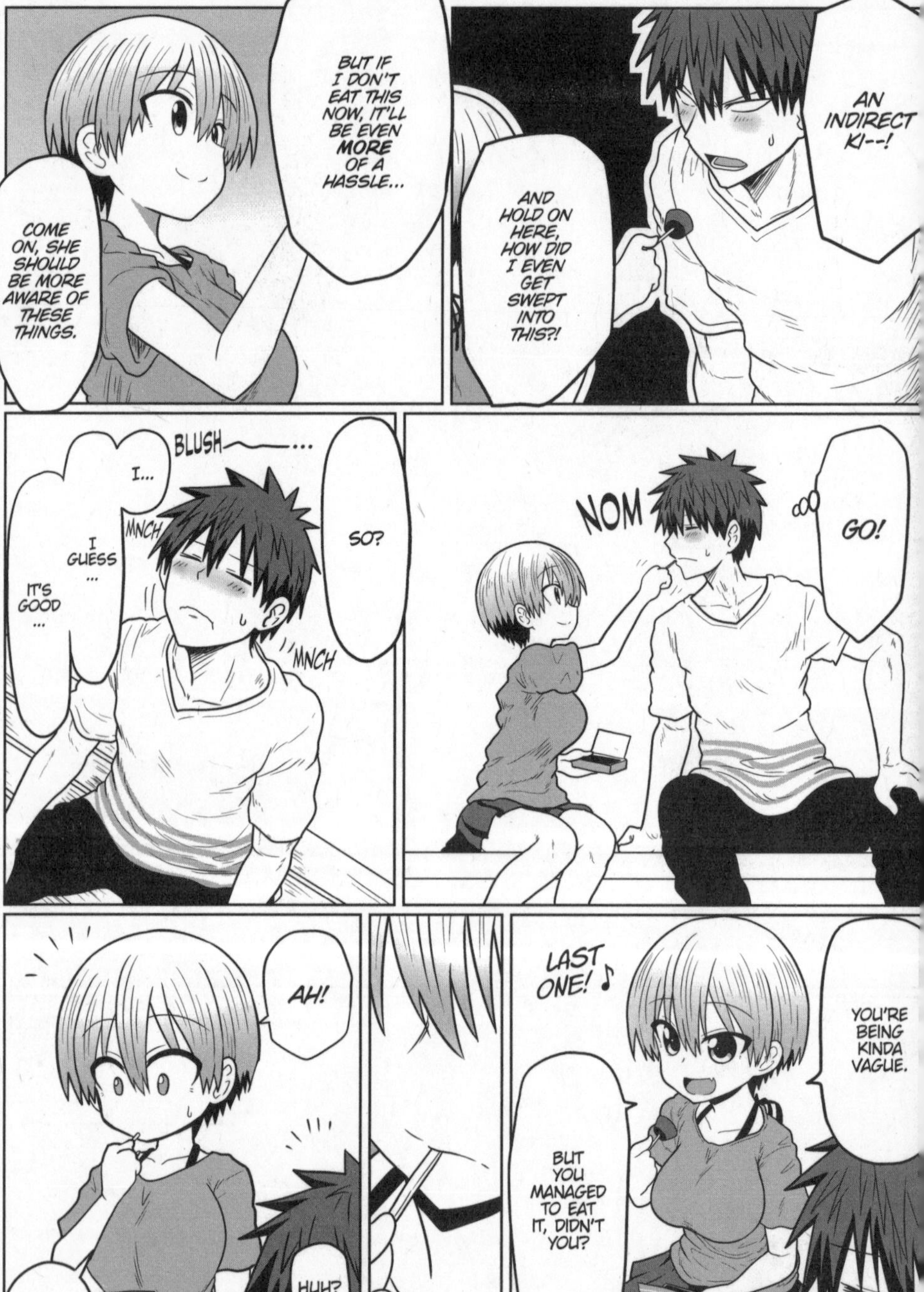
AN INDIRECT KI--!
AND HOLD ON HERE, HOW DID I EVEN GET SWEPT INTO THIS?!
BUT IF I DON'T EAT THIS NOW, IT'LL BE EVEN MORE OF A HASSLE...
COME ON, SHE SHOULD BE MORE AWARE OF THESE THINGS.
GO!
NOM
SO?
BLUSH—...
I...
MNCH
I GUESS...
IT'S GOOD...
MNCH
YOU'RE BEING KINDA VAGUE.
LAST ONE! ♪
BUT YOU MANAGED TO EAT IT, DIDN'T YOU?
AH!
HUH?
UH...

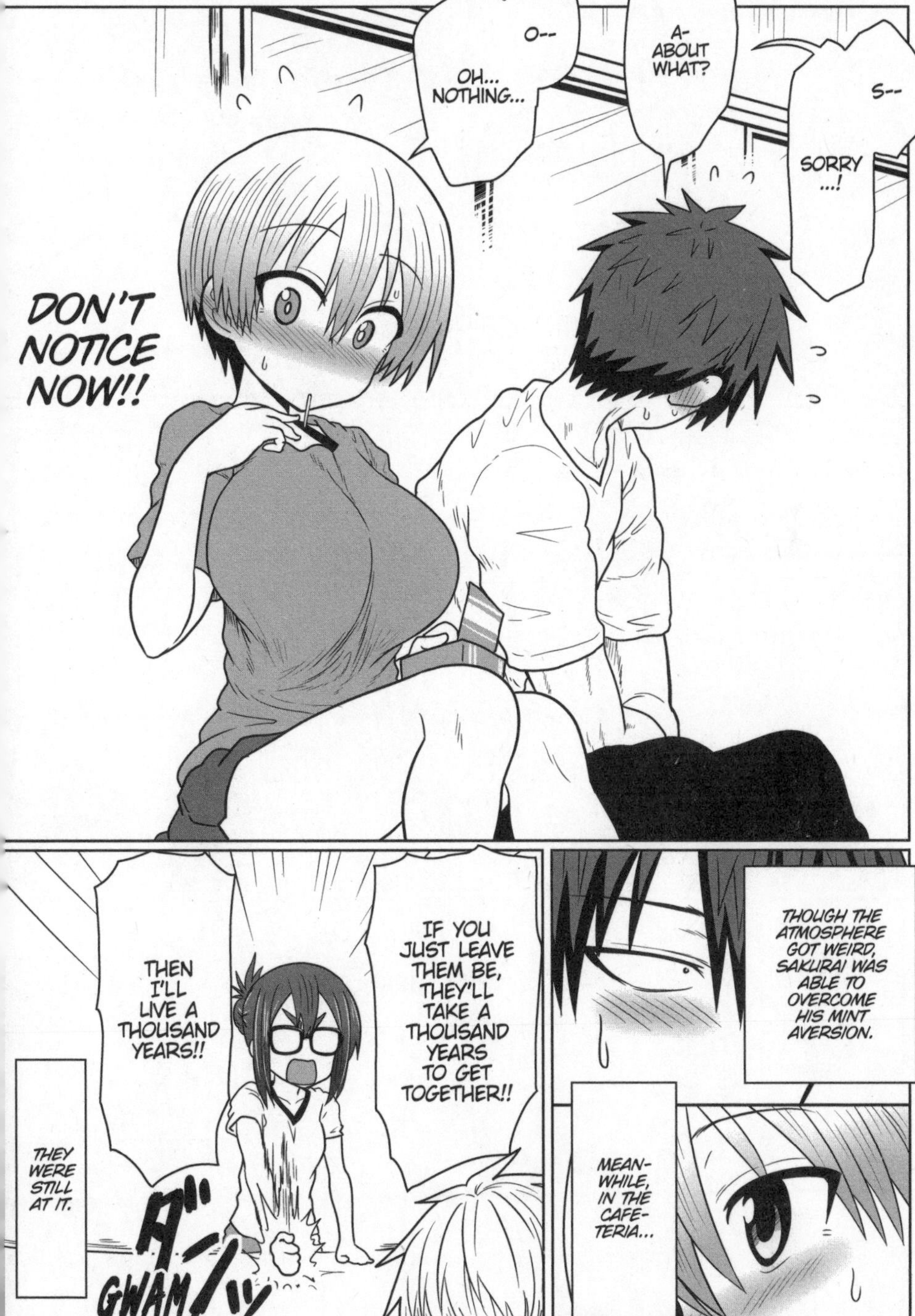
S--
SORRY ...!
A- ABOUT WHAT?
O--
OH... NOTHING...
DON'T NOTICE NOW!!
THOUGH THE ATMOSPHERE GOT WEIRD, SAKURAI WAS ABLE TO OVERCOME HIS MINT AVERSION.
MEAN-WHILE, IN THE CAFE-TERIA...
IF YOU JUST LEAVE THEM BE, THEY'LL TAKE A THOUSAND YEARS TO GET TOGETHER!!
THEN I'LL LIVE A THOUSAND YEARS!!
GWAM
THEY WERE STILL AT IT.

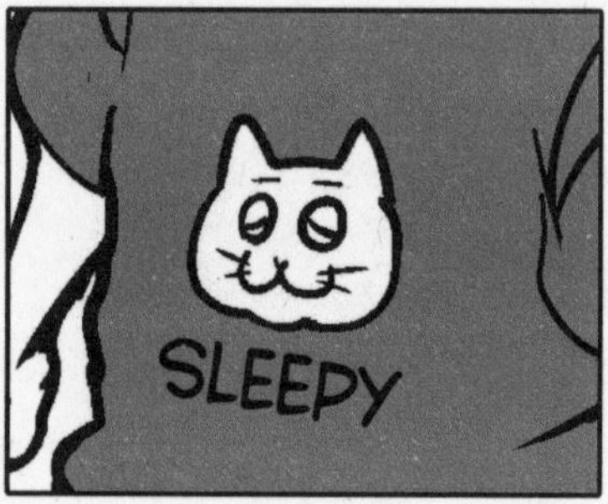
SLEEPY

**Uzaki-chan☆Wants to Hang Out!**

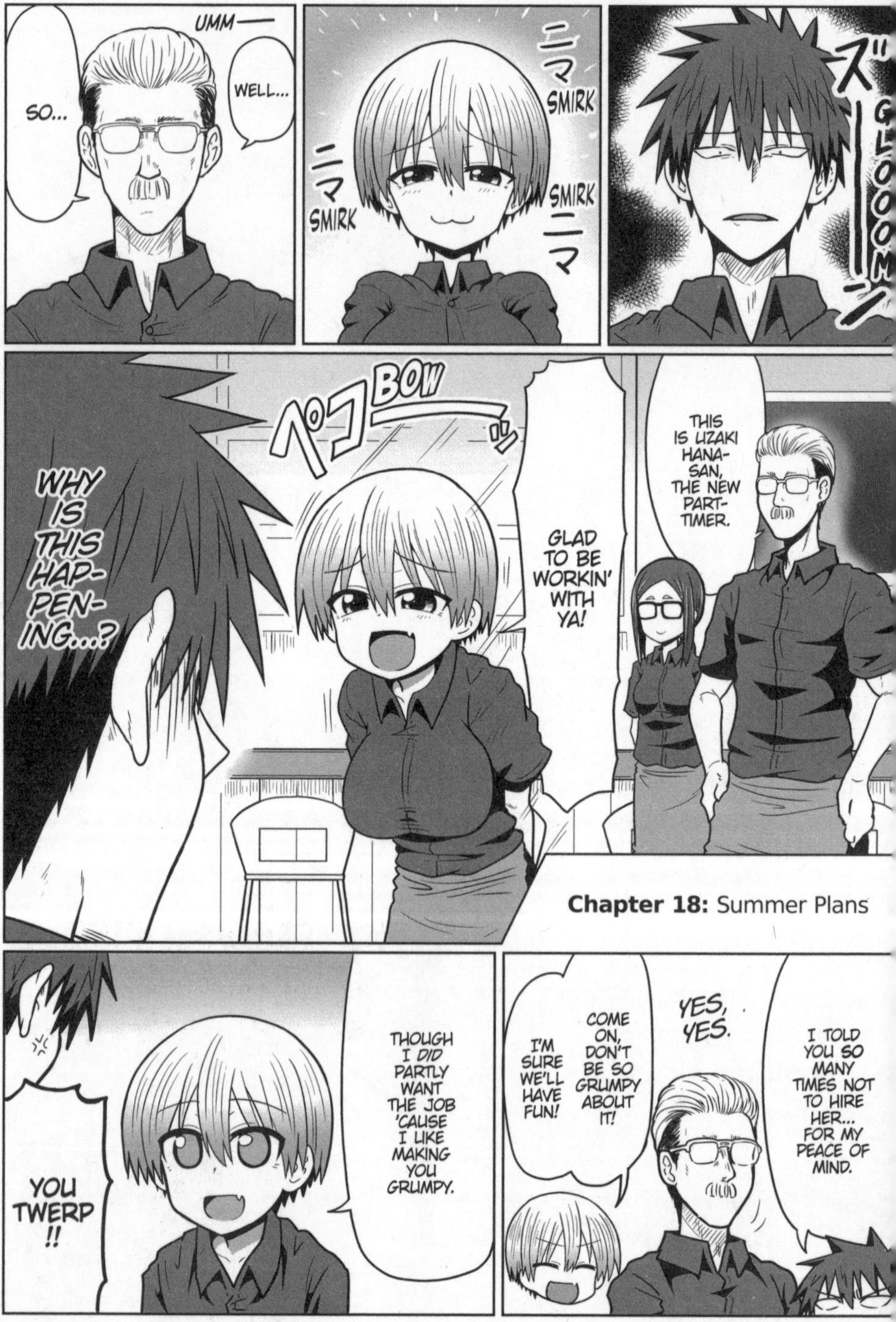
ズー
GLOOOOM
ニマ
SMIRK
SMIRK
ニマ
ニマ
SMIRK
UMM—
WELL...
SO...
THIS IS UZAKI HANA-SAN, THE NEW PART-TIMER.
GLAD TO BE WORKIN' WITH YA!
ペコ BOW
WHY IS THIS HAPPENING...?
Chapter 18: Summer Plans
I TOLD YOU SO MANY TIMES NOT TO HIRE HER... FOR MY PEACE OF MIND.
YES, YES.
COME ON, DON'T BE SO GRUMPY ABOUT IT!
I'M SURE WE'LL HAVE FUN!
THOUGH I DID PARTLY WANT THE JOB 'CAUSE I LIKE MAKING YOU GRUMPY.
YOU TWERP!!

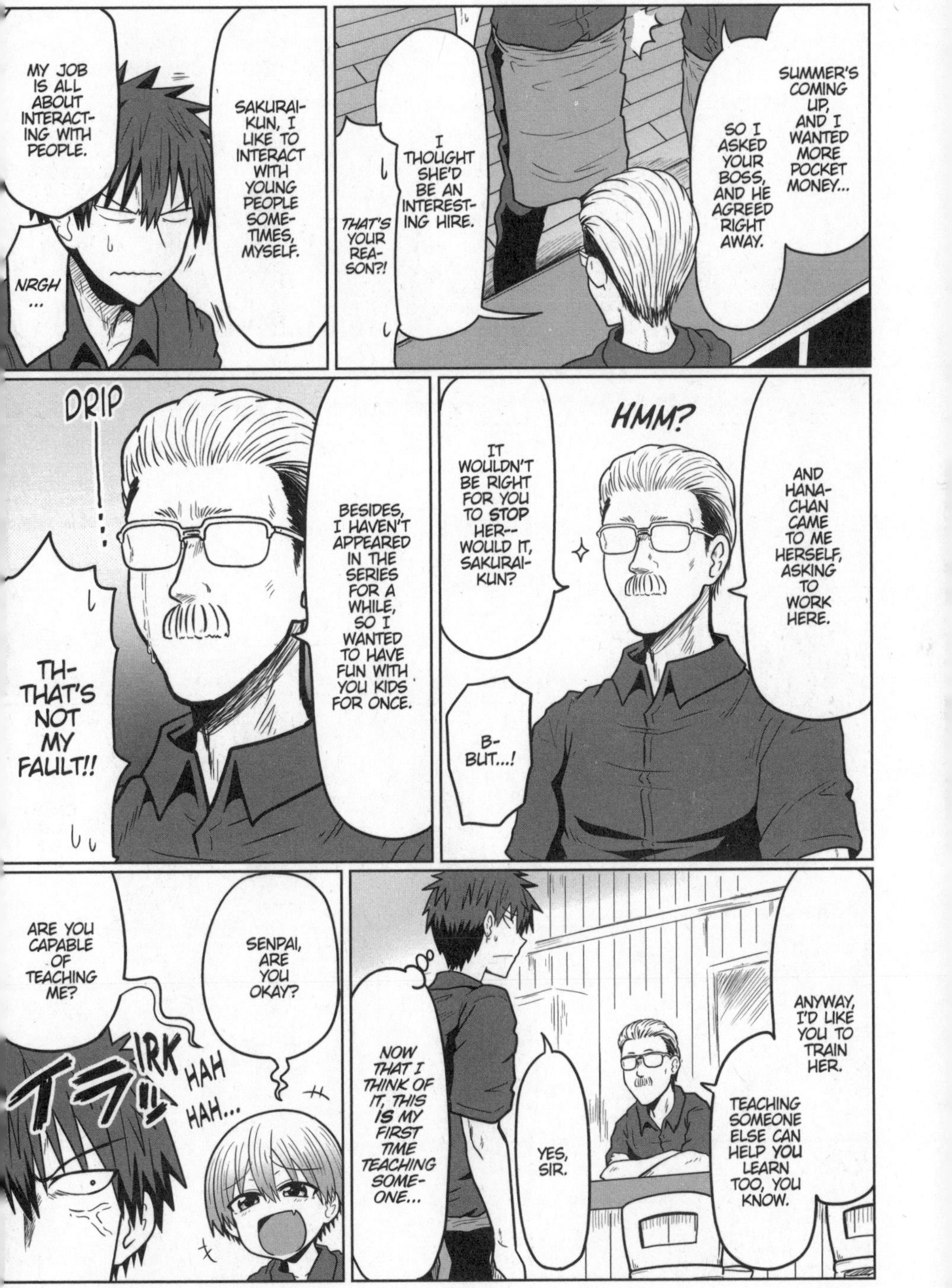
SUMMER'S COMING UP, AND I WANTED MORE POCKET MONEY...
SO I ASKED YOUR BOSS, AND HE AGREED RIGHT AWAY.
I THOUGHT SHE'D BE AN INTERESTING HIRE.
THAT'S YOUR REASON?!
SAKURAI-KUN, I LIKE TO INTERACT WITH YOUNG PEOPLE SOMETIMES, MYSELF.
MY JOB IS ALL ABOUT INTERACTING WITH PEOPLE.
NRGH...
AND HANA-CHAN CAME TO ME HERSELF, ASKING TO WORK HERE.
HMM?
IT WOULDN'T BE RIGHT FOR YOU TO STOP HER--WOULD IT, SAKURAI-KUN?
B-BUT...!
BESIDES, I HAVEN'T APPEARED IN THE SERIES FOR A WHILE, SO I WANTED TO HAVE FUN WITH YOU KIDS FOR ONCE.
DRIP
TH-THAT'S NOT MY FAULT!!
ANYWAY, I'D LIKE YOU TO TRAIN HER.
TEACHING SOMEONE ELSE CAN HELP YOU LEARN TOO, YOU KNOW.
YES, SIR.
NOW THAT I THINK OF IT, THIS IS MY FIRST TIME TEACHING SOMEONE...
SENPAI, ARE YOU OKAY?
ARE YOU CAPABLE OF TEACHING ME?
HAH HAH...
IRK

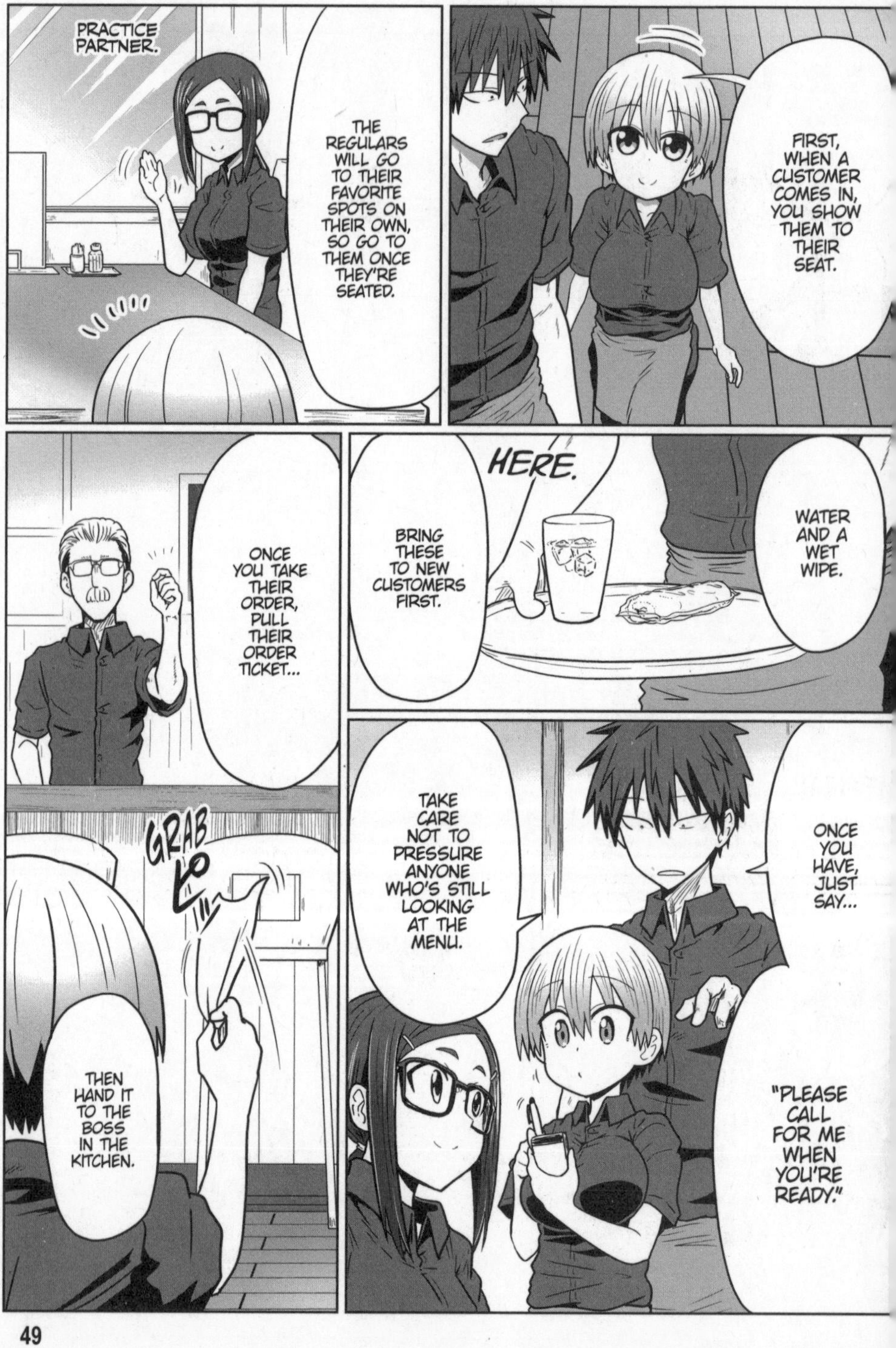
FIRST, WHEN A CUSTOMER COMES IN, YOU SHOW THEM TO THEIR SEAT.
THE REGULARS WILL GO TO THEIR FAVORITE SPOTS ON THEIR OWN, SO GO TO THEM ONCE THEY'RE SEATED.
PRACTICE PARTNER.
WATER AND A WET WIPE.
HERE.
BRING THESE TO NEW CUSTOMERS FIRST.
ONCE YOU HAVE, JUST SAY...
"PLEASE CALL FOR ME WHEN YOU'RE READY."
TAKE CARE NOT TO PRESSURE ANYONE WHO'S STILL LOOKING AT THE MENU.
ONCE YOU TAKE THEIR ORDER, PULL THEIR ORDER TICKET...
GRAB
THEN HAND IT TO THE BOSS IN THE KITCHEN.

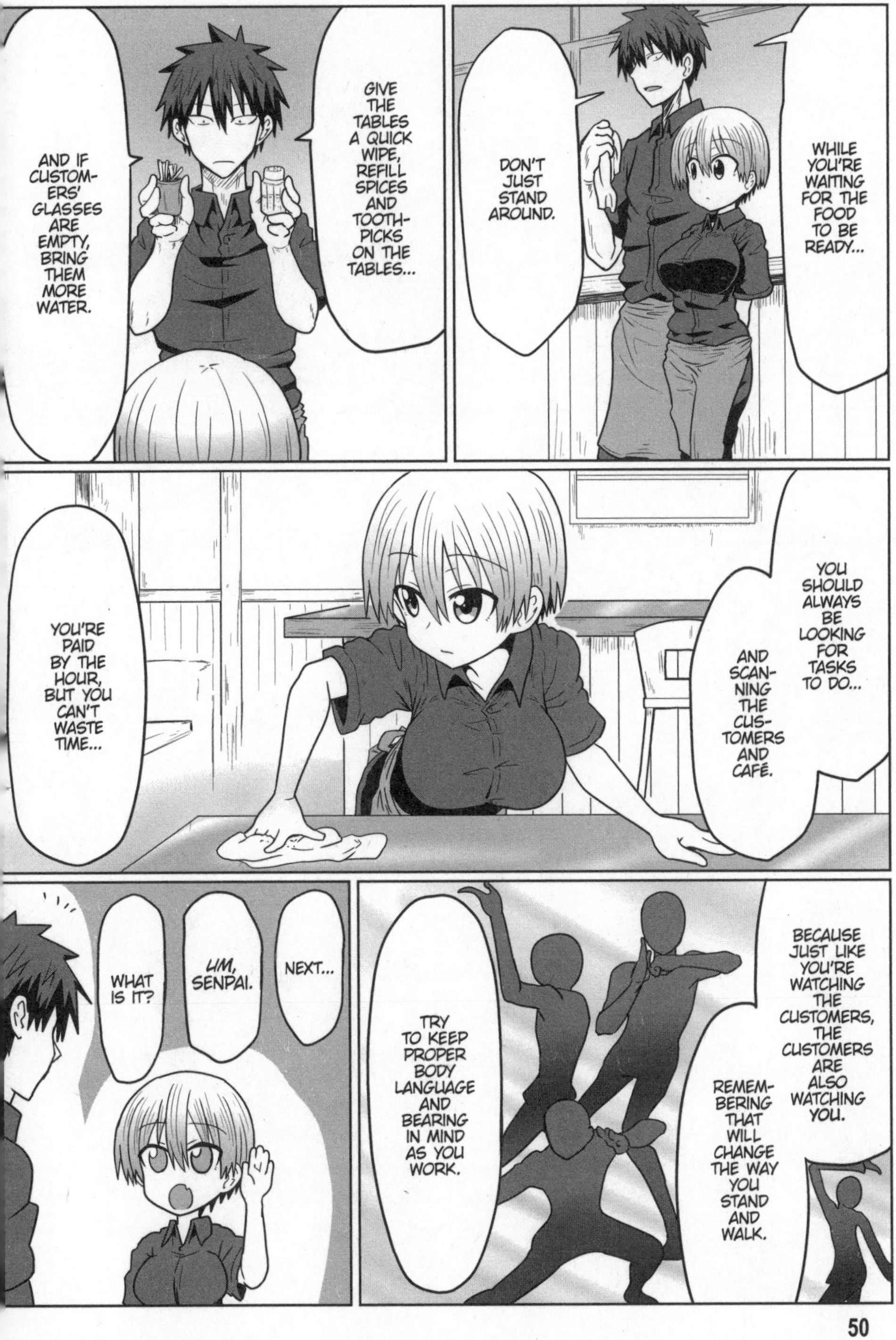

WHILE YOU'RE WAITING FOR THE FOOD TO BE READY...
DON'T JUST STAND AROUND.
GIVE THE TABLES A QUICK WIPE, REFILL SPICES AND TOOTHPICKS ON THE TABLES...
AND IF CUSTOMERS' GLASSES ARE EMPTY, BRING THEM MORE WATER.
YOU SHOULD ALWAYS BE LOOKING FOR TASKS TO DO...
AND SCANNING THE CUSTOMERS AND CAFÉ.
YOU'RE PAID BY THE HOUR, BUT YOU CAN'T WASTE TIME...
BECAUSE JUST LIKE YOU'RE WATCHING THE CUSTOMERS, THE CUSTOMERS ARE ALSO WATCHING YOU.
REMEMBERING THAT WILL CHANGE THE WAY YOU STAND AND WALK.
TRY TO KEEP PROPER BODY LANGUAGE AND BEARING IN MIND AS YOU WORK.
NEXT...
UM, SENPAI.
WHAT IS IT?

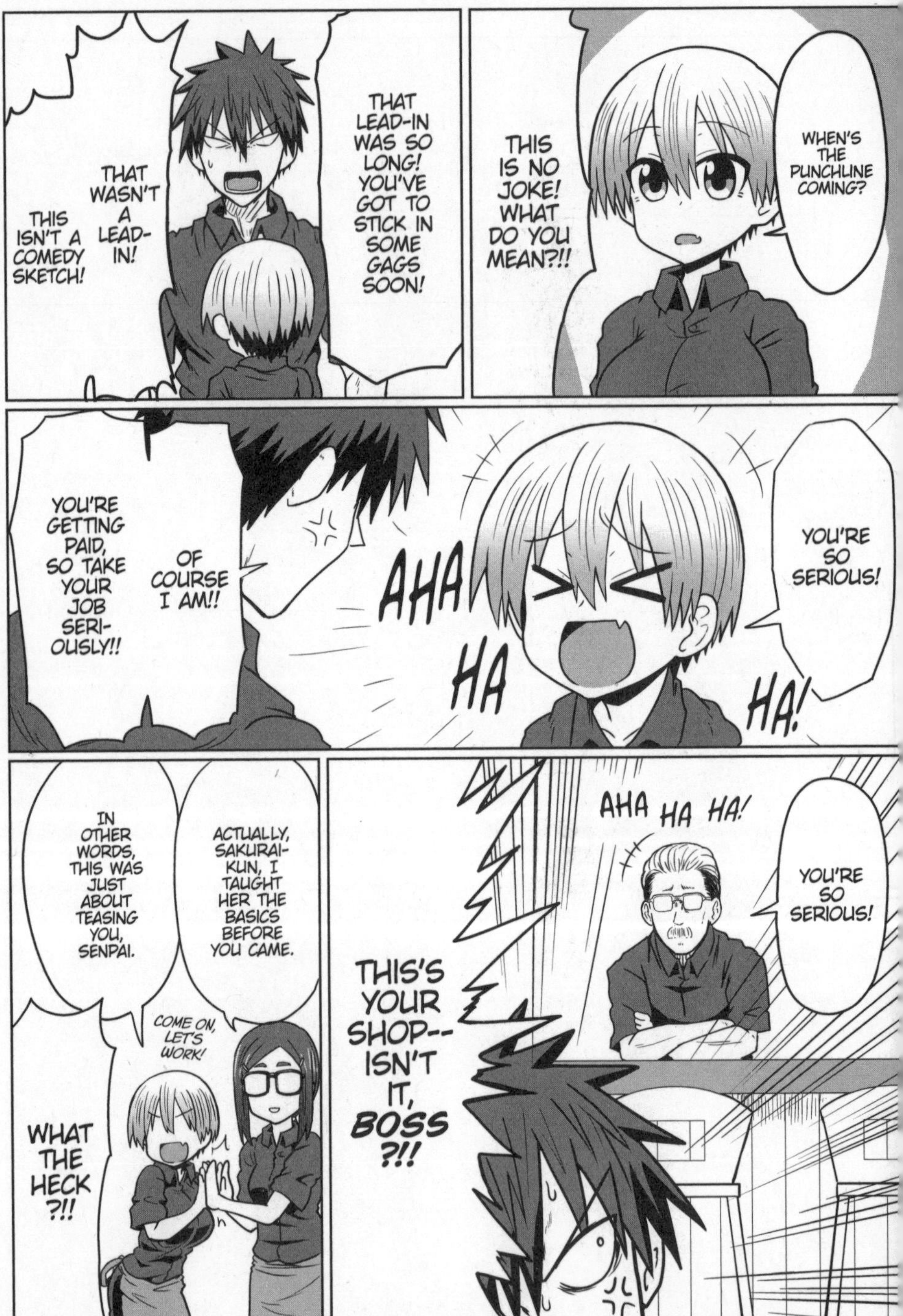
WHEN'S THE PUNCHLINE COMING?
THIS IS NO JOKE! WHAT DO YOU MEAN?!!
THAT LEAD-IN WAS SO LONG! YOU'VE GOT TO STICK IN SOME GAGS SOON!
THAT WASN'T A LEAD-IN!
THIS ISN'T A COMEDY SKETCH!
YOU'RE SO SERIOUS!
AHA HA HA!
OF COURSE I AM!!
YOU'RE GETTING PAID, SO TAKE YOUR JOB SERIOUSLY!!
YOU'RE SO SERIOUS!
AHA HA HA!
THIS'S YOUR SHOP--ISN'T IT, BOSS?!!
ACTUALLY, SAKURAI-KUN, I TAUGHT HER THE BASICS BEFORE YOU CAME.
IN OTHER WORDS, THIS WAS JUST ABOUT TEASING YOU, SENPAI.
COME ON, LET'S WORK!
WHAT THE HECK?!!

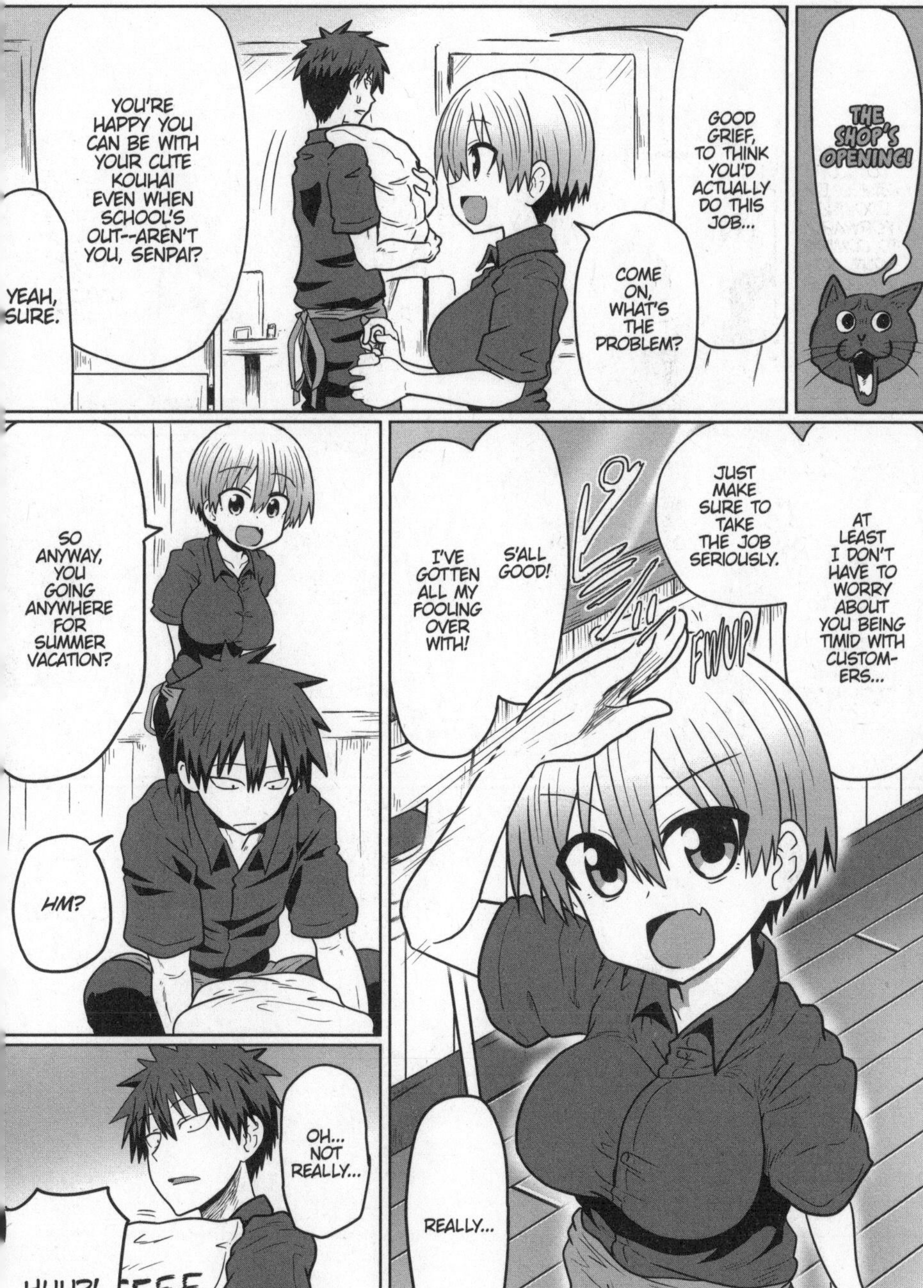
THE SHOP'S OPENING!
GOOD GRIEF, TO THINK YOU'D ACTUALLY DO THIS JOB...
COME ON, WHAT'S THE PROBLEM?
YOU'RE HAPPY YOU CAN BE WITH YOUR CUTE KOUHAI EVEN WHEN SCHOOL'S OUT--AREN'T YOU, SENPAI?
YEAH, SURE.
AT LEAST I DON'T HAVE TO WORRY ABOUT YOU BEING TIMID WITH CUSTOMERS...
JUST MAKE SURE TO TAKE THE JOB SERIOUSLY.
S'ALL GOOD!
I'VE GOTTEN ALL MY FOOLING OVER WITH!
FWUP
REALLY...
SO ANYWAY, YOU GOING ANYWHERE FOR SUMMER VACATION?
HM?
OH... NOT REALLY...
HUH?!
FFEE
20Kg

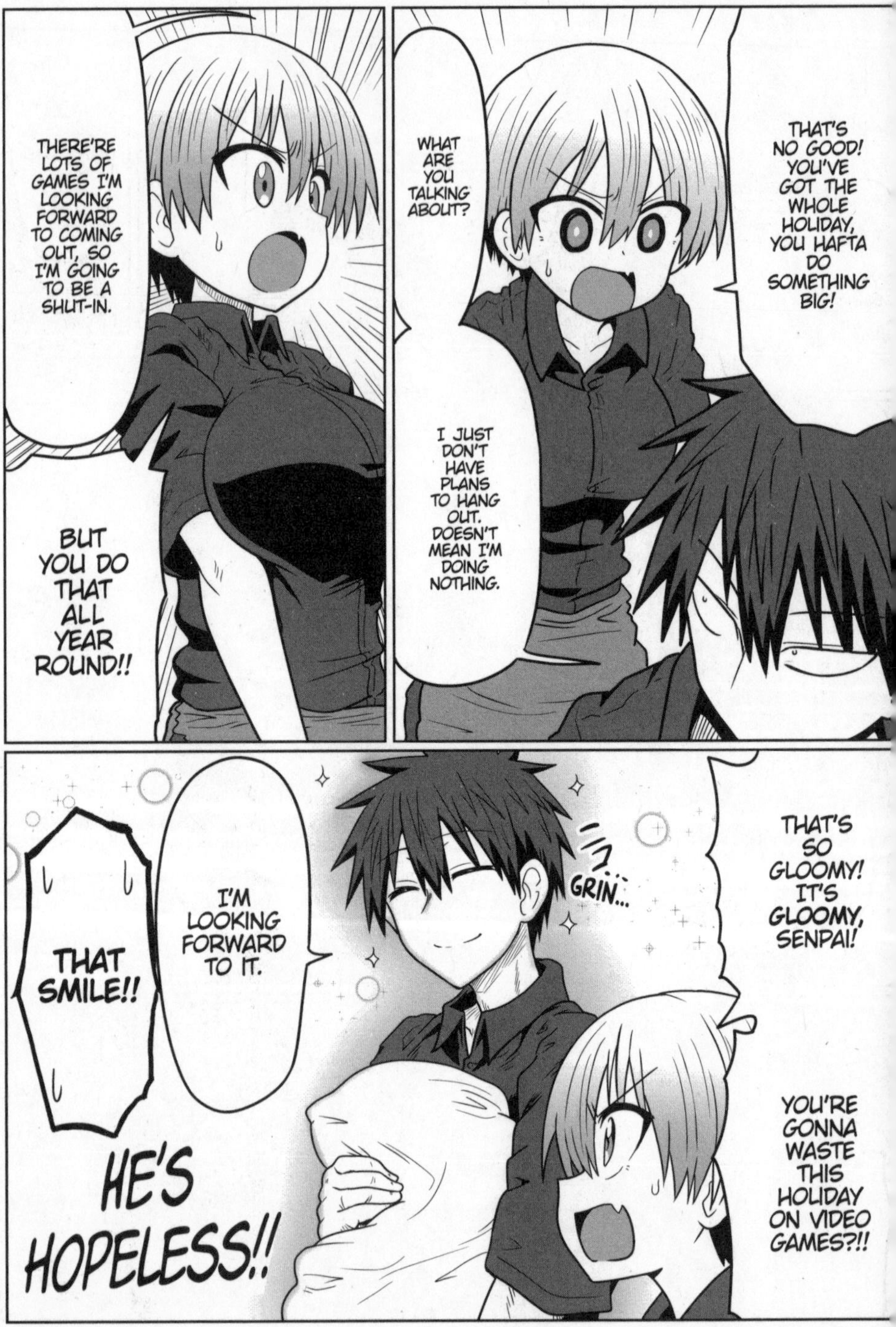
THAT'S NO GOOD! YOU'VE GOT THE WHOLE HOLIDAY, YOU HAFTA DO SOMETHING BIG!
WHAT ARE YOU TALKING ABOUT?
I JUST DON'T HAVE PLANS TO HANG OUT. DOESN'T MEAN I'M DOING NOTHING.
THERE'RE LOTS OF GAMES I'M LOOKING FORWARD TO COMING OUT, SO I'M GOING TO BE A SHUT-IN.
BUT YOU DO THAT ALL YEAR ROUND!!
THAT'S SO GLOOMY! IT'S GLOOMY, SENPAI!
GRIN...
I'M LOOKING FORWARD TO IT.
THAT SMILE!!
YOU'RE GONNA WASTE THIS HOLIDAY ON VIDEO GAMES?!!
HE'S HOPELESS!!

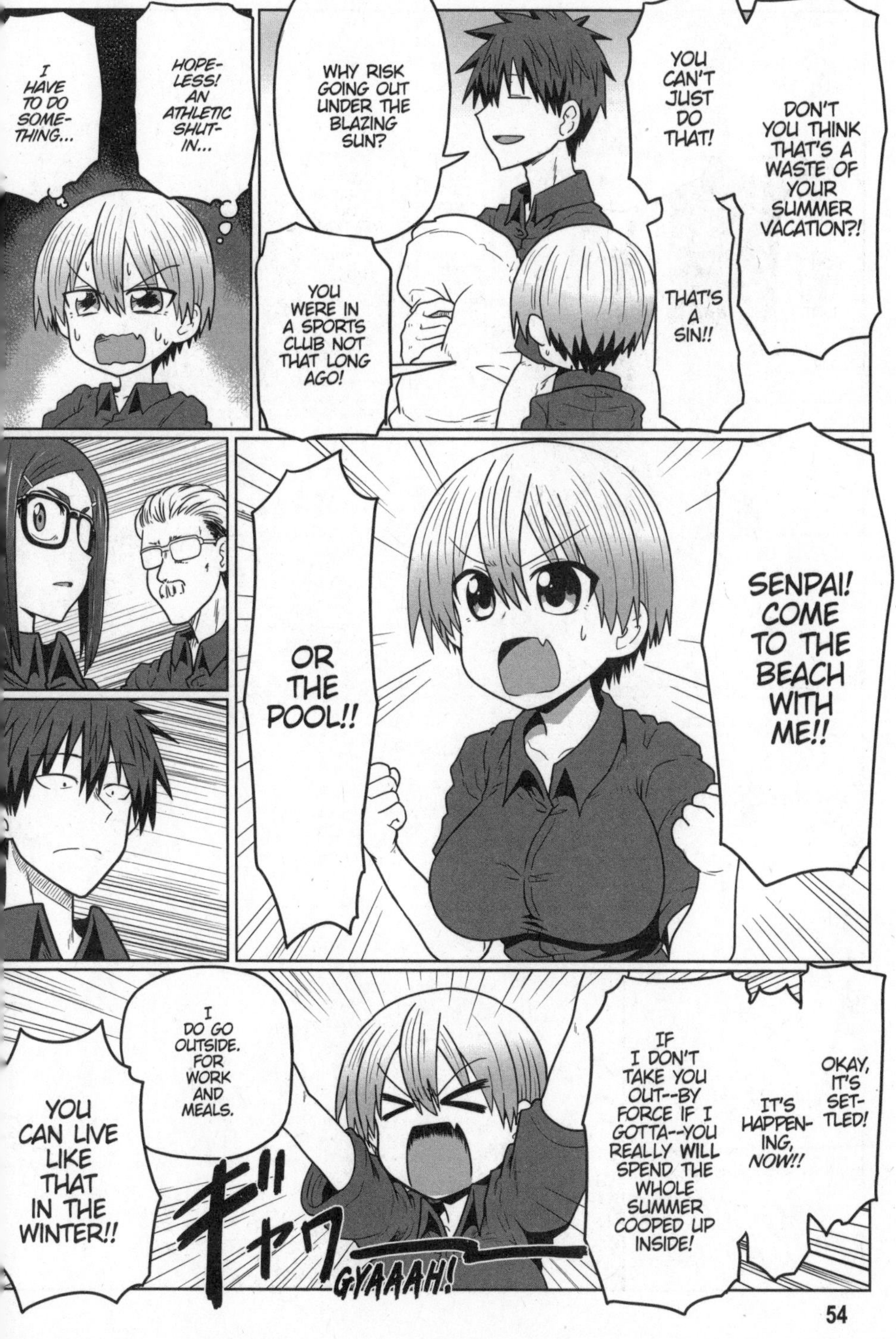
DON'T YOU THINK THAT'S A WASTE OF YOUR SUMMER VACATION?!
YOU CAN'T JUST DO THAT!
THAT'S A SIN!!
WHY RISK GOING OUT UNDER THE BLAZING SUN?
YOU WERE IN A SPORTS CLUB NOT THAT LONG AGO!
HOPE-LESS! AN ATHLETIC SHUT-IN...
I HAVE TO DO SOME-THING...
SENPAI! COME TO THE BEACH WITH ME!!
OR THE POOL!!
OKAY, IT'S SET-TLED!
IT'S HAPPEN-ING, NOW!!
IF I DON'T TAKE YOU OUT--BY FORCE IF I GOTTA--YOU REALLY WILL SPEND THE WHOLE SUMMER COOPED UP INSIDE!
I DO GO OUTSIDE. FOR WORK AND MEALS.
YOU CAN LIVE LIKE THAT IN THE WINTER!!
ギャウ
GYAAAH!

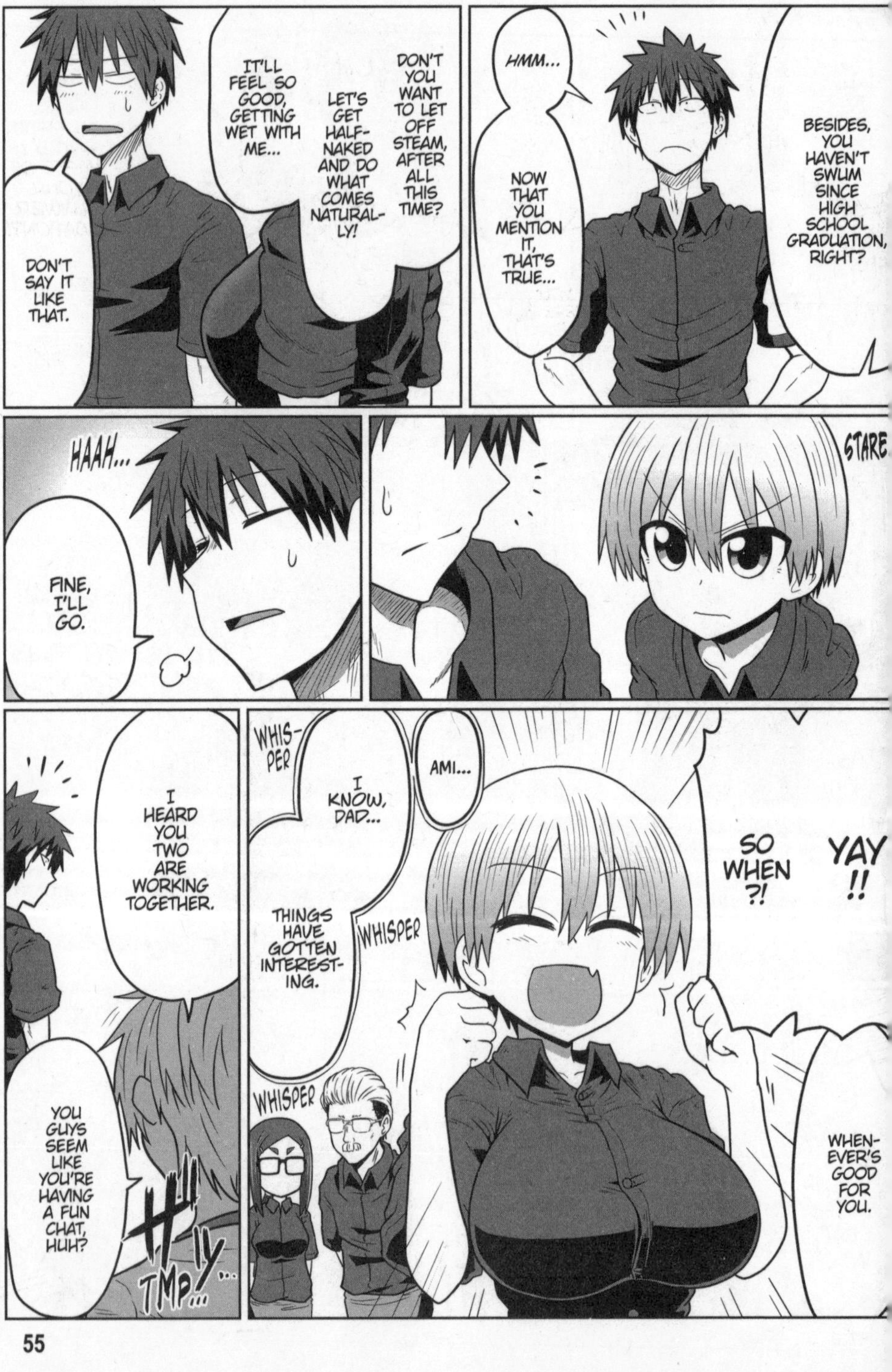
BESIDES, YOU HAVEN'T SWUM SINCE HIGH SCHOOL GRADUATION, RIGHT?
HMM...
NOW THAT YOU MENTION IT, THAT'S TRUE...
DON'T YOU WANT TO LET OFF STEAM, AFTER ALL THIS TIME?
LET'S GET HALF-NAKED AND DO WHAT COMES NATURALLY!
IT'LL FEEL SO GOOD, GETTING WET WITH ME...
DON'T SAY IT LIKE THAT.
STARE
HAAH...
FINE, I'LL GO.
YAY!!
SO WHEN?!
WHENEVER'S GOOD FOR YOU.
AMI...
I KNOW, DAD...
WHISPER
WHISPER
THINGS HAVE GOTTEN INTERESTING.
WHISPER
I HEARD YOU TWO ARE WORKING TOGETHER.
YOU GUYS SEEM LIKE YOU'RE HAVING A FUN CHAT, HUH?
TMP!...

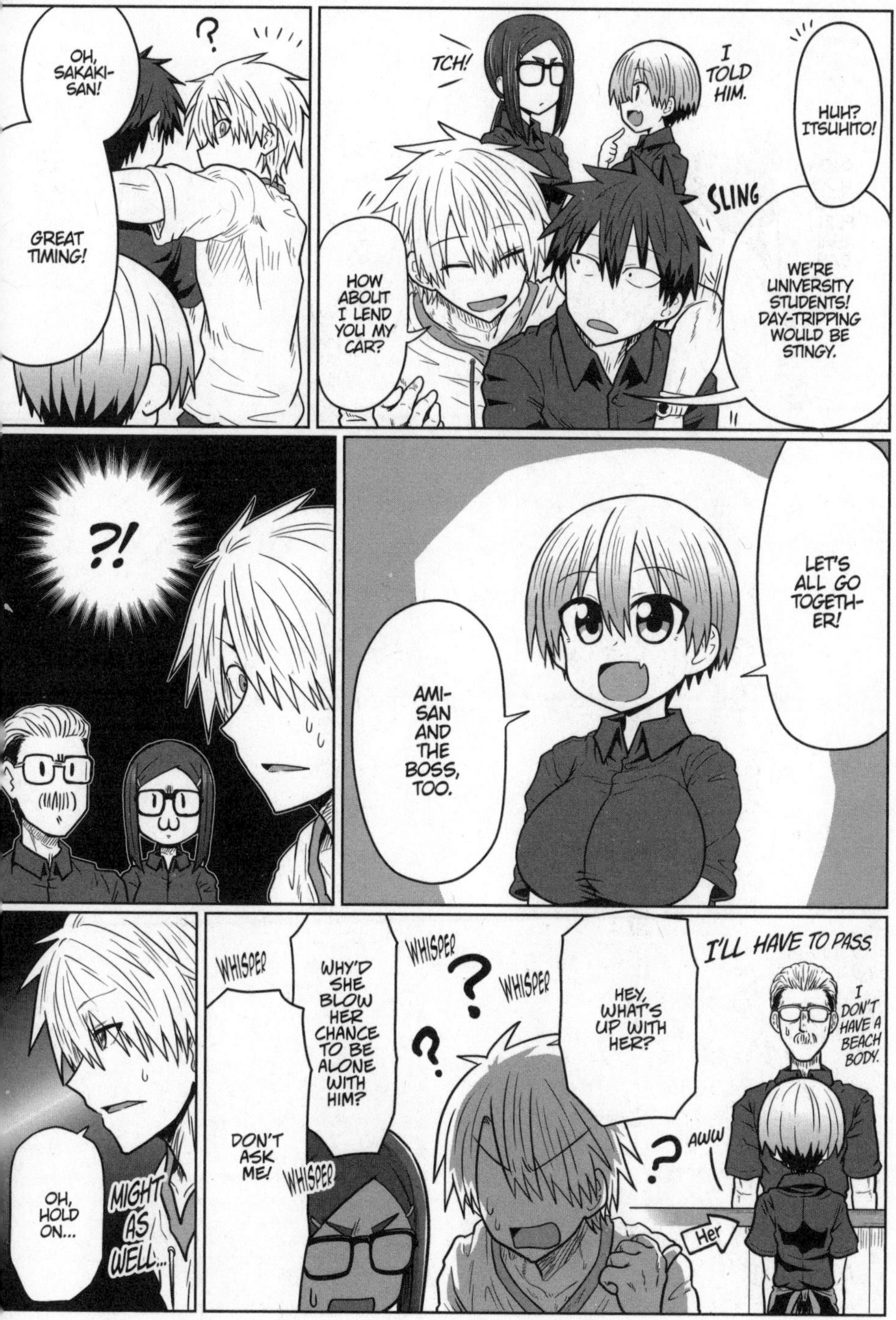
HUH? ITSUHITO!
SLING
WE'RE UNIVERSITY STUDENTS! DAY-TRIPPING WOULD BE STINGY.
I TOLD HIM.
TCH!
HOW ABOUT I LEND YOU MY CAR?
?
OH, SAKAKI-SAN!
GREAT TIMING!
LET'S ALL GO TOGETH-ER!
AMI-SAN AND THE BOSS, TOO.
?!
I'LL HAVE TO PASS.
I DON'T HAVE A BEACH BODY.
AWW
Her
HEY, WHAT'S UP WITH HER?
WHISPER
WHISPER
WHY'D SHE BLOW HER CHANCE TO BE ALONE WITH HIM?
WHISPER
DON'T ASK ME!
MIGHT AS WELL...
OH, HOLD ON...

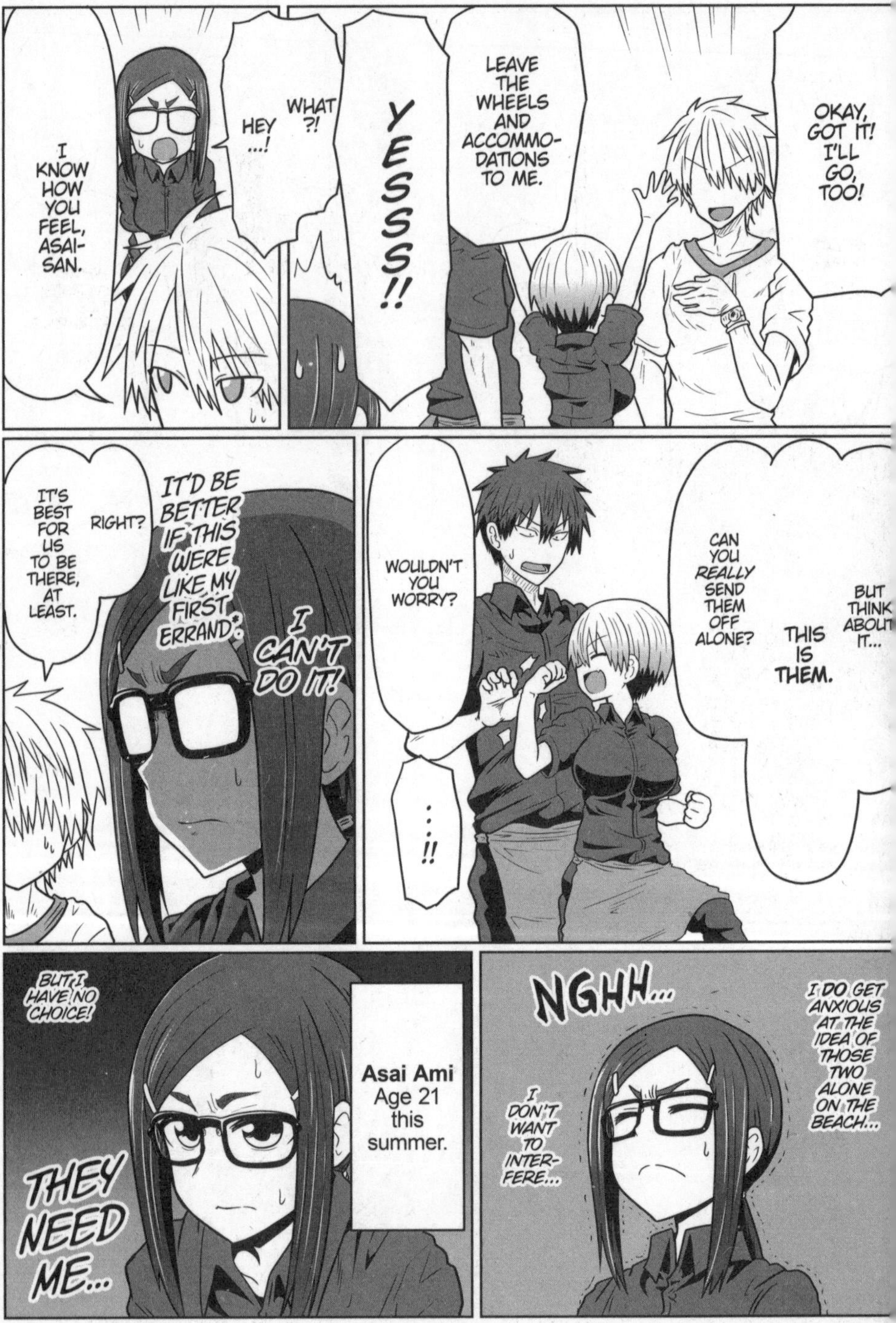
OKAY, GOT IT! I'LL GO, TOO!
LEAVE THE WHEELS AND ACCOMMODATIONS TO ME.
YESSS!!
WHAT ?!
HEY ...!
I KNOW HOW YOU FEEL, ASAI-SAN.
BUT THINK ABOUT IT...
THIS IS THEM.
CAN YOU REALLY SEND THEM OFF ALONE?
WOULDN'T YOU WORRY?
...!!
IT'D BE BETTER IF THIS WERE LIKE MY FIRST ERRAND*.
I CAN'T DO IT!
RIGHT?
IT'S BEST FOR US TO BE THERE, AT LEAST.
I DO GET ANXIOUS AT THE IDEA OF THOSE TWO ALONE ON THE BEACH...
NGHH...
I DON'T WANT TO INTERFERE...
Asai Ami Age 21 this summer.
BUT, I HAVE NO CHOICE!
THEY NEED ME...

*A variety show that films young children going out to perform their first errand, and their general confusion and inexperience.

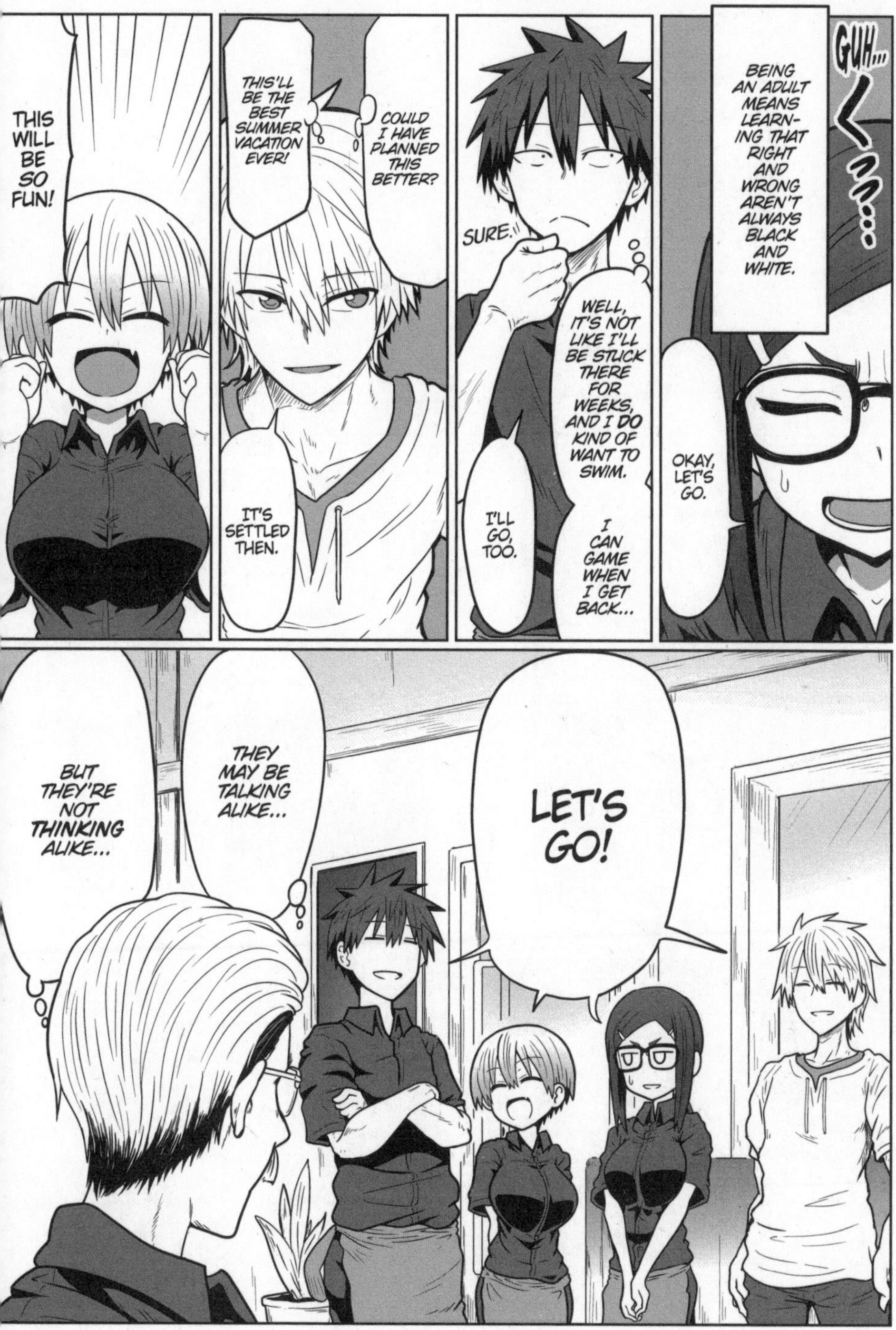
GUH...
くっ...
BEING AN ADULT MEANS LEARNING THAT RIGHT AND WRONG AREN'T ALWAYS BLACK AND WHITE.
OKAY, LET'S GO.
SURE.
WELL, IT'S NOT LIKE I'LL BE STUCK THERE FOR WEEKS, AND I DO KIND OF WANT TO SWIM.
I CAN GAME WHEN I GET BACK...
I'LL GO, TOO.
COULD I HAVE PLANNED THIS BETTER?
THIS'LL BE THE BEST SUMMER VACATION EVER!
IT'S SETTLED THEN.
THIS WILL BE SO FUN!
LET'S GO!
THEY MAY BE TALKING ALIKE...
BUT THEY'RE NOT THINKING ALIKE...

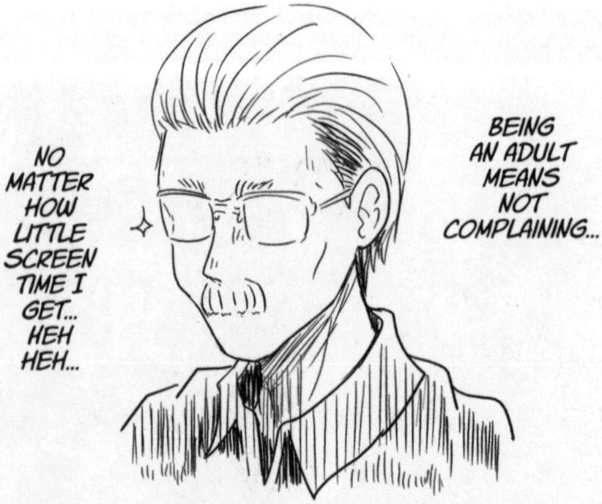
BEING AN ADULT MEANS NOT COMPLAINING...
NO MATTER HOW LITTLE SCREEN TIME I GET... HEH HEH...

**Uzaki-chan ☆ Wants to Hang Out!**

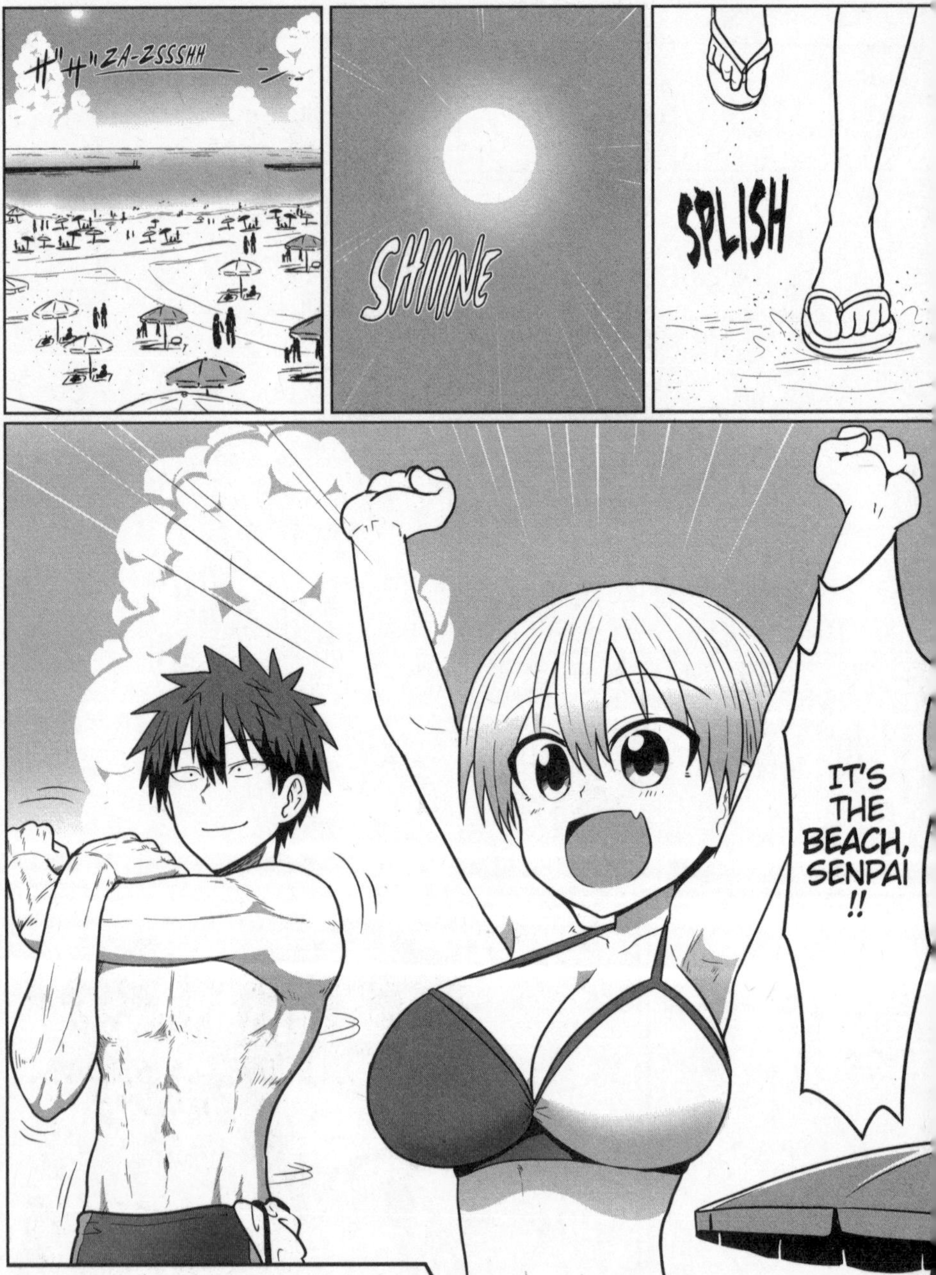
SPLISH
SHIIINE
ZA-ZSSSHH
IT'S THE BEACH, SENPAI!!

**Chapter 19:**
How I Began My Summer Vacation

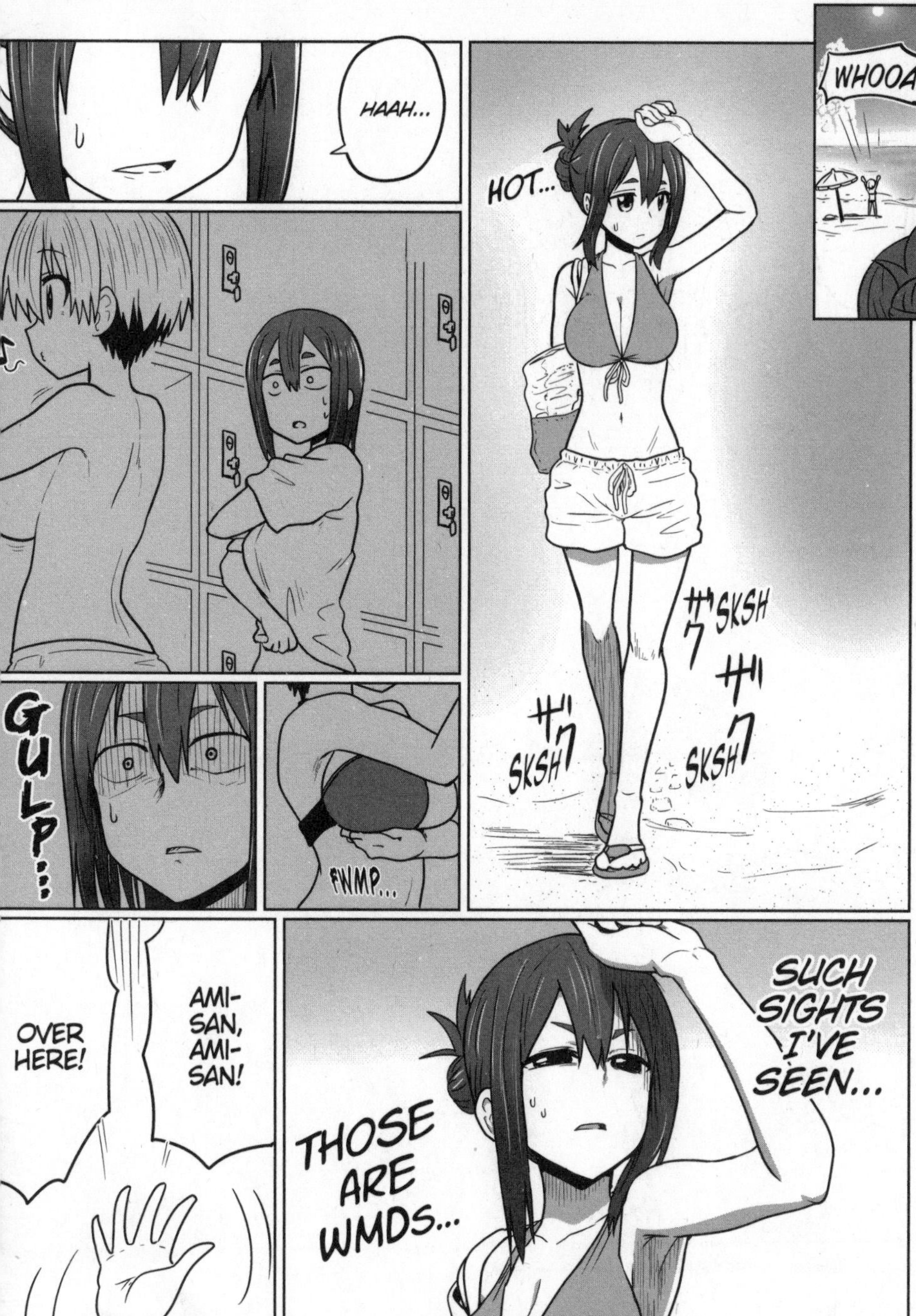
WHOOA!!
HOT...
ザク SKSH
ザク SKSH
ザク SKSH
HAAH...
FWMP...
GULP...
SUCH SIGHTS I'VE SEEN...
THOSE ARE WMDS...
AMI-SAN, AMI-SAN!
OVER HERE!

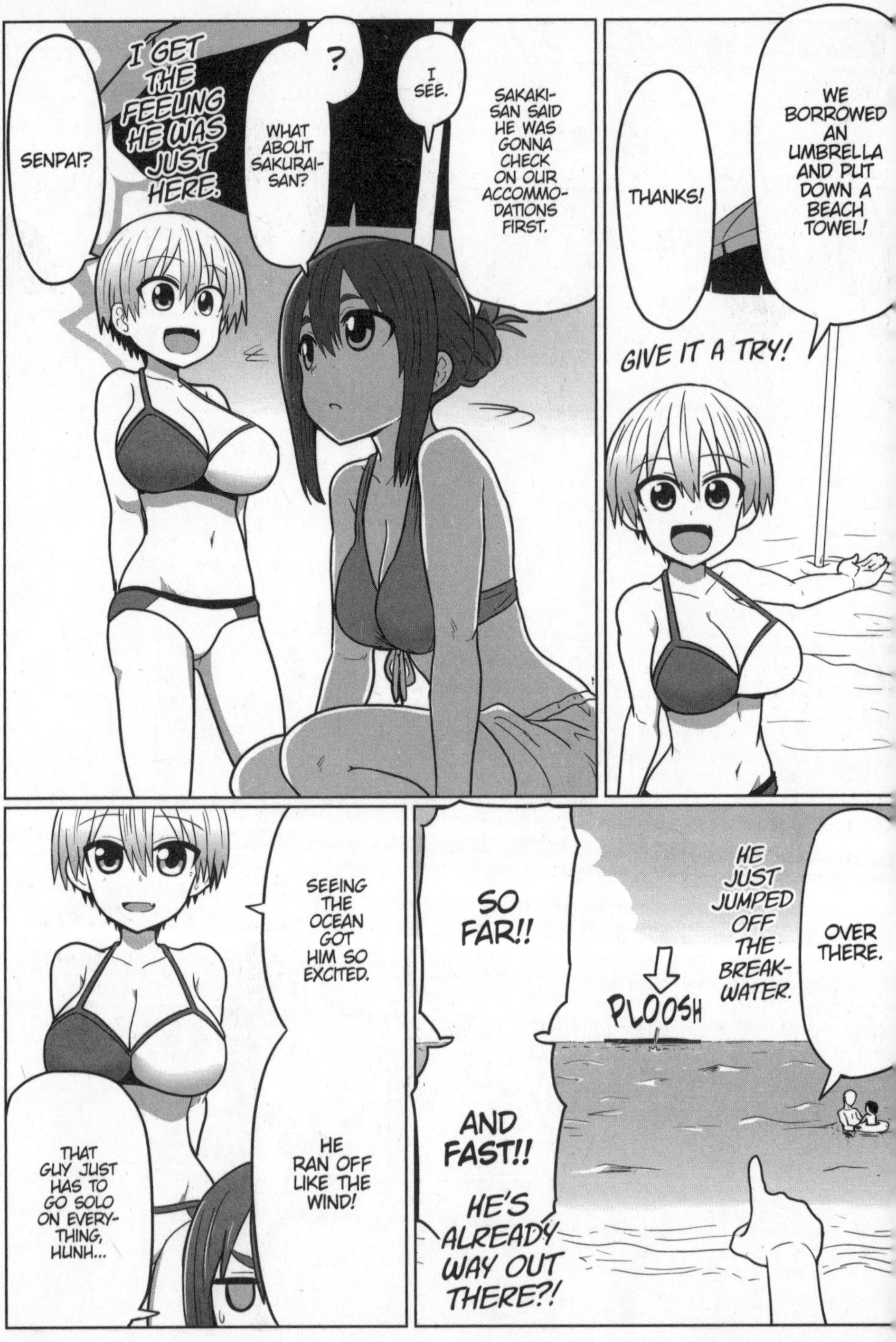
WE BORROWED AN UMBRELLA AND PUT DOWN A BEACH TOWEL!
GIVE IT A TRY!
THANKS!
SAKAKI-SAN SAID HE WAS GONNA CHECK ON OUR ACCOMMODATIONS FIRST.
I SEE.
WHAT ABOUT SAKURAI-SAN?
?
I GET THE FEELING HE WAS JUST HERE.
SENPAI?
OVER THERE.
HE JUST JUMPED OFF THE BREAKWATER.
PLOOSH
SO FAR!!
AND FAST!!
HE'S ALREADY WAY OUT THERE?!
SEEING THE OCEAN GOT HIM SO EXCITED.
HE RAN OFF LIKE THE WIND!
THAT GUY JUST HAS TO GO SOLO ON EVERYTHING, HUNH...

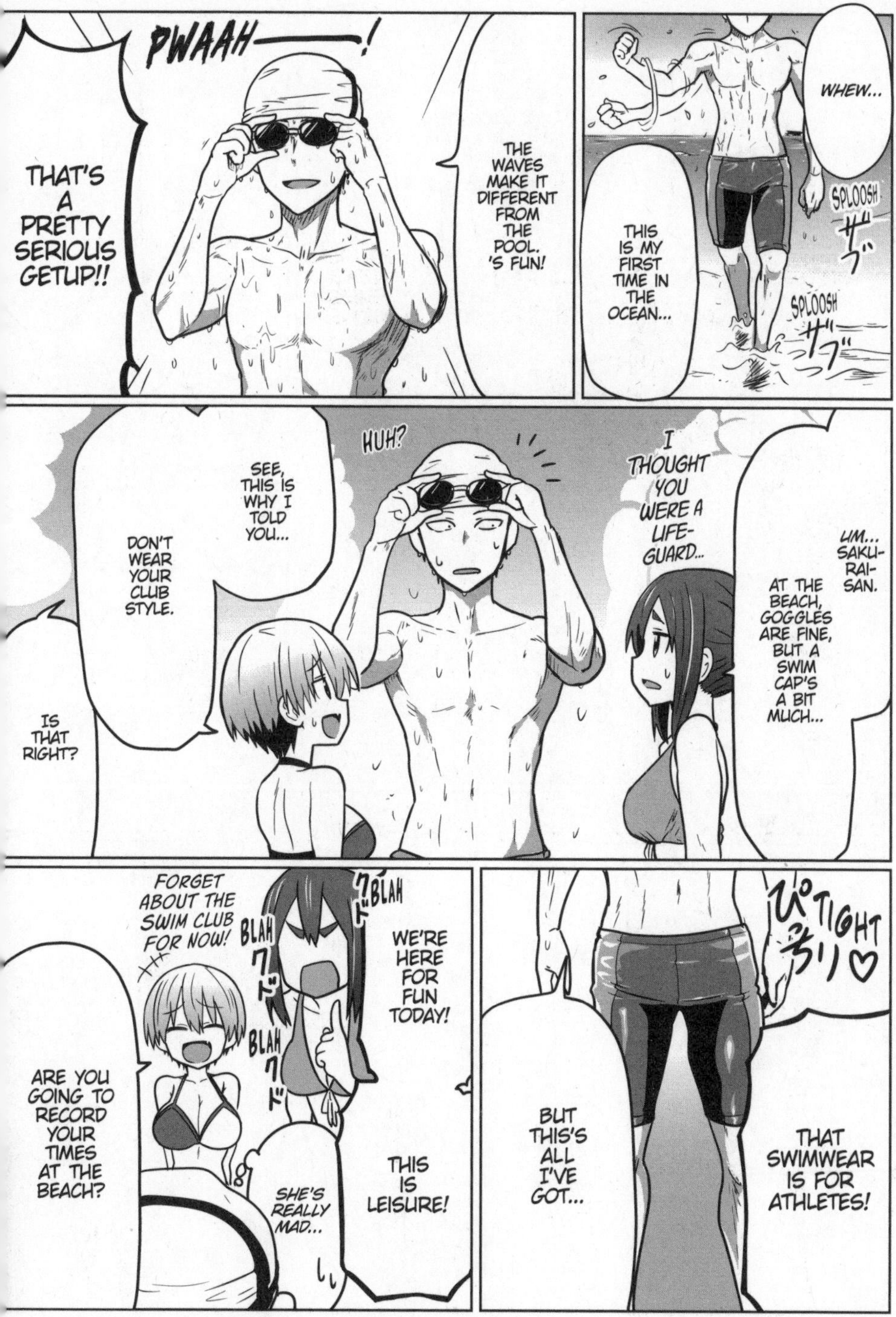
WHEW...
THIS IS MY FIRST TIME IN THE OCEAN...
SPLOOSH
SPLOOSH
PWAAH———!
THE WAVES MAKE IT DIFFERENT FROM THE POOL. 'S FUN!
THAT'S A PRETTY SERIOUS GETUP!!
UM... SAKURAI-SAN.
AT THE BEACH, GOGGLES ARE FINE, BUT A SWIM CAP'S A BIT MUCH...
I THOUGHT YOU WERE A LIFEGUARD...
HUH?
SEE, THIS IS WHY I TOLD YOU...
DON'T WEAR YOUR CLUB STYLE.
IS THAT RIGHT?
TIGHT
THAT SWIMWEAR IS FOR ATHLETES!
BUT THIS'S ALL I'VE GOT...
FORGET ABOUT THE SWIM CLUB FOR NOW!
WE'RE HERE FOR FUN TODAY!
BLAH
BLAH
BLAH
THIS IS LEISURE!
SHE'S REALLY MAD...
ARE YOU GOING TO RECORD YOUR TIMES AT THE BEACH?

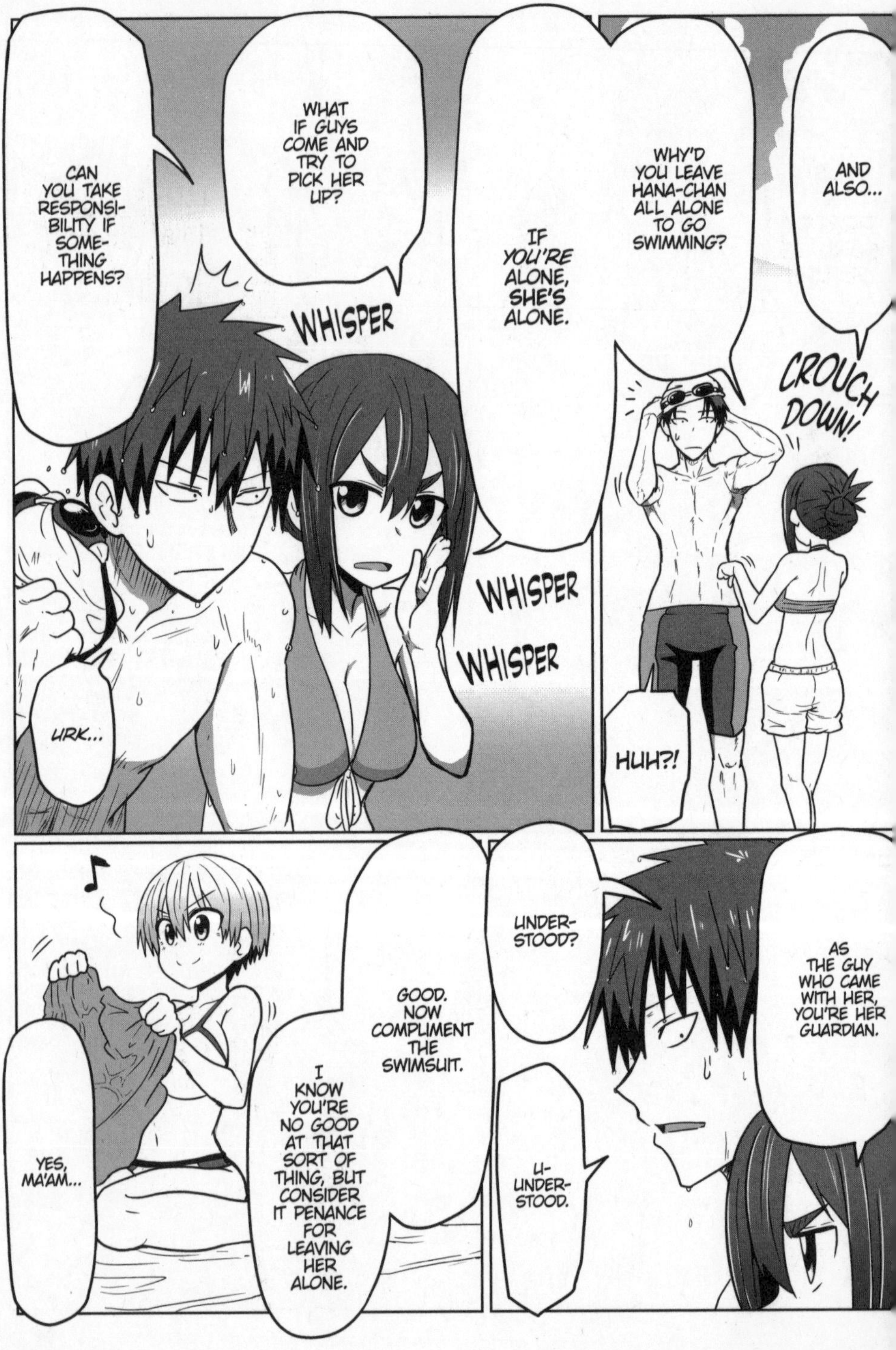
AND ALSO...
WHY'D YOU LEAVE HANA-CHAN ALL ALONE TO GO SWIMMING?
CROUCH DOWN!
HUH?!
IF YOU'RE ALONE, SHE'S ALONE.
WHAT IF GUYS COME AND TRY TO PICK HER UP?
CAN YOU TAKE RESPONSIBILITY IF SOMETHING HAPPENS?
WHISPER
WHISPER
WHISPER
URK...
AS THE GUY WHO CAME WITH HER, YOU'RE HER GUARDIAN.
UNDERSTOOD?
U-UNDERSTOOD.
GOOD. NOW COMPLIMENT THE SWIMSUIT.
I KNOW YOU'RE NO GOOD AT THAT SORT OF THING, BUT CONSIDER IT PENANCE FOR LEAVING HER ALONE.
YES, MA'AM...

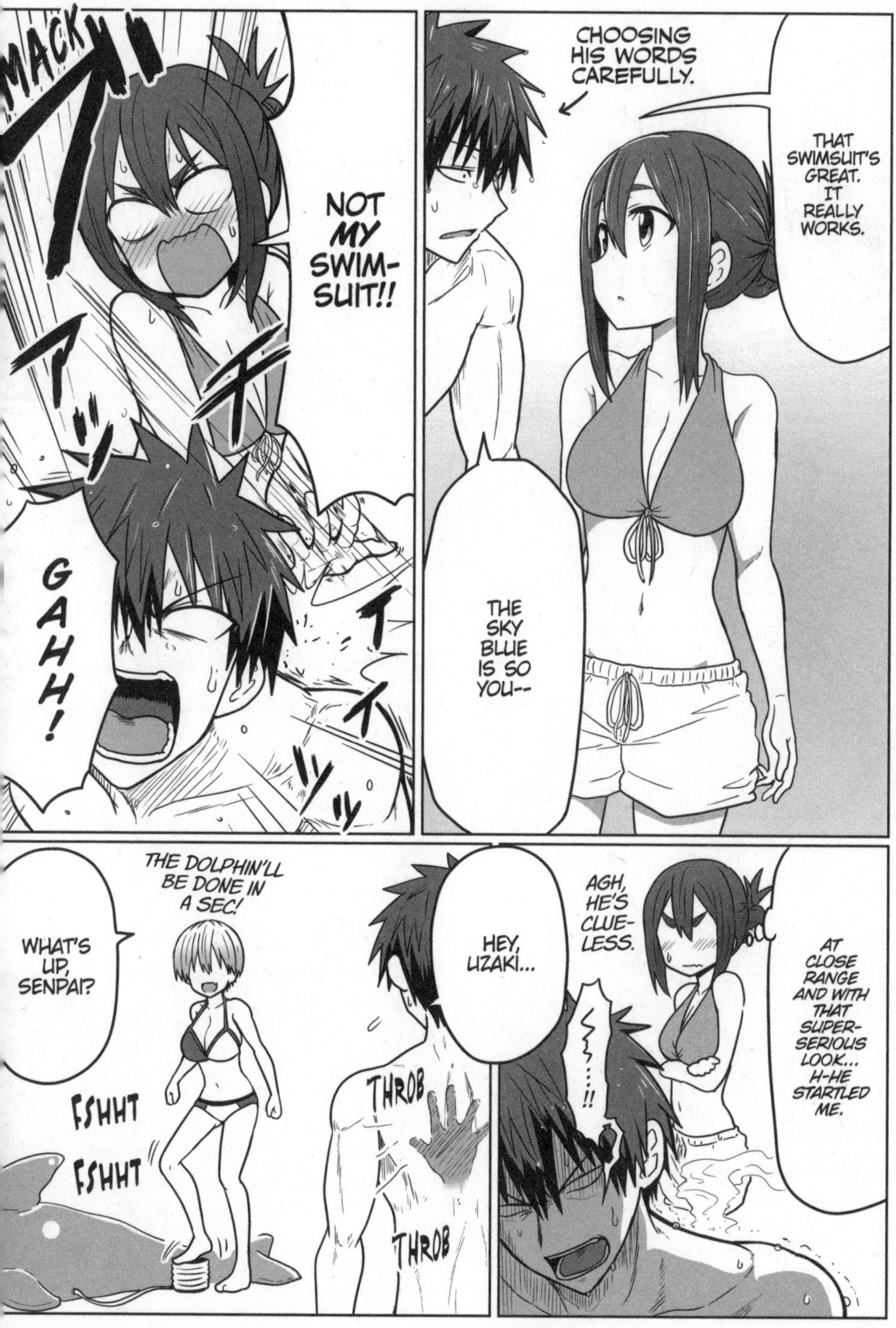
THAT SWIMSUIT'S GREAT. IT REALLY WORKS.
CHOOSING HIS WORDS CAREFULLY.
THE SKY BLUE IS SO YOU--
MACK
NOT MY SWIM-SUIT!!
GAHH!
AT CLOSE RANGE AND WITH THAT SUPER-SERIOUS LOOK... H-HE STARTLED ME.
AGH, HE'S CLUELESS.
HEY, UZAKI...
THROB
THROB
THE DOLPHIN'LL BE DONE IN A SEC!
WHAT'S UP, SENPAI?
FSHHT
FSHHT

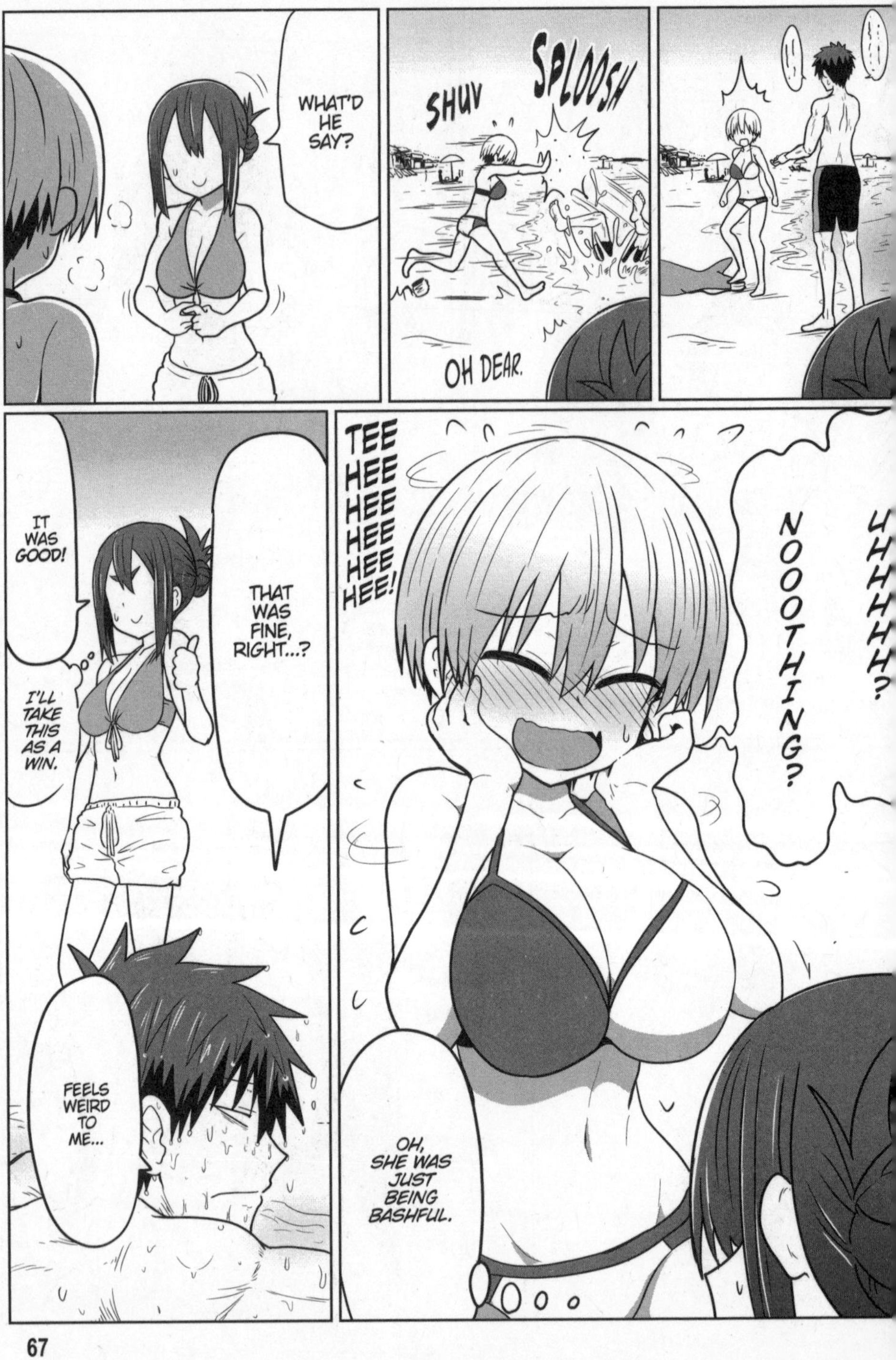
SHUV
SPLOOSH
OH DEAR.
WHAT'D HE SAY?
UHHHHHH?
NOOOTHING?
TEE HEE HEE HEE HEE HEE HEE!
OH, SHE WAS JUST BEING BASHFUL.
THAT WAS FINE, RIGHT...?
IT WAS GOOD!
I'LL TAKE THIS AS A WIN.
FEELS WEIRD TO ME...

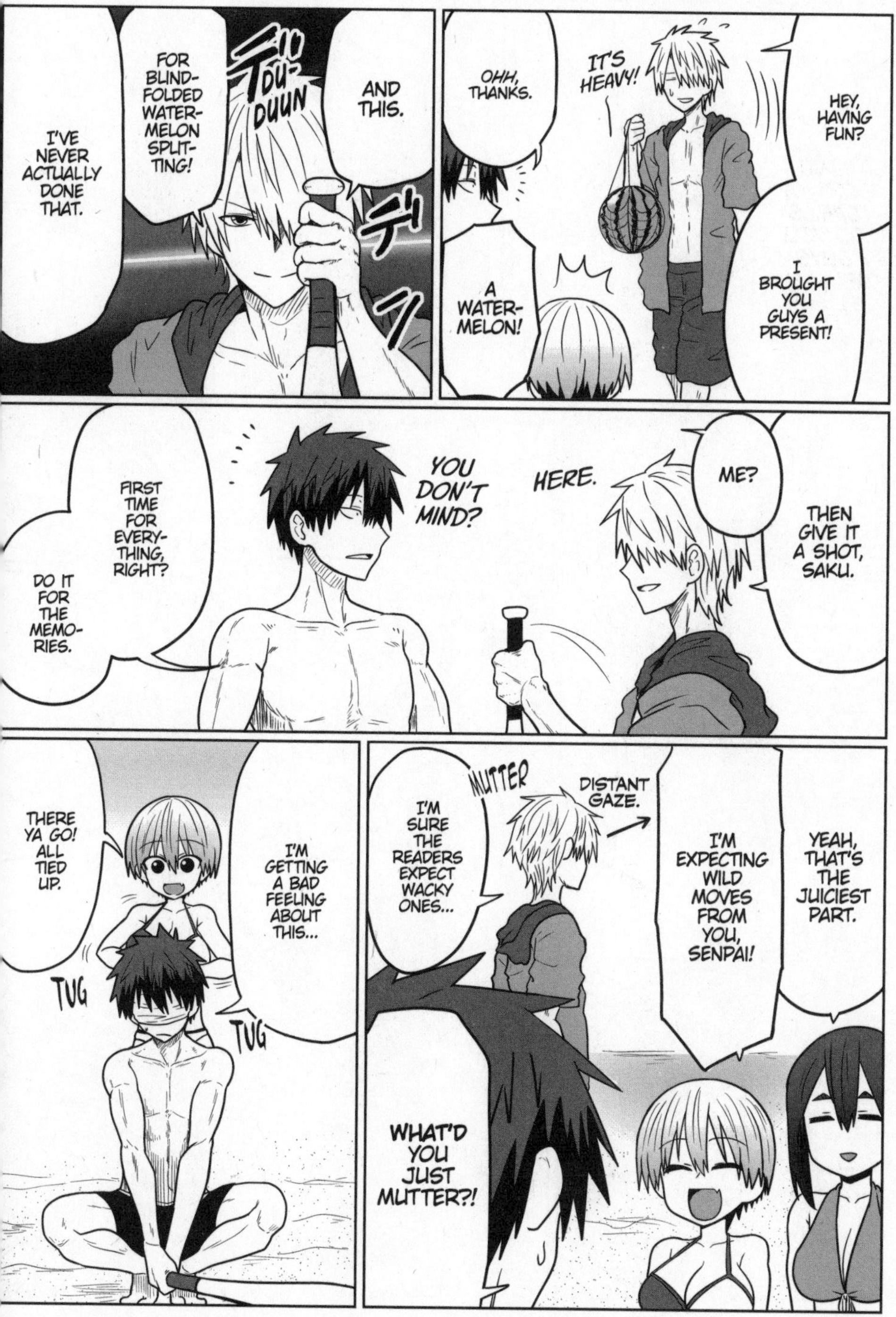
HEY, HAVING FUN?
I BROUGHT YOU GUYS A PRESENT!
IT'S HEAVY!
OHH, THANKS.
A WATER-MELON!
AND THIS.
DU-DUUN
FOR BLIND-FOLDED WATER-MELON SPLIT-TING!
I'VE NEVER ACTUALLY DONE THAT.
ME?
THEN GIVE IT A SHOT, SAKU.
HERE.
YOU DON'T MIND?
FIRST TIME FOR EVERY-THING, RIGHT?
DO IT FOR THE MEMO-RIES.
YEAH, THAT'S THE JUICIEST PART.
I'M EXPECTING WILD MOVES FROM YOU, SENPAI!
DISTANT GAZE.
MUTTER
I'M SURE THE READERS EXPECT WACKY ONES...
WHAT'D YOU JUST MUTTER?!
I'M GETTING A BAD FEELING ABOUT THIS...
THERE YA GO! ALL TIED UP.
TUG
TUG

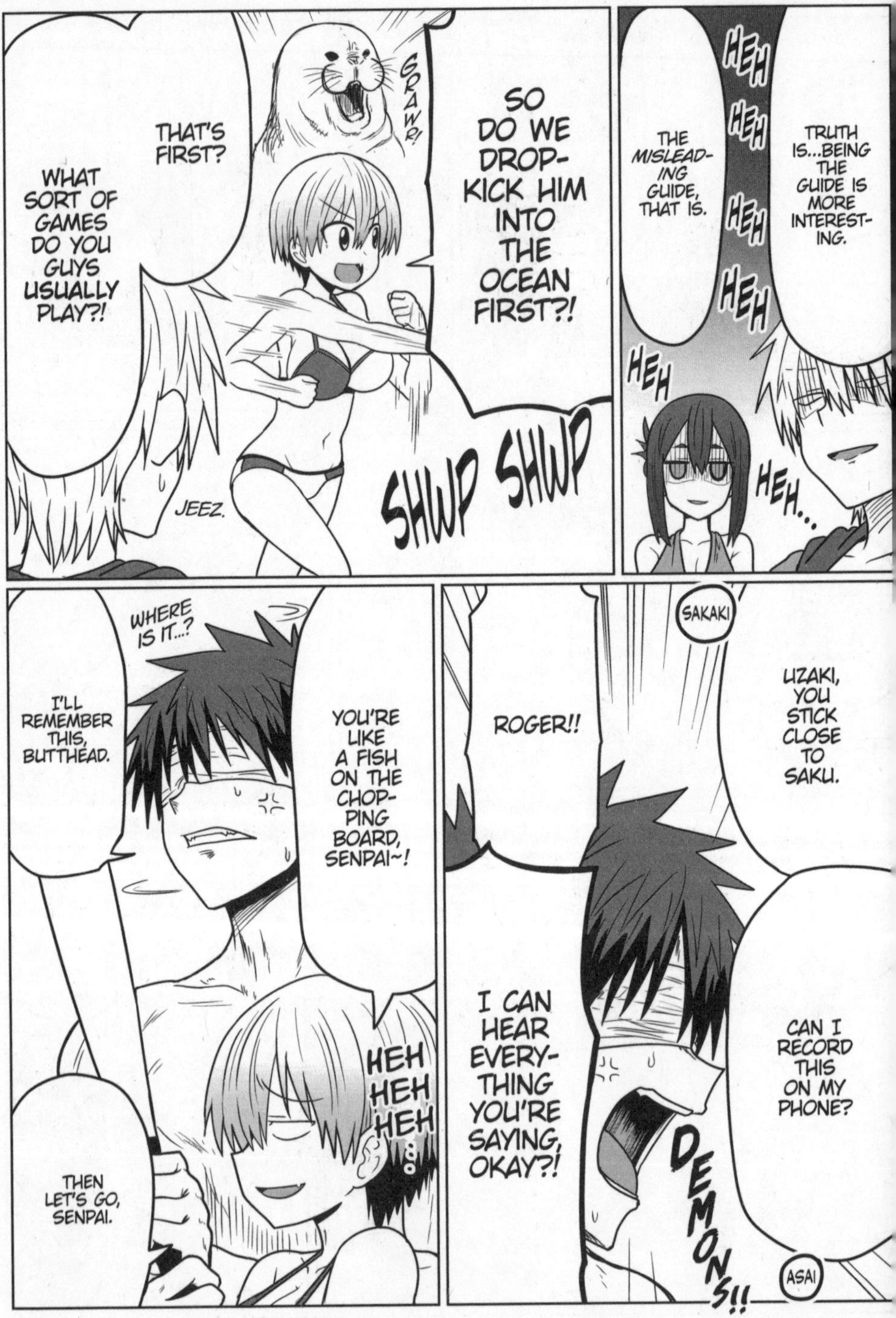
TRUTH IS...BEING THE GUIDE IS MORE INTERESTING.
THE MISLEADING GUIDE, THAT IS.
HEH HEH HEH HEH
HEH
HEH...
SO DO WE DROP-KICK HIM INTO THE OCEAN FIRST?!
GRAWR!
THAT'S FIRST?
WHAT SORT OF GAMES DO YOU GUYS USUALLY PLAY?!
SHWP SHWP
JEEZ.
SAKAKI
UZAKI, YOU STICK CLOSE TO SAKU.
ROGER!!
CAN I RECORD THIS ON MY PHONE?
ASAI
I CAN HEAR EVERYTHING YOU'RE SAYING, OKAY?!
DEMONS!!
YOU'RE LIKE A FISH ON THE CHOPPING BOARD, SENPAI~!
WHERE IS IT...?
I'LL REMEMBER THIS, BUTTHEAD.
HEH HEH HEH
THEN LET'S GO, SENPAI.

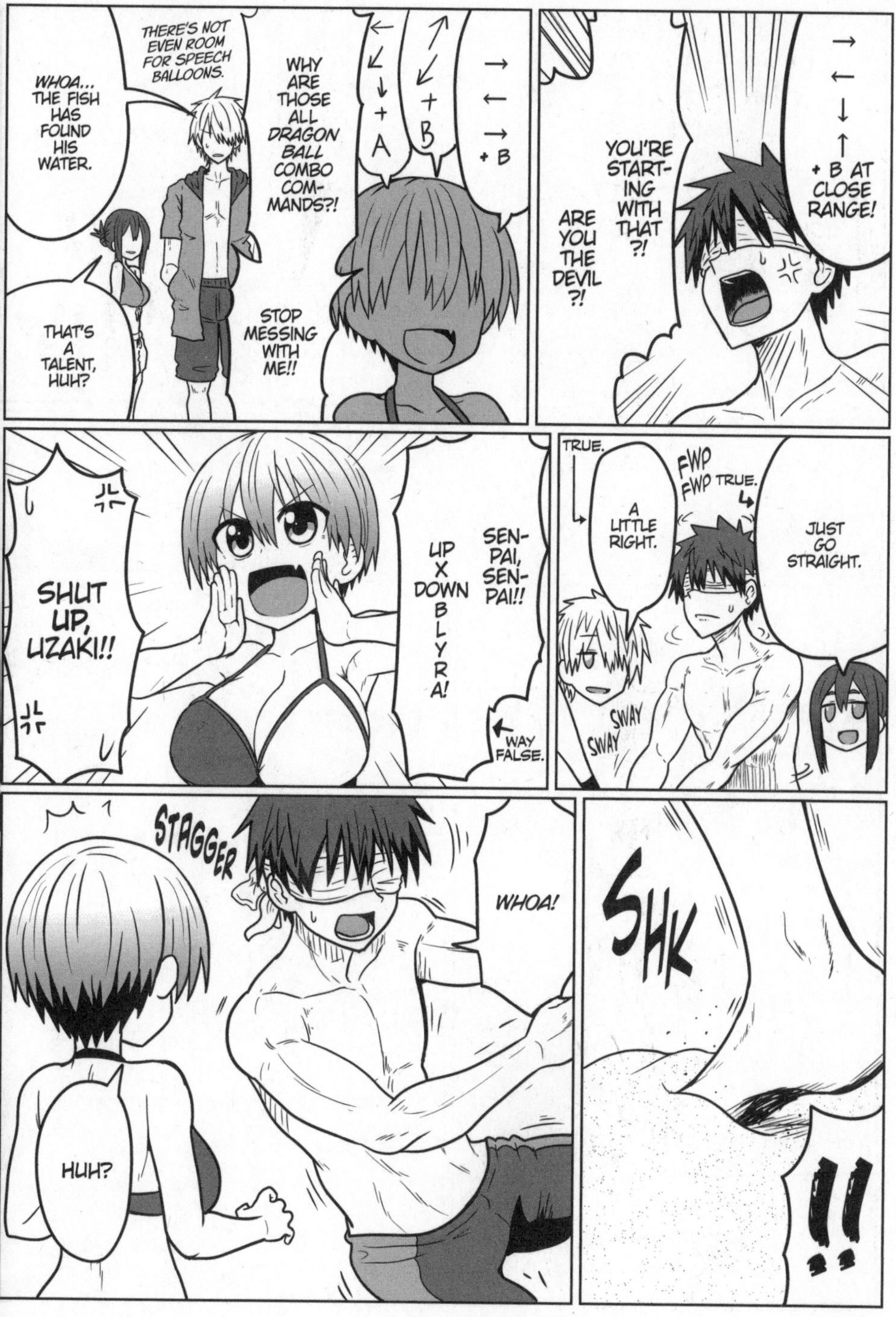

→ ← ↓ ↑ + B AT CLOSE RANGE!
YOU'RE STARTING WITH THAT?!
ARE YOU THE DEVIL?!
→ ← → + B
↗ ↙ + B
← ↙ ↓ + A
WHY ARE THOSE ALL DRAGON BALL COMBO COMMANDS?!
THERE'S NOT EVEN ROOM FOR SPEECH BALLOONS.
STOP MESSING WITH ME!!
WHOA... THE FISH HAS FOUND HIS WATER.
THAT'S A TALENT, HUH?
JUST GO STRAIGHT.
TRUE.
FWP FWP
A LITTLE RIGHT.
TRUE.
SWAY SWAY
SEN-PAI, SEN-PAI!!
UP X DOWN BLYRA!
WAY FALSE.
SHUT UP, UZAKI!!
SHK
!!
WHOA!
STAGGER
HUH?

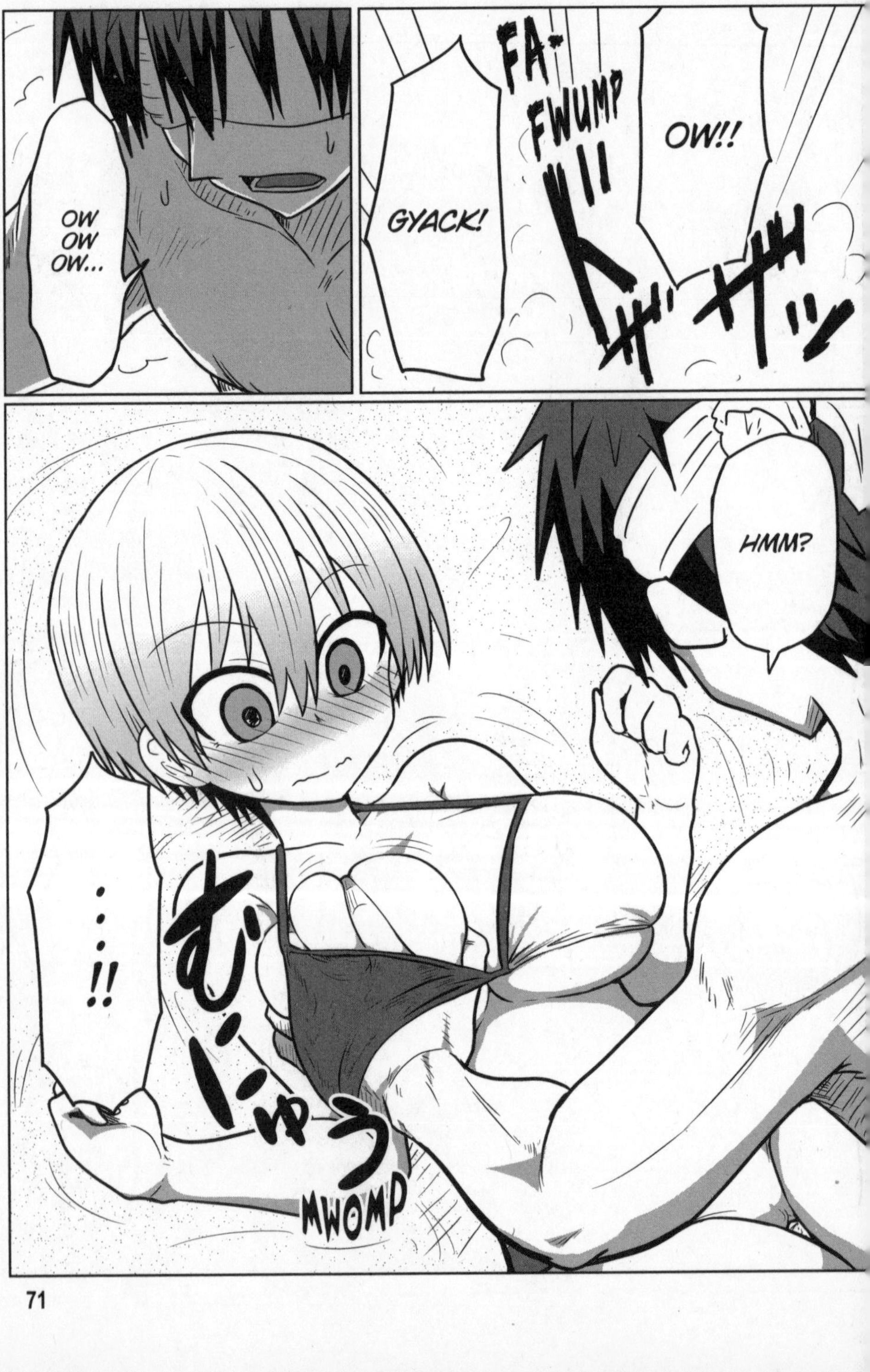

OW!!
FA-FWUMP
ドザザッ
GYACK!
OW OW OW...
HMM?
...!!
むにゅう
MWOMP

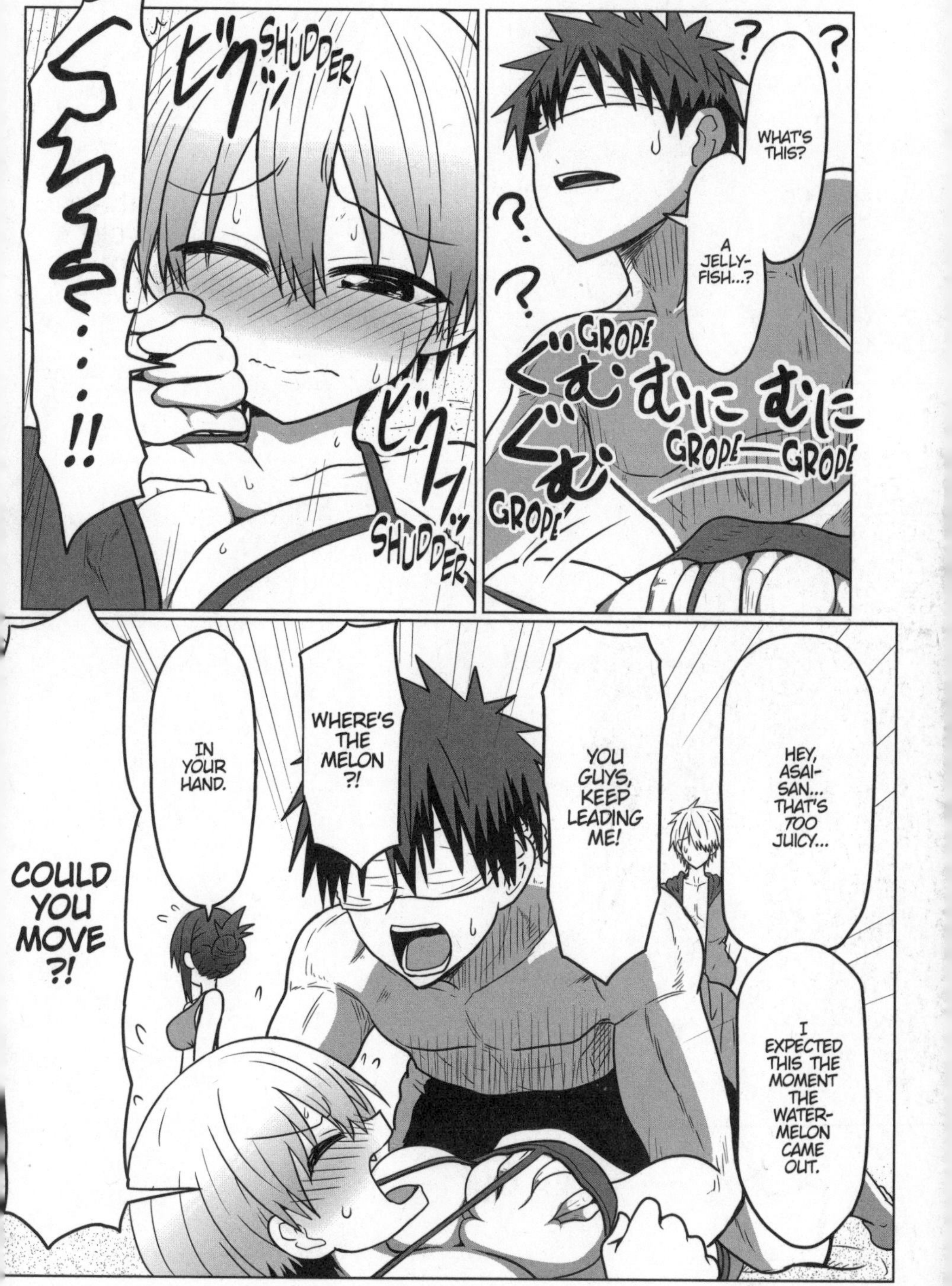
??
WHAT'S THIS?
A JELLY-FISH...?
??
GROPE
GROPE
GROPE
GROPE
SHUDDER
SHUDDER
...!!
HEY, ASAI-SAN... THAT'S *TOO* JUICY...
I EXPECTED THIS THE MOMENT THE WATER-MELON CAME OUT.
YOU GUYS, KEEP LEADING ME!
WHERE'S THE MELON ?!
IN YOUR HAND.
COULD YOU MOVE ?!

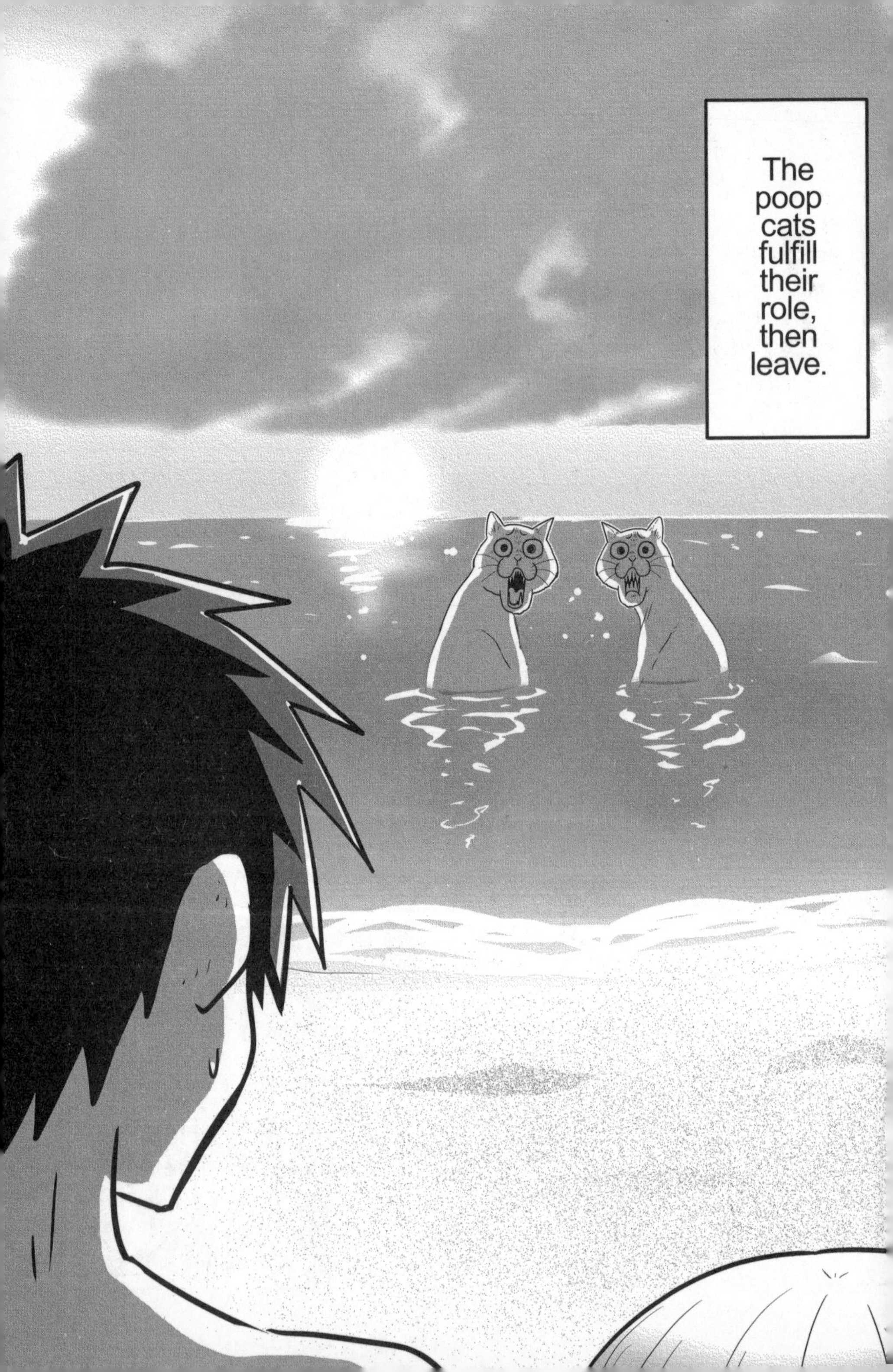
The poop cats fulfill their role, then leave.

Uzaki-chan ✪ Wants to Hang Out!

## Chapter 20: Night in the Wilderness

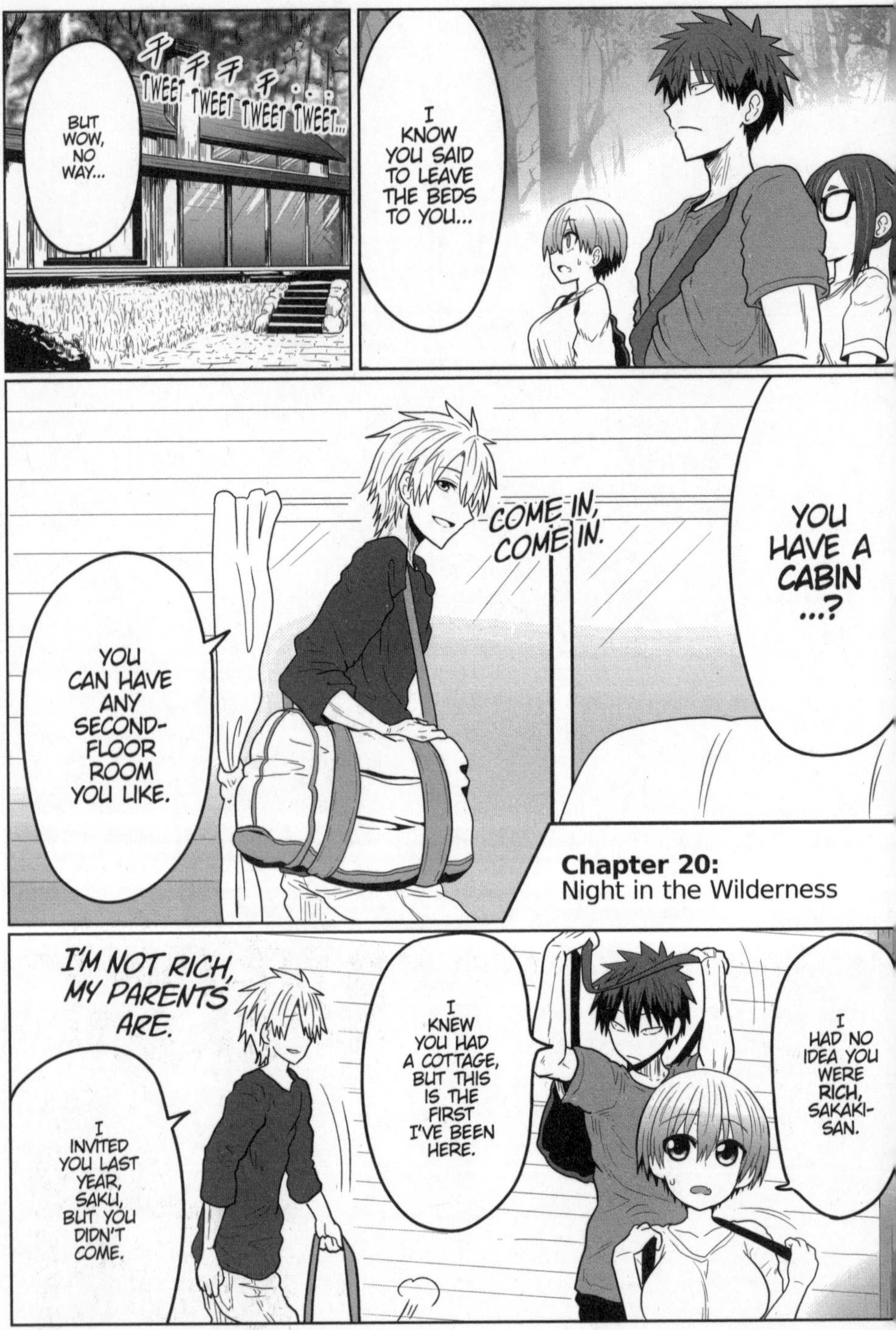
I KNOW YOU SAID TO LEAVE THE BEDS TO YOU...
TWEET TWEET TWEET TWEET...
BUT WOW, NO WAY...
YOU HAVE A CABIN ...?
COME IN, COME IN.
YOU CAN HAVE ANY SECOND-FLOOR ROOM YOU LIKE.
I HAD NO IDEA YOU WERE RICH, SAKAKI-SAN.
I KNEW YOU HAD A COTTAGE, BUT THIS IS THE FIRST I'VE BEEN HERE.
I'M NOT RICH, MY PARENTS ARE.
I INVITED YOU LAST YEAR, SAKU, BUT YOU DIDN'T COME.

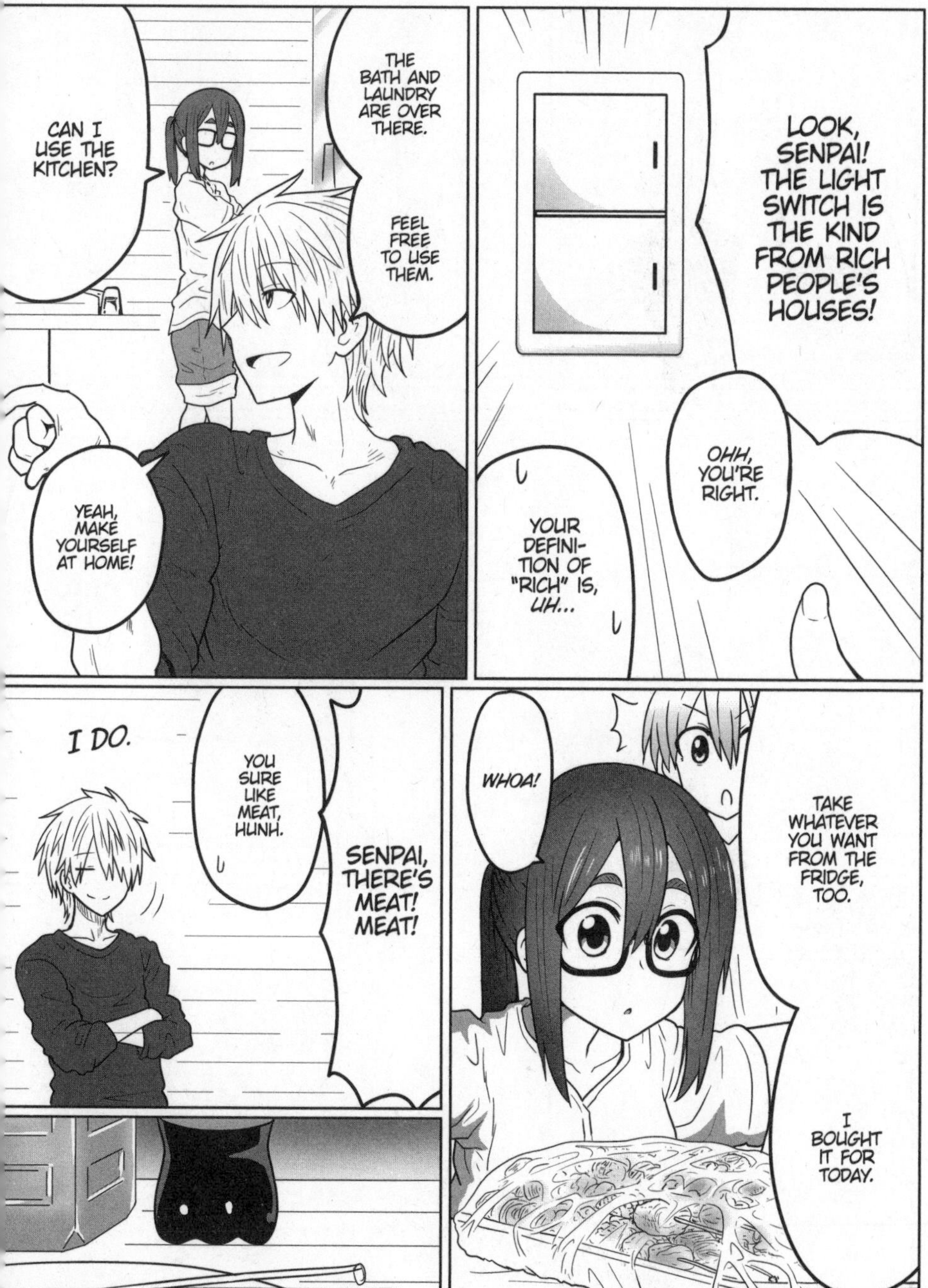
LOOK, SENPAI! THE LIGHT SWITCH IS THE KIND FROM RICH PEOPLE'S HOUSES!
OHH, YOU'RE RIGHT.
YOUR DEFINITION OF "RICH" IS, UH...
THE BATH AND LAUNDRY ARE OVER THERE.
FEEL FREE TO USE THEM.
CAN I USE THE KITCHEN?
YEAH, MAKE YOURSELF AT HOME!
TAKE WHATEVER YOU WANT FROM THE FRIDGE, TOO.
WHOA!
I BOUGHT IT FOR TODAY.
SENPAI, THERE'S MEAT! MEAT!
YOU SURE LIKE MEAT, HUNH.
I DO.

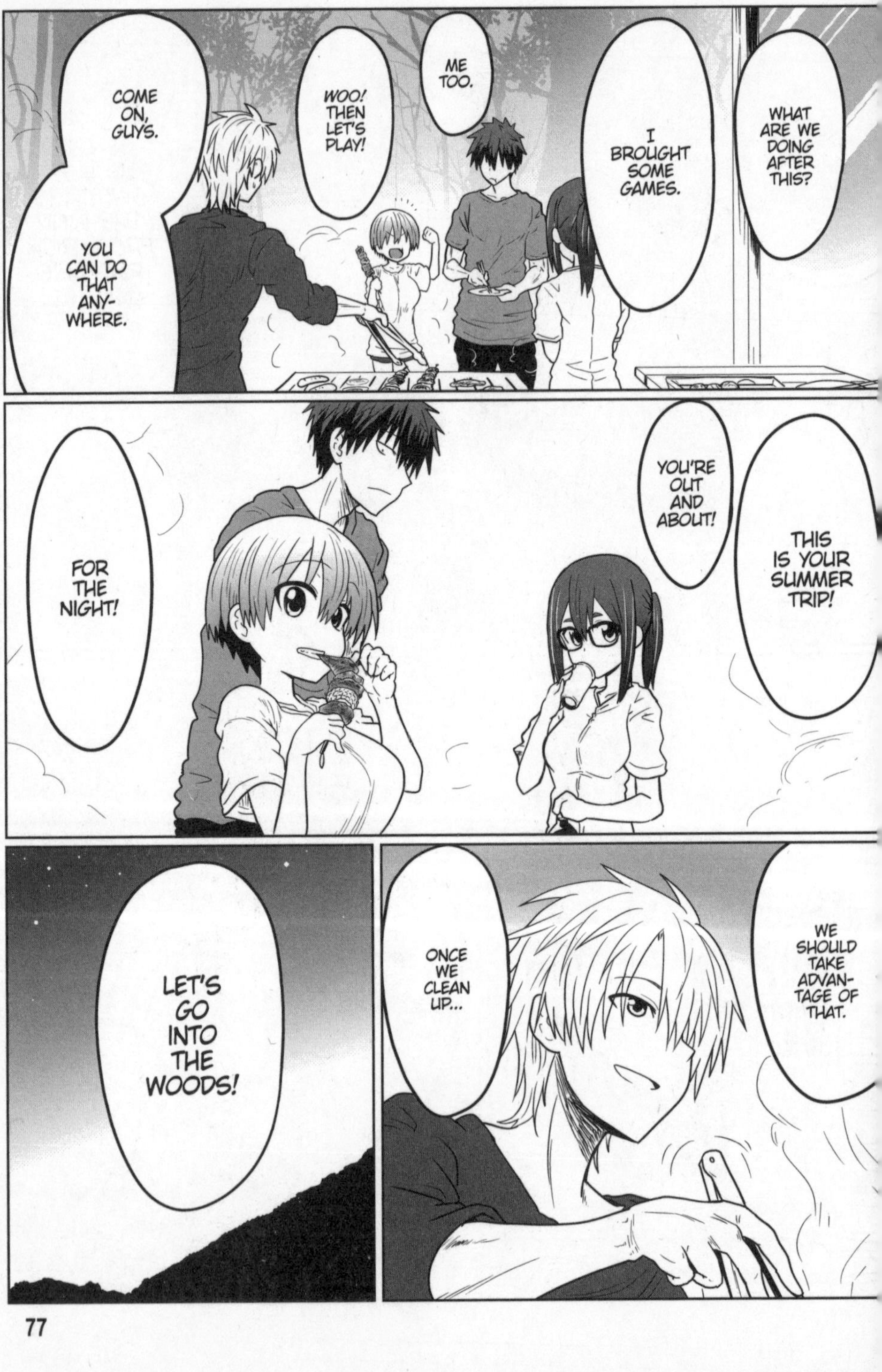
WHAT ARE WE DOING AFTER THIS?
I BROUGHT SOME GAMES.
ME TOO.
WOO! THEN LET'S PLAY!
COME ON, GUYS.
YOU CAN DO THAT ANY-WHERE.
THIS IS YOUR SUMMER TRIP!
YOU'RE OUT AND ABOUT!
FOR THE NIGHT!
WE SHOULD TAKE ADVAN-TAGE OF THAT.
ONCE WE CLEAN UP...
LET'S GO INTO THE WOODS!

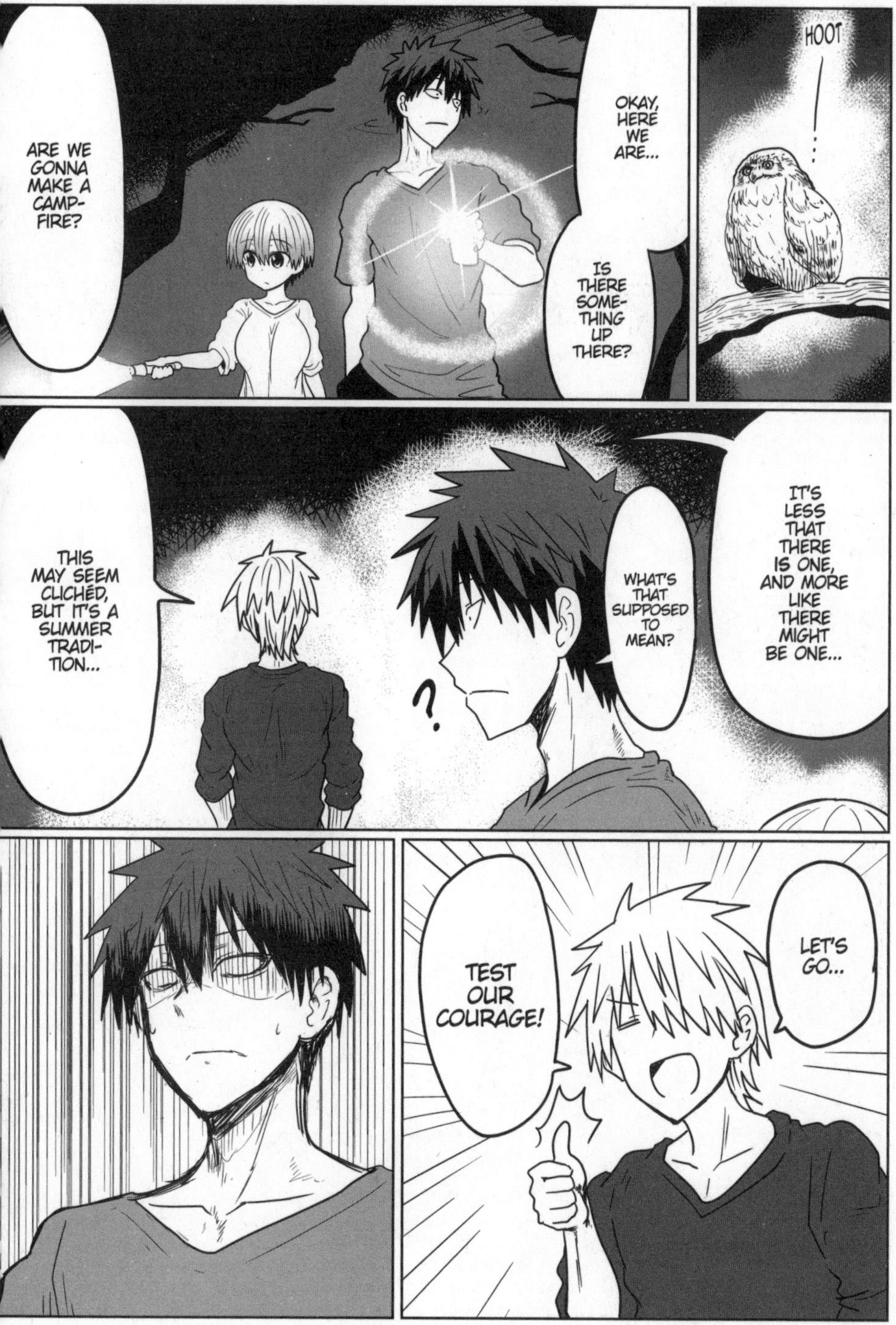

HOOT
OKAY, HERE WE ARE...
IS THERE SOMETHING UP THERE?
ARE WE GONNA MAKE A CAMPFIRE?
IT'S LESS THAT THERE IS ONE, AND MORE LIKE THERE MIGHT BE ONE...
WHAT'S THAT SUPPOSED TO MEAN?
?
THIS MAY SEEM CLICHÉD, BUT IT'S A SUMMER TRADITION...
LET'S GO...
TEST OUR COURAGE!

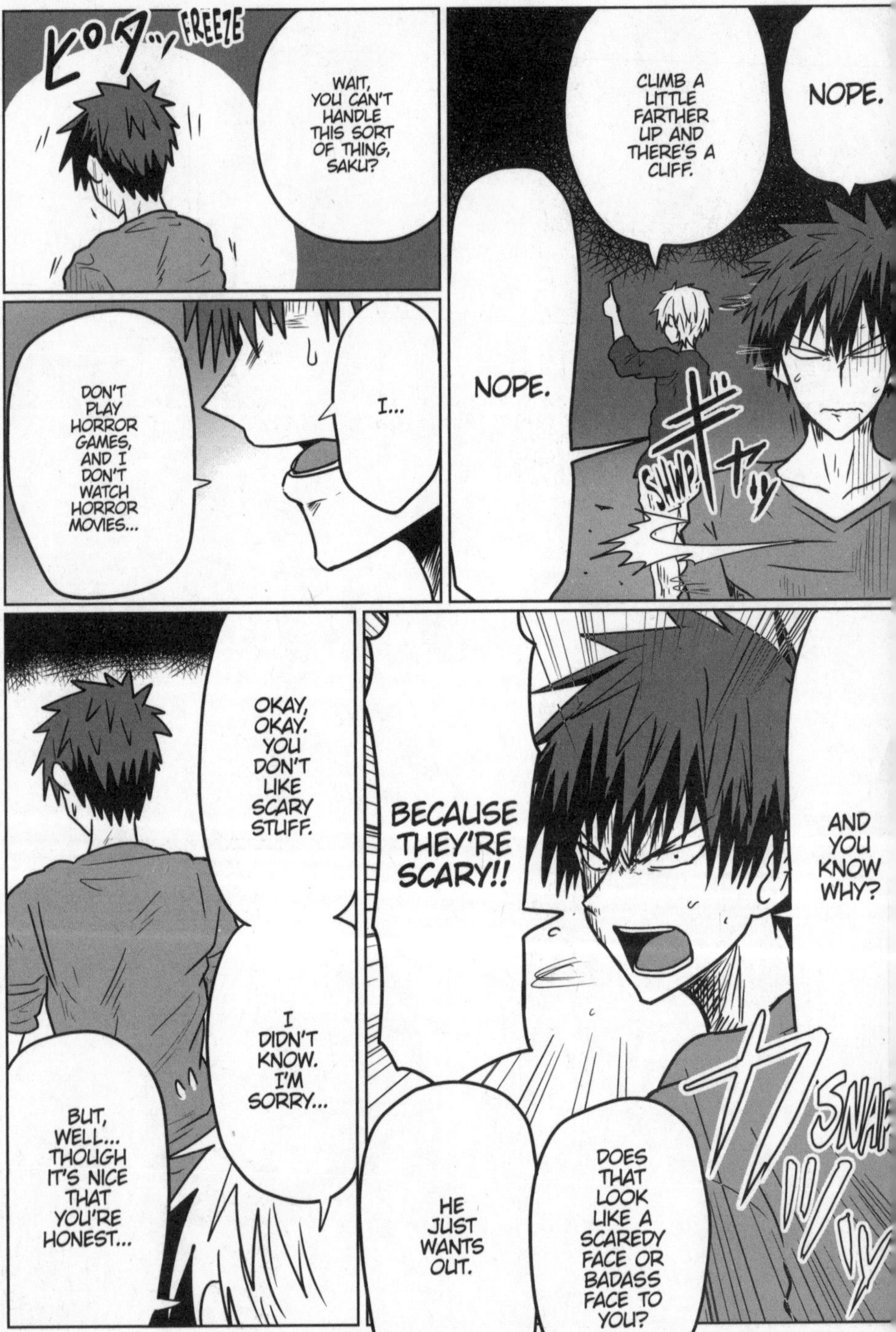
NOPE.
CLIMB A LITTLE FARTHER UP AND THERE'S A CLIFF.
SHWIP
NOPE.
WAIT, YOU CAN'T HANDLE THIS SORT OF THING, SAKU?
FREEZE
I...
DON'T PLAY HORROR GAMES, AND I DON'T WATCH HORROR MOVIES...
AND YOU KNOW WHY?
BECAUSE THEY'RE SCARY!!
SNA
DOES THAT LOOK LIKE A SCAREDY FACE OR BADASS FACE TO YOU?
HE JUST WANTS OUT.
OKAY, OKAY. YOU DON'T LIKE SCARY STUFF.
I DIDN'T KNOW. I'M SORRY...
BUT, WELL... THOUGH IT'S NICE THAT YOU'RE HONEST...

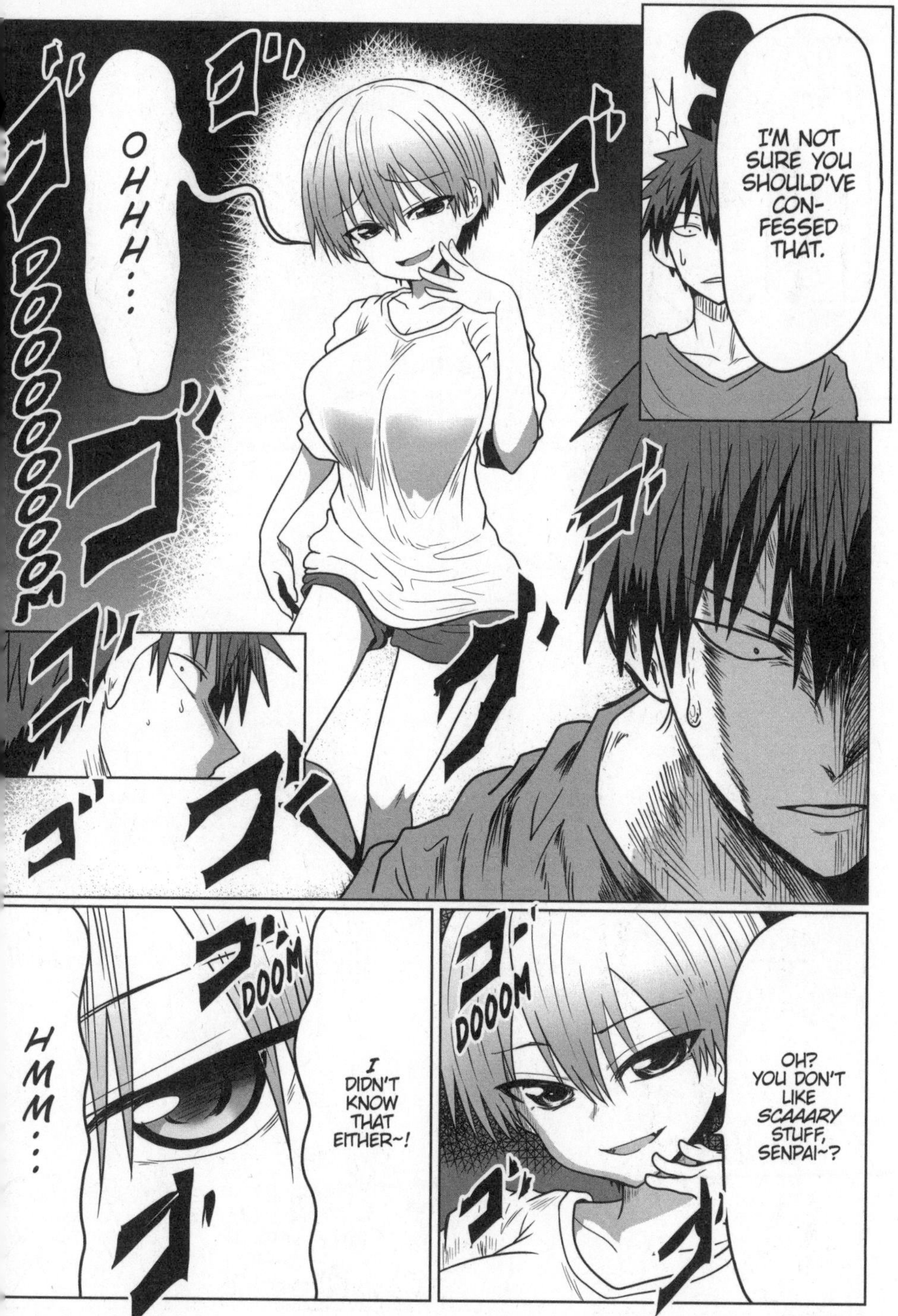
I'M NOT SURE YOU SHOULD'VE CON-FESSED THAT.
OHHH...
DOOOOOOOOOM
OH? YOU DON'T LIKE SCAAARY STUFF, SENPAI~?
DOOOM
I DIDN'T KNOW THAT EITHER~!
DOOM
HMM...

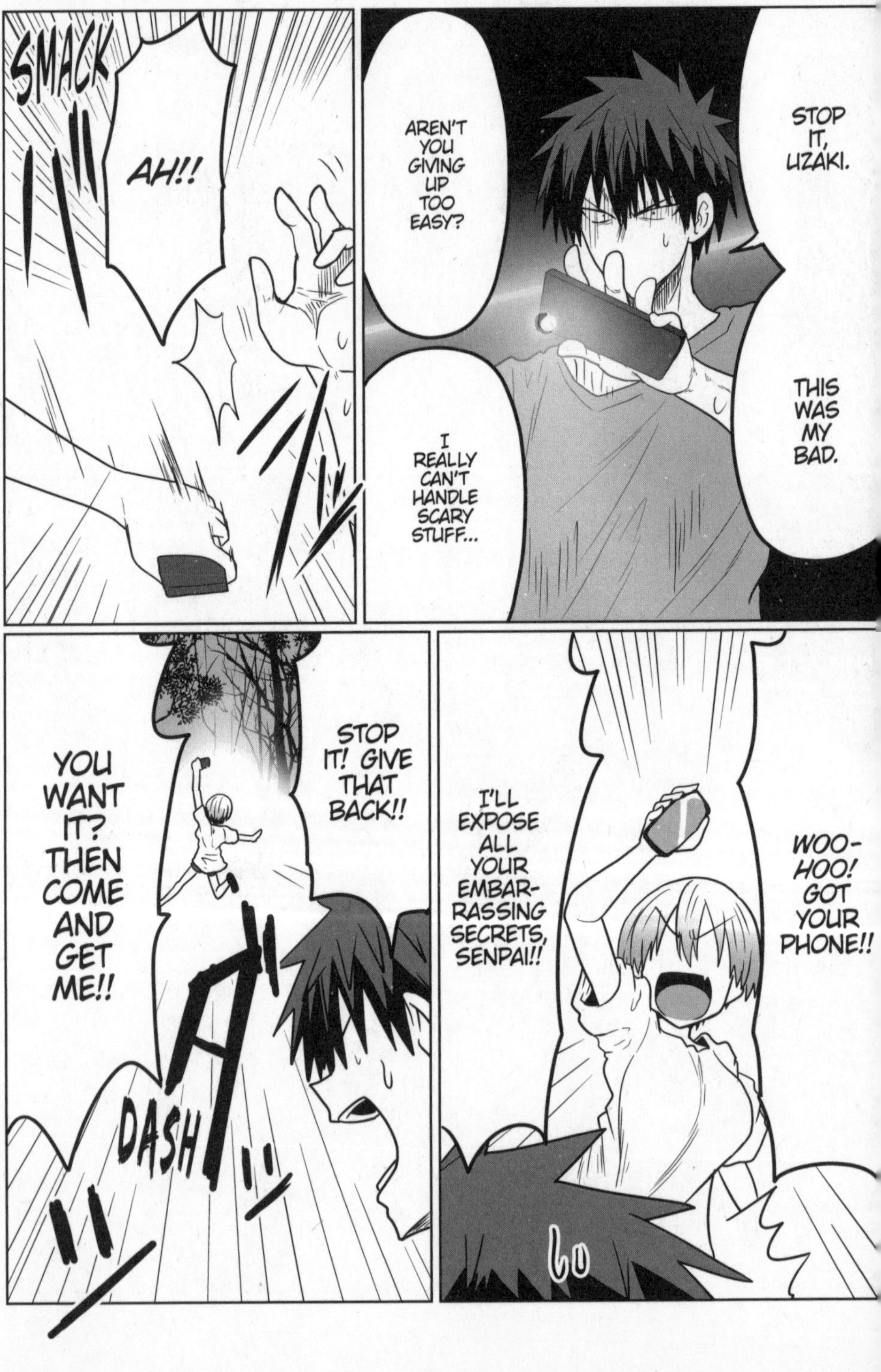
STOP IT, UZAKI.
AREN'T YOU GIVING UP TOO EASY?
THIS WAS MY BAD.
I REALLY CAN'T HANDLE SCARY STUFF...
SMACK
AH!!
WOO-HOO! GOT YOUR PHONE!!
I'LL EXPOSE ALL YOUR EMBARRASSING SECRETS, SENPAI!!
STOP IT! GIVE THAT BACK!!
YOU WANT IT? THEN COME AND GET ME!!
DASH

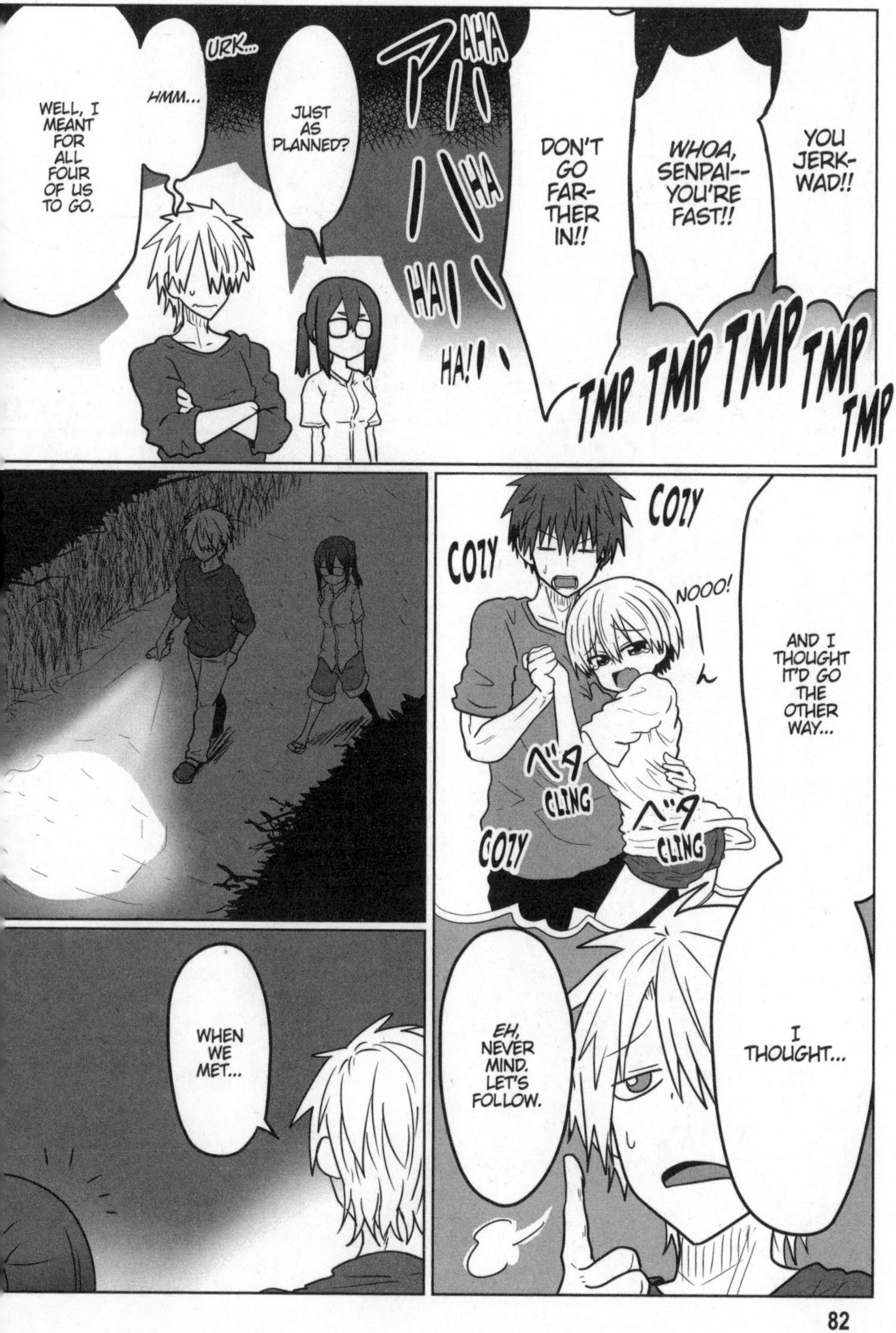
YOU JERK-WAD!!
WHOA, SENPAI-- YOU'RE FAST!!
DON'T GO FAR-THER IN!!
TMP TMP TMP TMP TMP
AHA HA HA HA!
JUST AS PLANNED?
URK...
HMM...
WELL, I MEANT FOR ALL FOUR OF US TO GO.
AND I THOUGHT IT'D GO THE OTHER WAY...
COZY
NOOO!
COZY
ベタ CLING
ベタ CLING
COZY
I THOUGHT...
EH, NEVER MIND. LET'S FOLLOW.
WHEN WE MET...

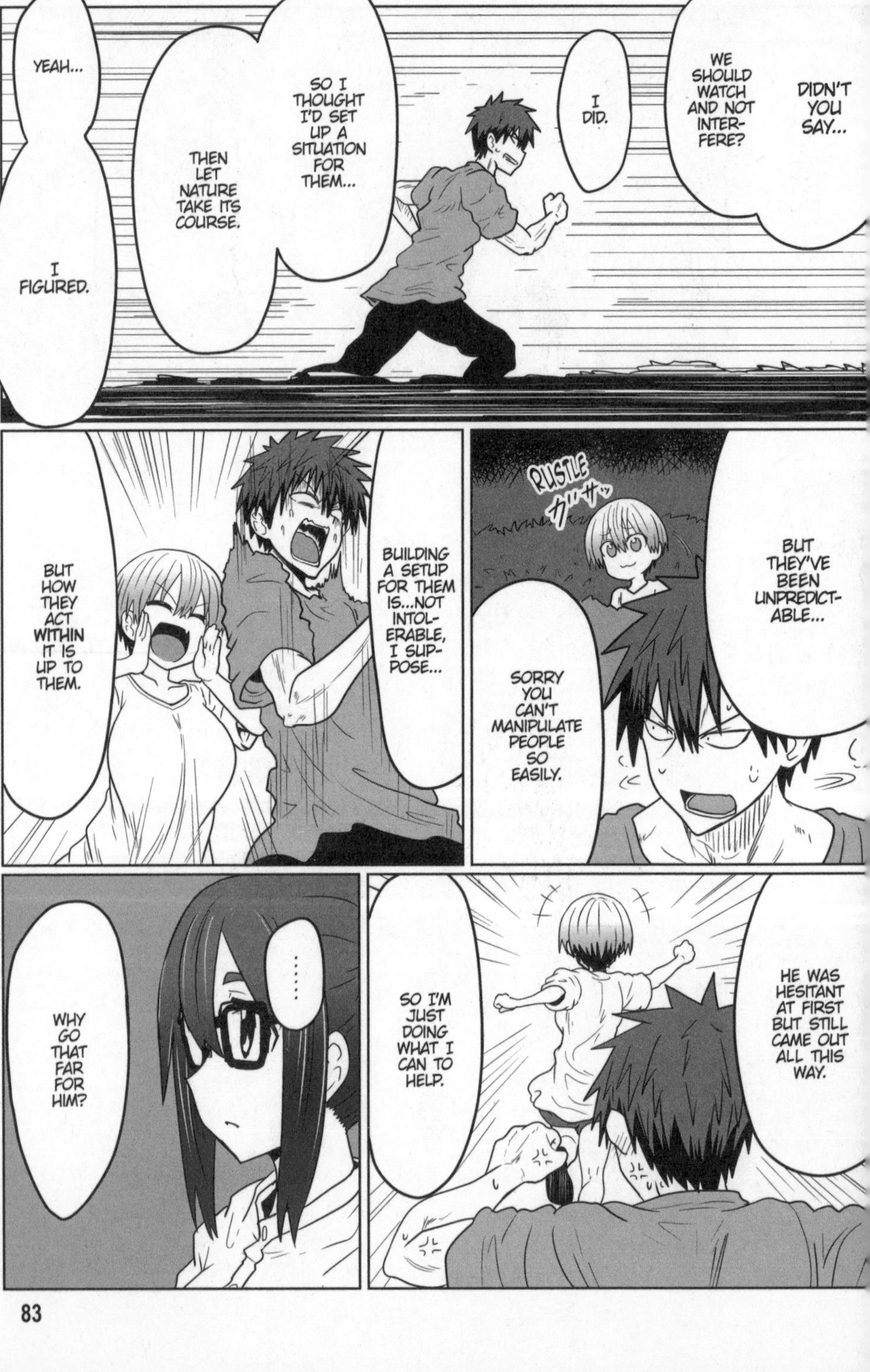
DIDN'T YOU SAY...
WE SHOULD WATCH AND NOT INTERFERE?
I DID.
SO I THOUGHT I'D SET UP A SITUATION FOR THEM...
THEN LET NATURE TAKE ITS COURSE.
YEAH...
I FIGURED.
RUSTLE
ガサッ
BUT THEY'VE BEEN UNPREDICTABLE...
SORRY YOU CAN'T MANIPULATE PEOPLE SO EASILY.
BUILDING A SETUP FOR THEM IS...NOT INTOLERABLE, I SUPPOSE...
BUT HOW THEY ACT WITHIN IT IS UP TO THEM.
HE WAS HESITANT AT FIRST BUT STILL CAME OUT ALL THIS WAY.
SO I'M JUST DOING WHAT I CAN TO HELP.
......
WHY GO THAT FAR FOR HIM?

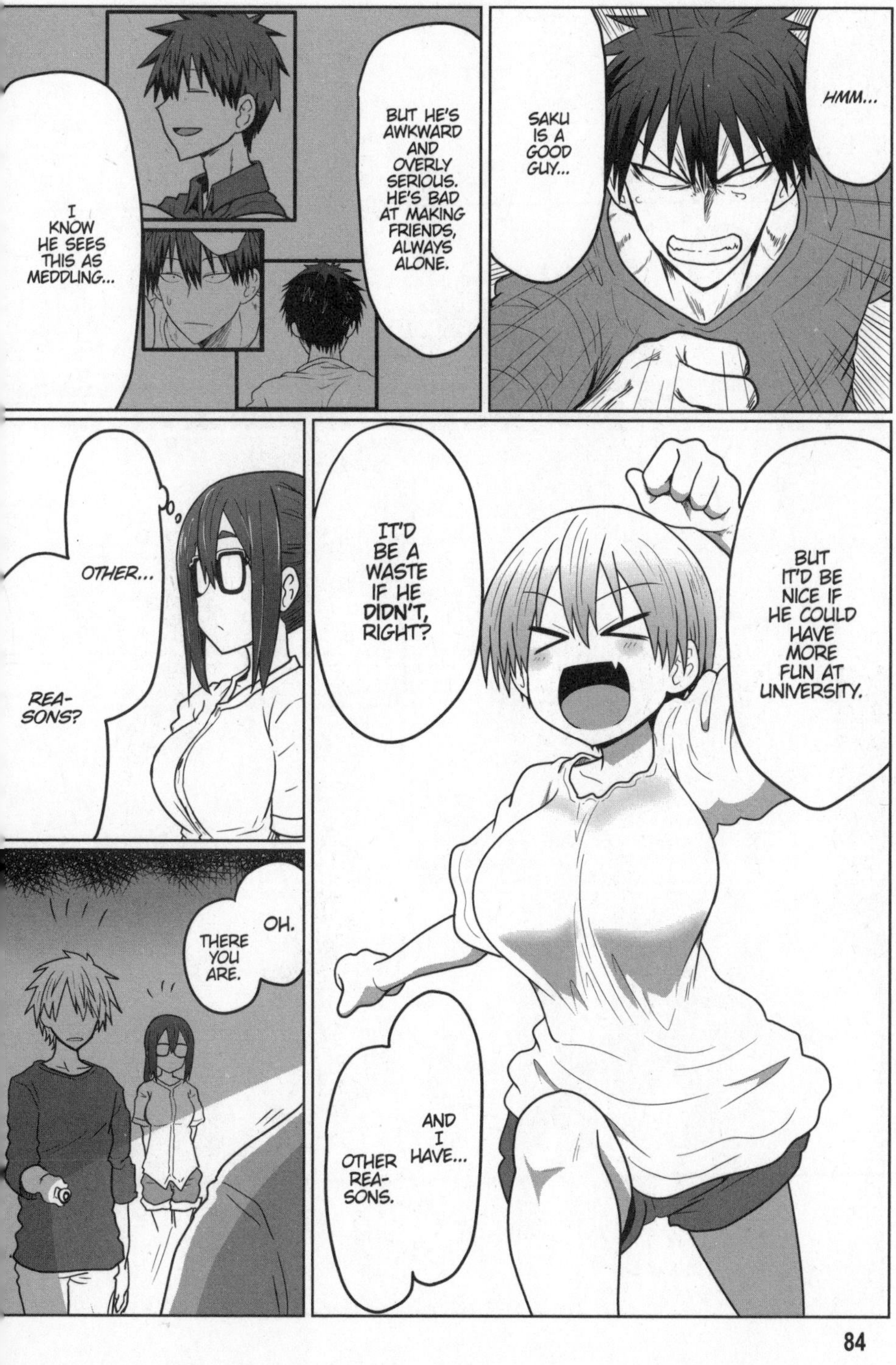
HMM...
SAKU IS A GOOD GUY...
BUT HE'S AWKWARD AND OVERLY SERIOUS. HE'S BAD AT MAKING FRIENDS, ALWAYS ALONE.
I KNOW HE SEES THIS AS MEDDLING...
BUT IT'D BE NICE IF HE COULD HAVE MORE FUN AT UNIVERSITY.
IT'D BE A WASTE IF HE DIDN'T, RIGHT?
AND I HAVE...
OTHER REASONS.
OTHER...
REASONS?
OH.
THERE YOU ARE.

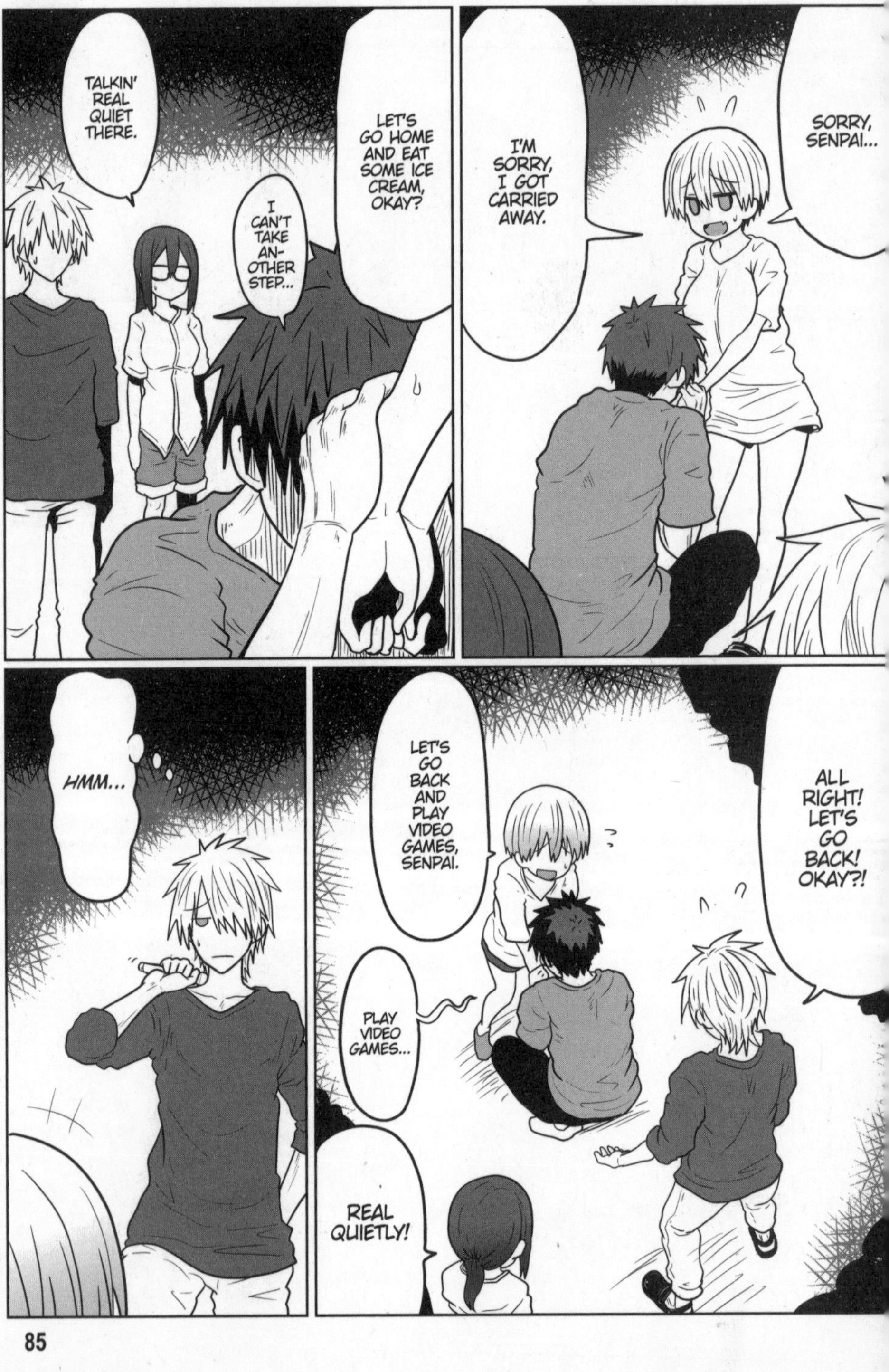
SORRY, SENPAI...
I'M SORRY, I GOT CARRIED AWAY.
LET'S GO HOME AND EAT SOME ICE CREAM, OKAY?
I CAN'T TAKE AN-OTHER STEP...
TALKIN' REAL QUIET THERE.
ALL RIGHT! LET'S GO BACK! OKAY?!
LET'S GO BACK AND PLAY VIDEO GAMES, SENPAI.
PLAY VIDEO GAMES...
REAL QUIETLY!
HMM...

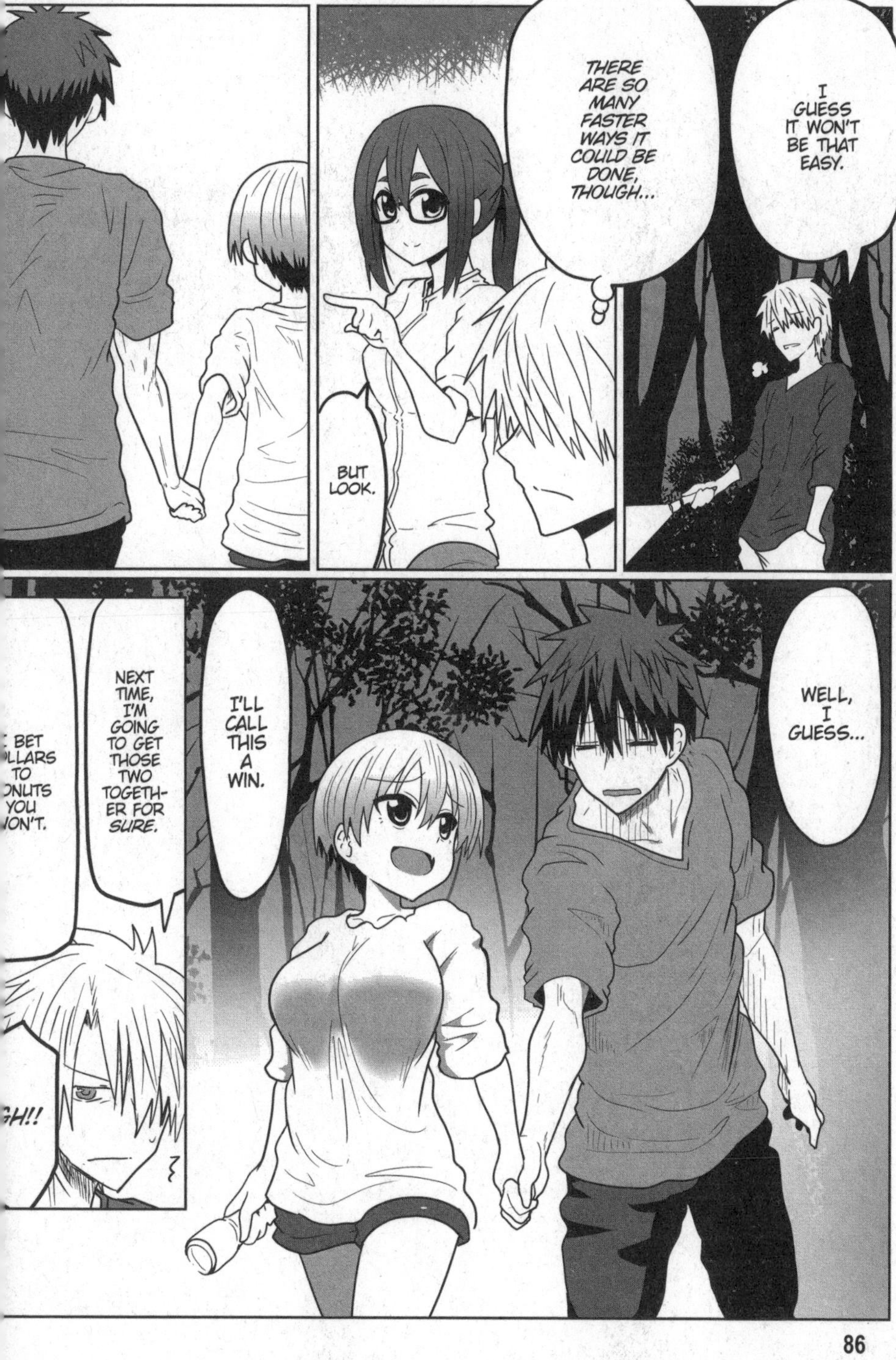

I GUESS IT WON'T BE THAT EASY.
THERE ARE SO MANY FASTER WAYS IT COULD BE DONE, THOUGH...
BUT LOOK.
WELL, I GUESS...
I'LL CALL THIS A WIN.
NEXT TIME, I'M GOING TO GET THOSE TWO TOGETHER FOR SURE.
BET
TO
YOU

FWOO...

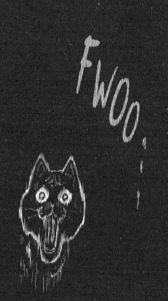

Uzaki-chan
chan ✦
Wants
to Hang
Out!

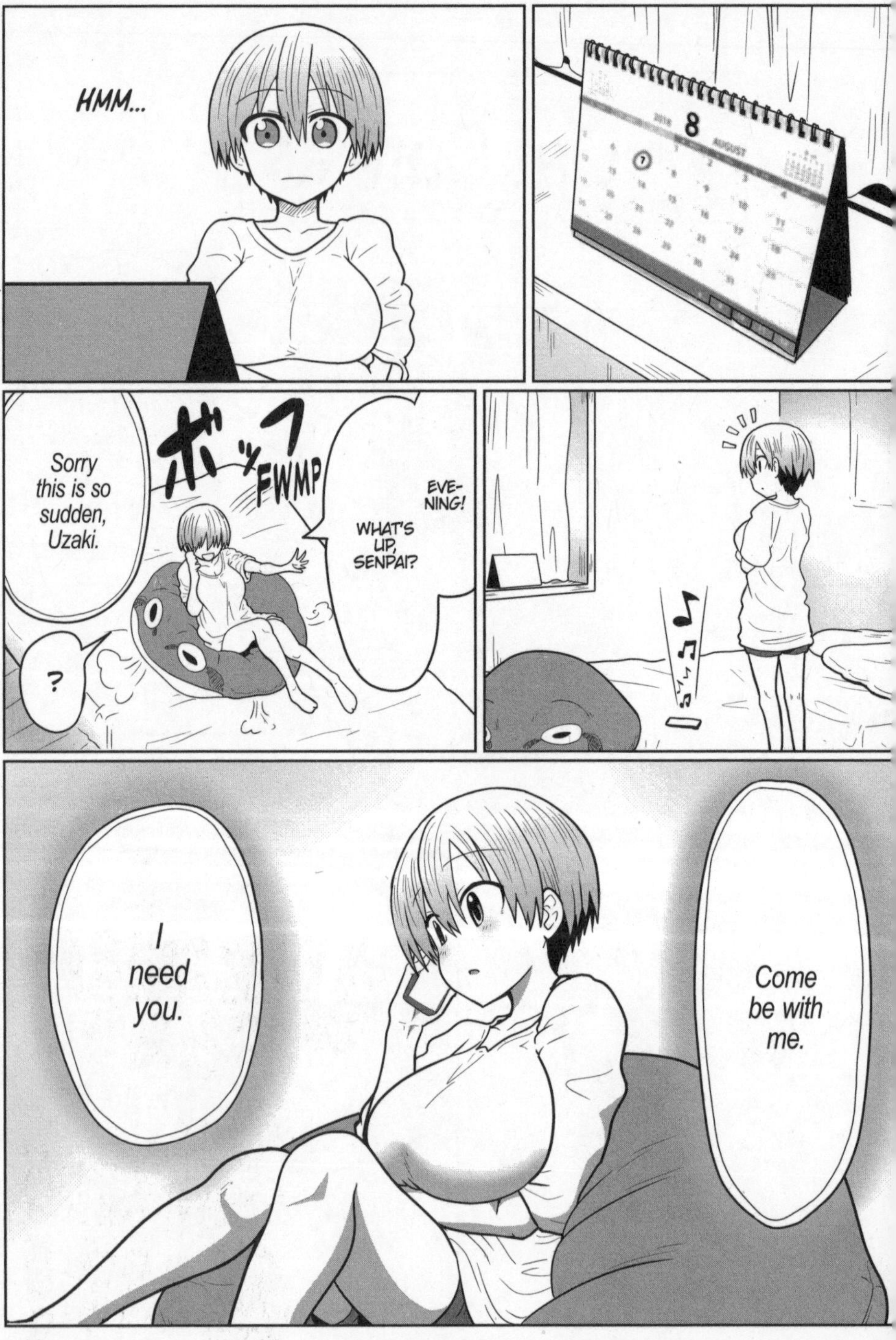
HMM...
EVE-NING! WHAT'S UP, SENPAI?
ボッ FWMP
Sorry this is so sudden, Uzaki.
?
Come be with me.
I need you.

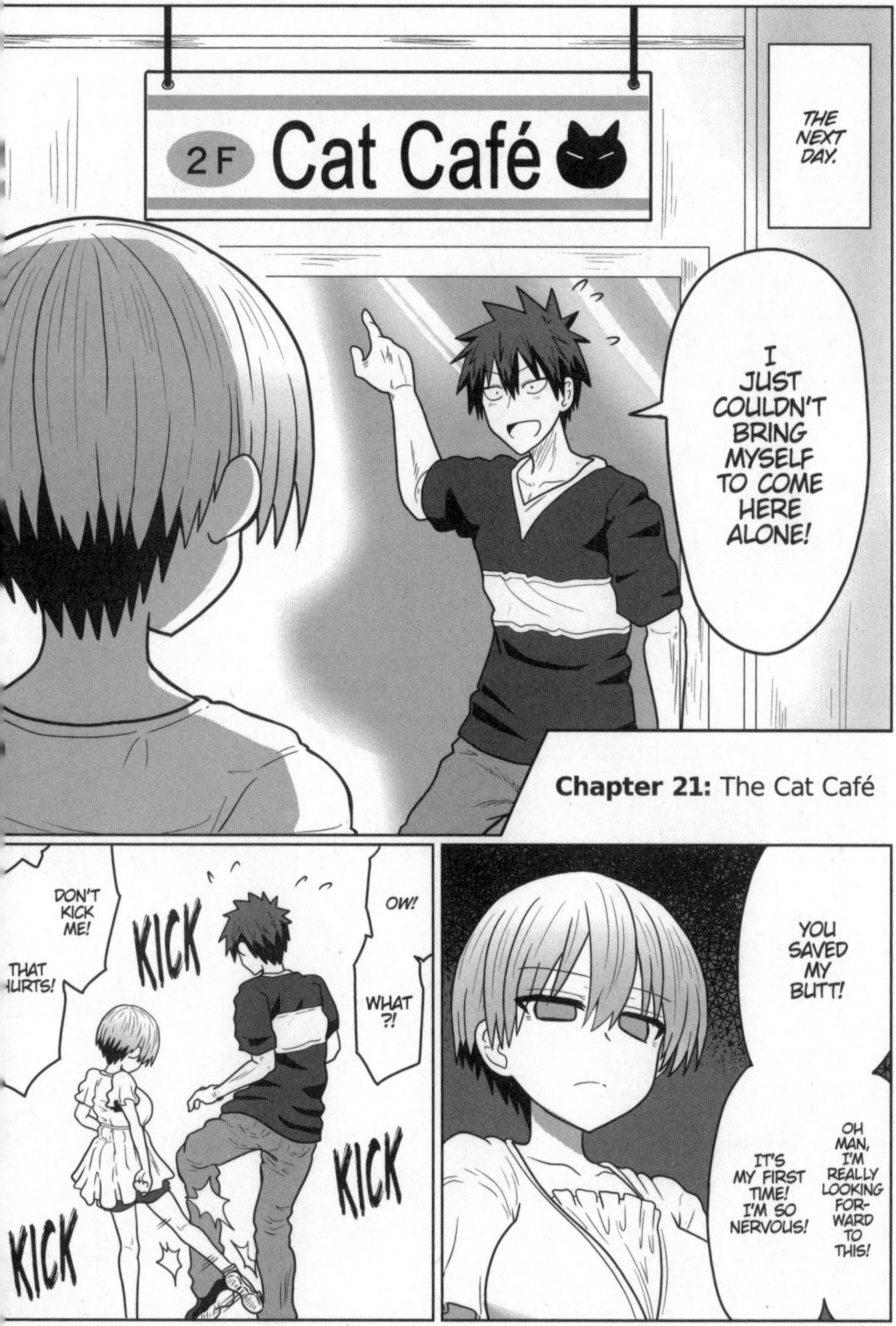
2F Cat Café
THE NEXT DAY.
I JUST COULDN'T BRING MYSELF TO COME HERE ALONE!
YOU SAVED MY BUTT!
OH MAN, I'M REALLY LOOKING FOR-WARD TO THIS!
IT'S MY FIRST TIME! I'M SO NERVOUS!
OW!
WHAT?!
KICK
KICK
DON'T KICK ME!
THAT HURTS!
KICK

## Chapter 21: The Cat Café

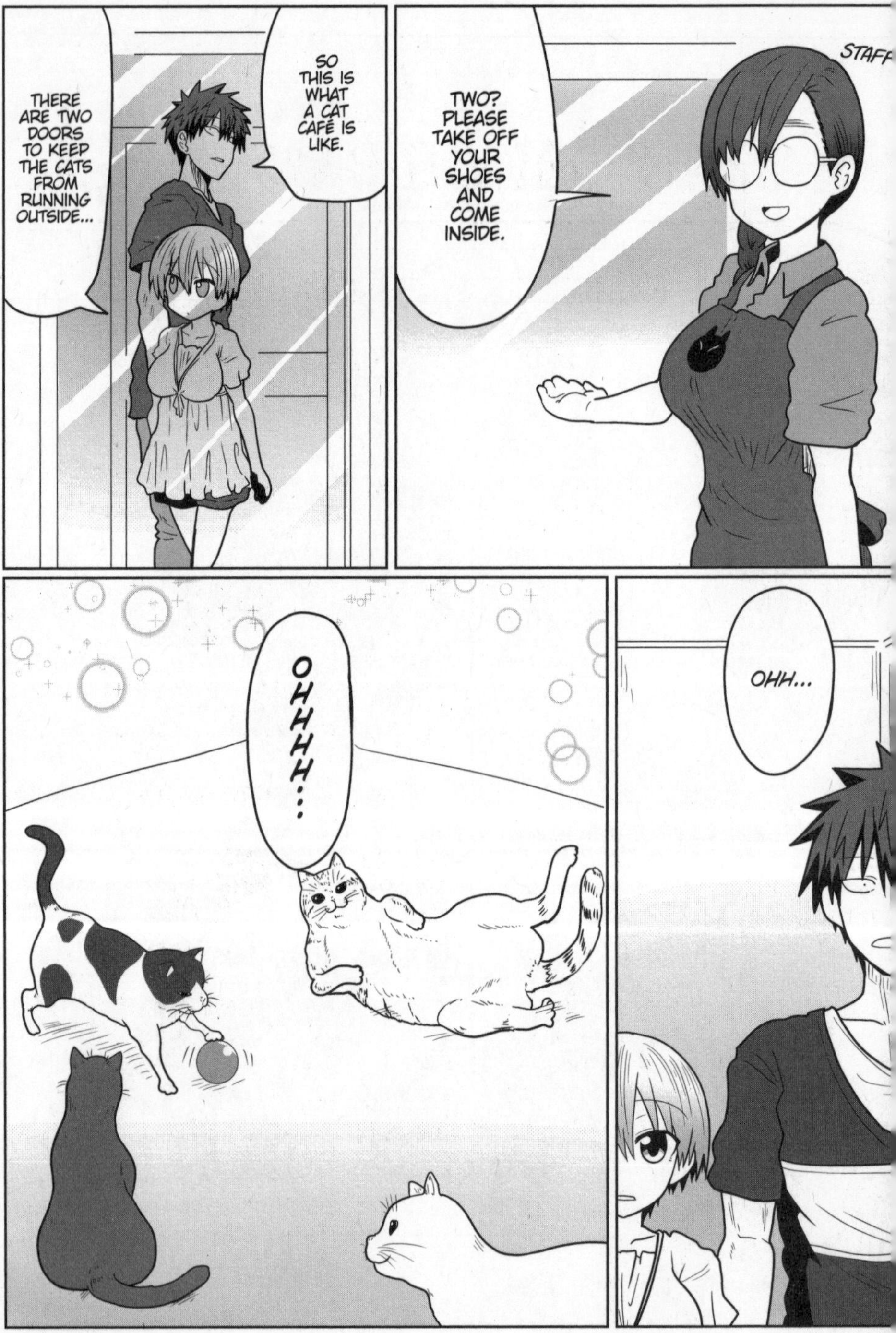
STAFF
TWO? PLEASE TAKE OFF YOUR SHOES AND COME INSIDE.
SO THIS IS WHAT A CAT CAFÉ IS LIKE.
THERE ARE TWO DOORS TO KEEP THE CATS FROM RUNNING OUTSIDE...
OHH...
OHHHH...

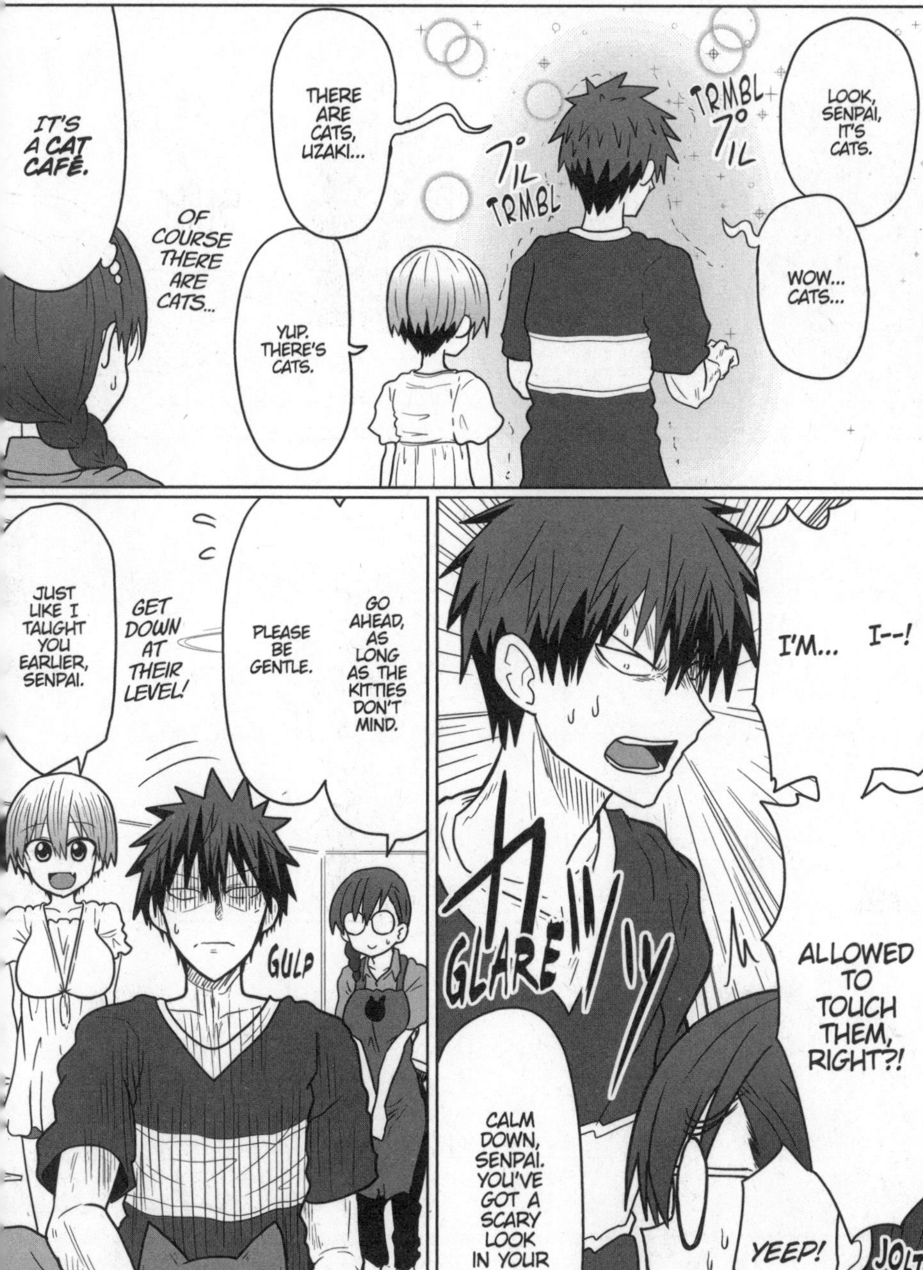
LOOK, SENPAI, IT'S CATS.
TRMBL プル
TRMBL プル
WOW... CATS...
THERE ARE CATS, UZAKI...
YUP. THERE'S CATS.
OF COURSE THERE ARE CATS...
IT'S A CAT CAFÉ.
I'M... I--!
ALLOWED TO TOUCH THEM, RIGHT?!
GLARE カッ
CALM DOWN, SENPAI. YOU'VE GOT A SCARY LOOK IN YOUR EYE.
YEEP!
JOLT ビクッ
GO AHEAD, AS LONG AS THE KITTIES DON'T MIND.
PLEASE BE GENTLE.
GET DOWN AT THEIR LEVEL!
JUST LIKE I TAUGHT YOU EARLIER, SENPAI.
GULP

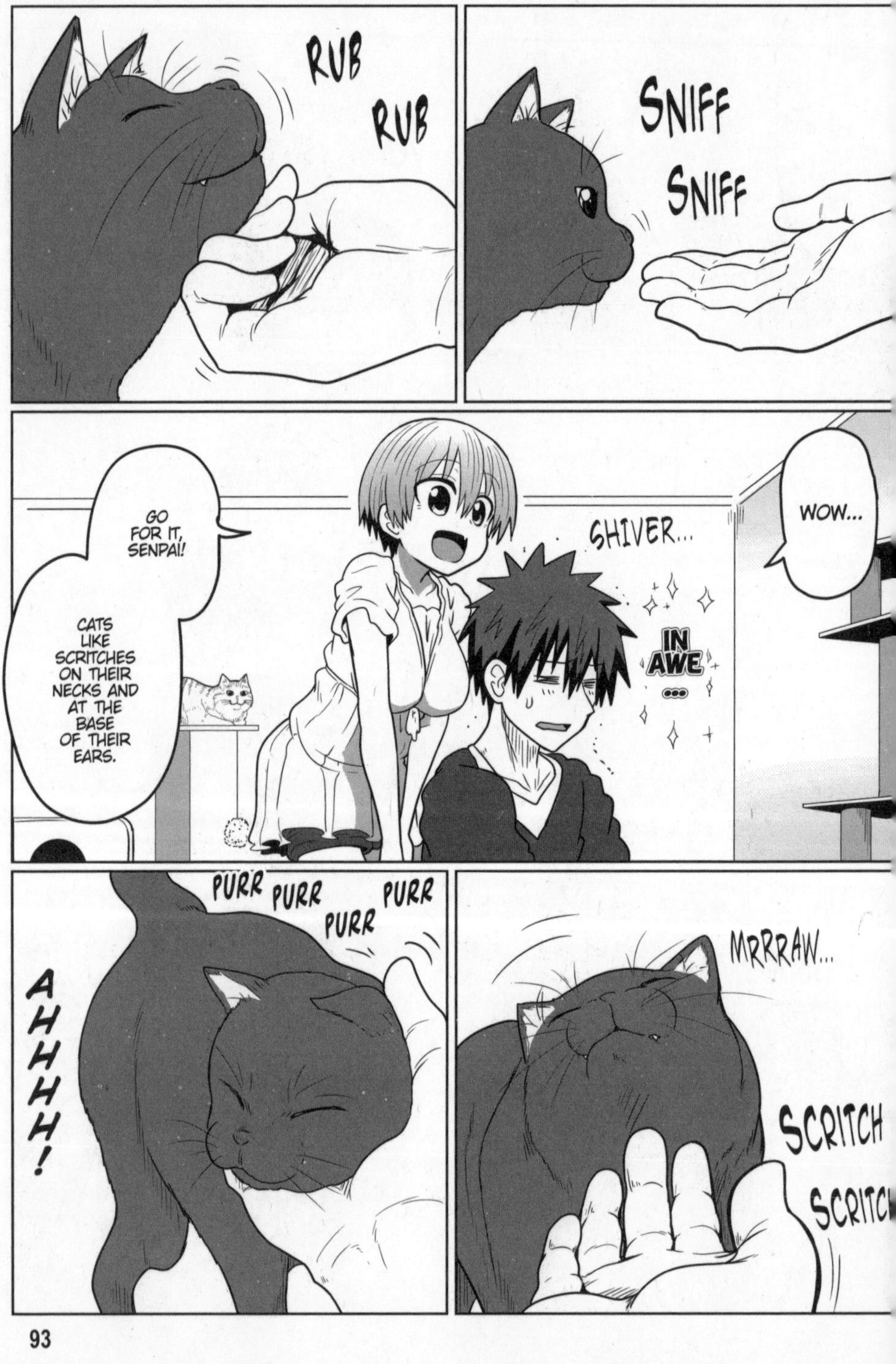
SNIFF
SNIFF
RUB
RUB
WOW...
SHIVER...
IN AWE...
GO FOR IT, SENPAI!
CATS LIKE SCRITCHES ON THEIR NECKS AND AT THE BASE OF THEIR EARS.
MRRRAW...
SCRITCH
PURR
PURR
PURR
PURR
AHHHHH!

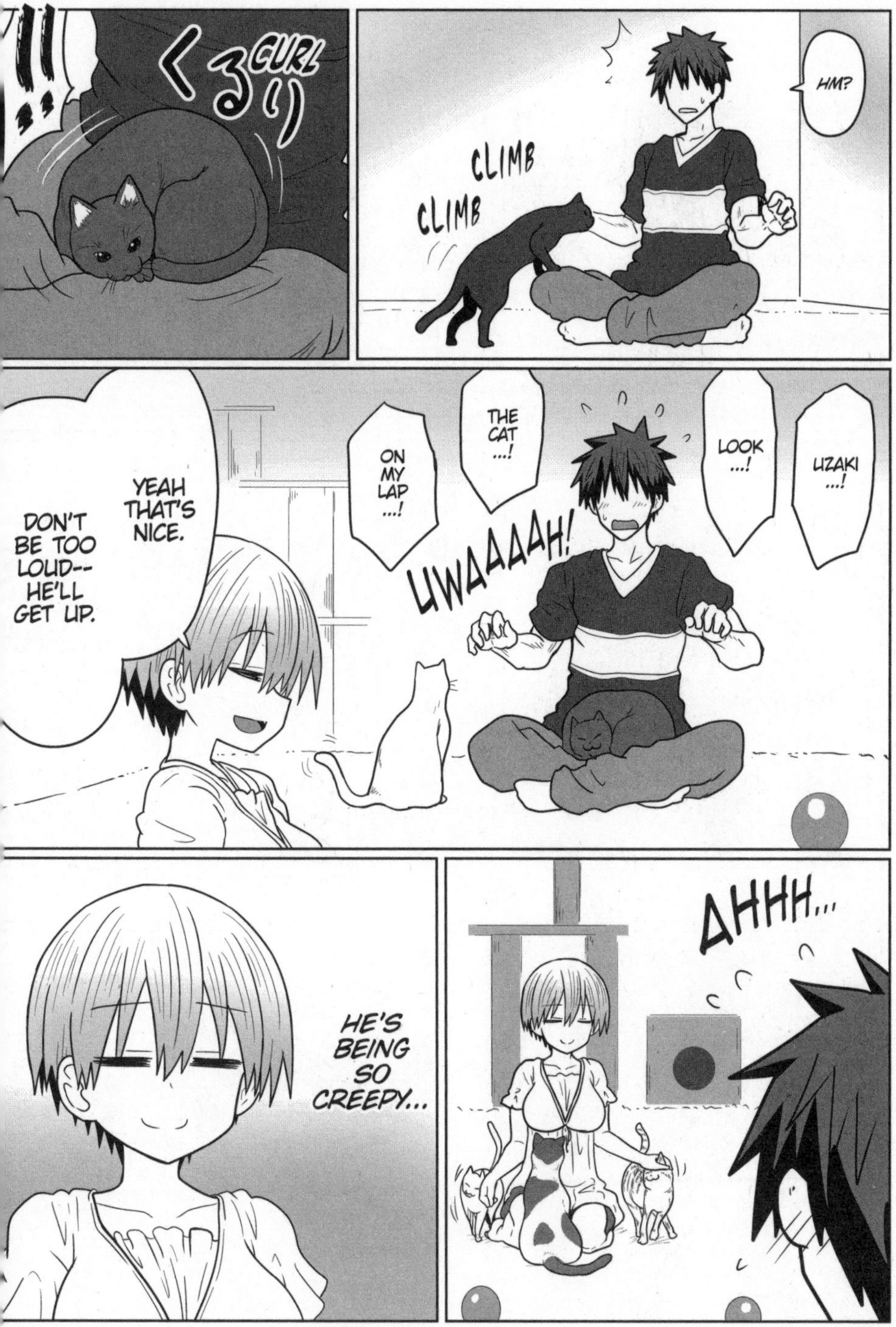
HM?
CLIMB
CLIMB
くるり CURL
UZAKI...!
LOOK...!
THE CAT...!
ON MY LAP...!
UWAAAAH!
YEAH THAT'S NICE.
DON'T BE TOO LOUD-- HE'LL GET UP.
AHHH...
HE'S BEING SO CREEPY...

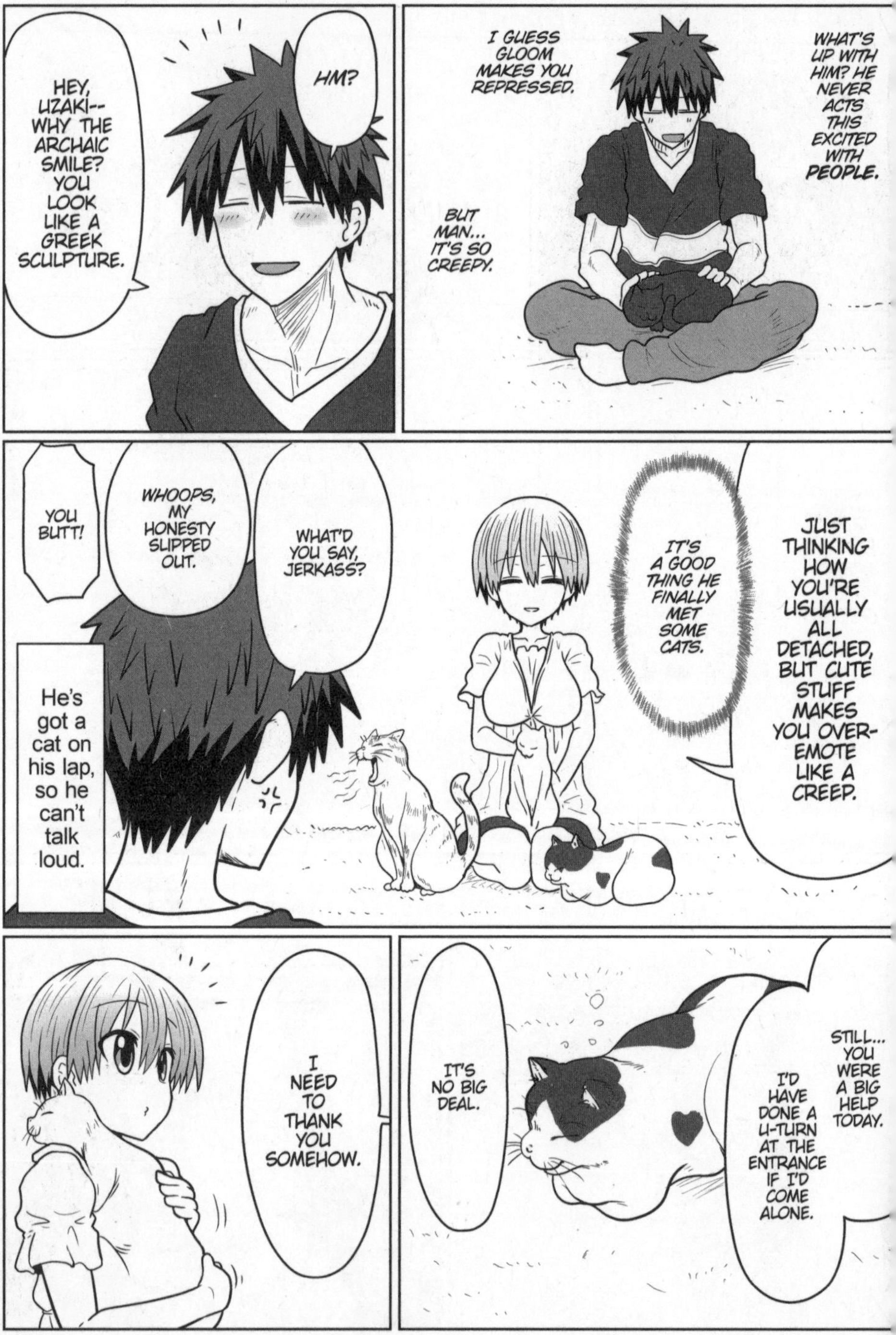
WHAT'S UP WITH HIM? HE NEVER ACTS THIS EXCITED WITH **PEOPLE**.
I GUESS GLOOM MAKES YOU REPRESSED.
BUT MAN... IT'S SO CREEPY.
HM?
HEY, UZAKI-- WHY THE ARCHAIC SMILE? YOU LOOK LIKE A GREEK SCULPTURE.
JUST THINKING HOW YOU'RE USUALLY ALL DETACHED, BUT CUTE STUFF MAKES YOU OVER-EMOTE LIKE A CREEP.
IT'S A GOOD THING HE FINALLY MET SOME CATS.
WHAT'D YOU SAY, JERKASS?
WHOOPS, MY HONESTY SLIPPED OUT.
YOU BUTT!
He's got a cat on his lap, so he can't talk loud.
STILL... YOU WERE A BIG HELP TODAY.
I'D HAVE DONE A U-TURN AT THE ENTRANCE IF I'D COME ALONE.
IT'S NO BIG DEAL.
I NEED TO THANK YOU SOMEHOW.

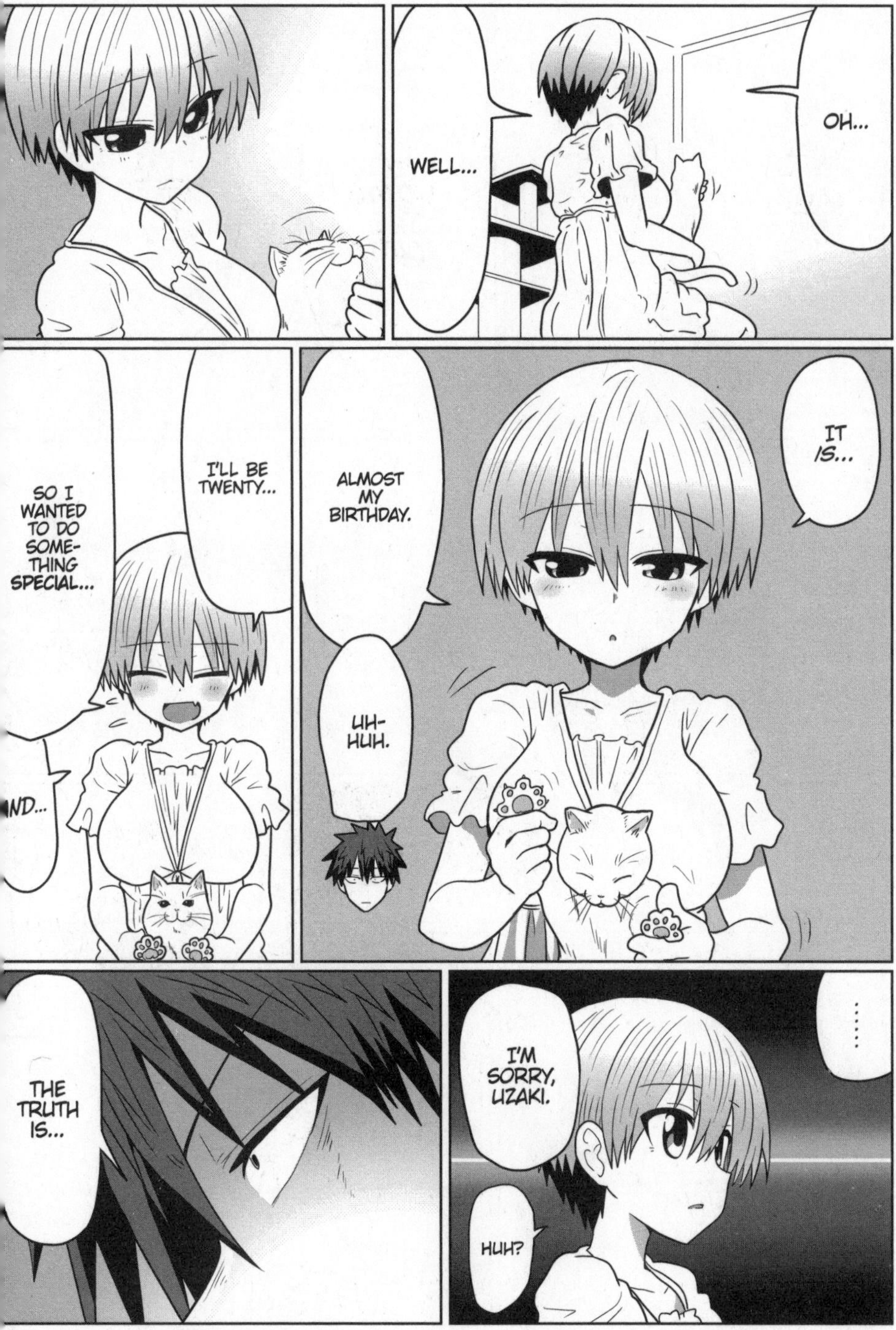
OH...
WELL...
IT IS...
ALMOST MY BIRTHDAY.
UH-HUH.
I'LL BE TWENTY...
SO I WANTED TO DO SOME-THING SPECIAL...
ND...
......
I'M SORRY, UZAKI.
HUH?
THE TRUTH IS...

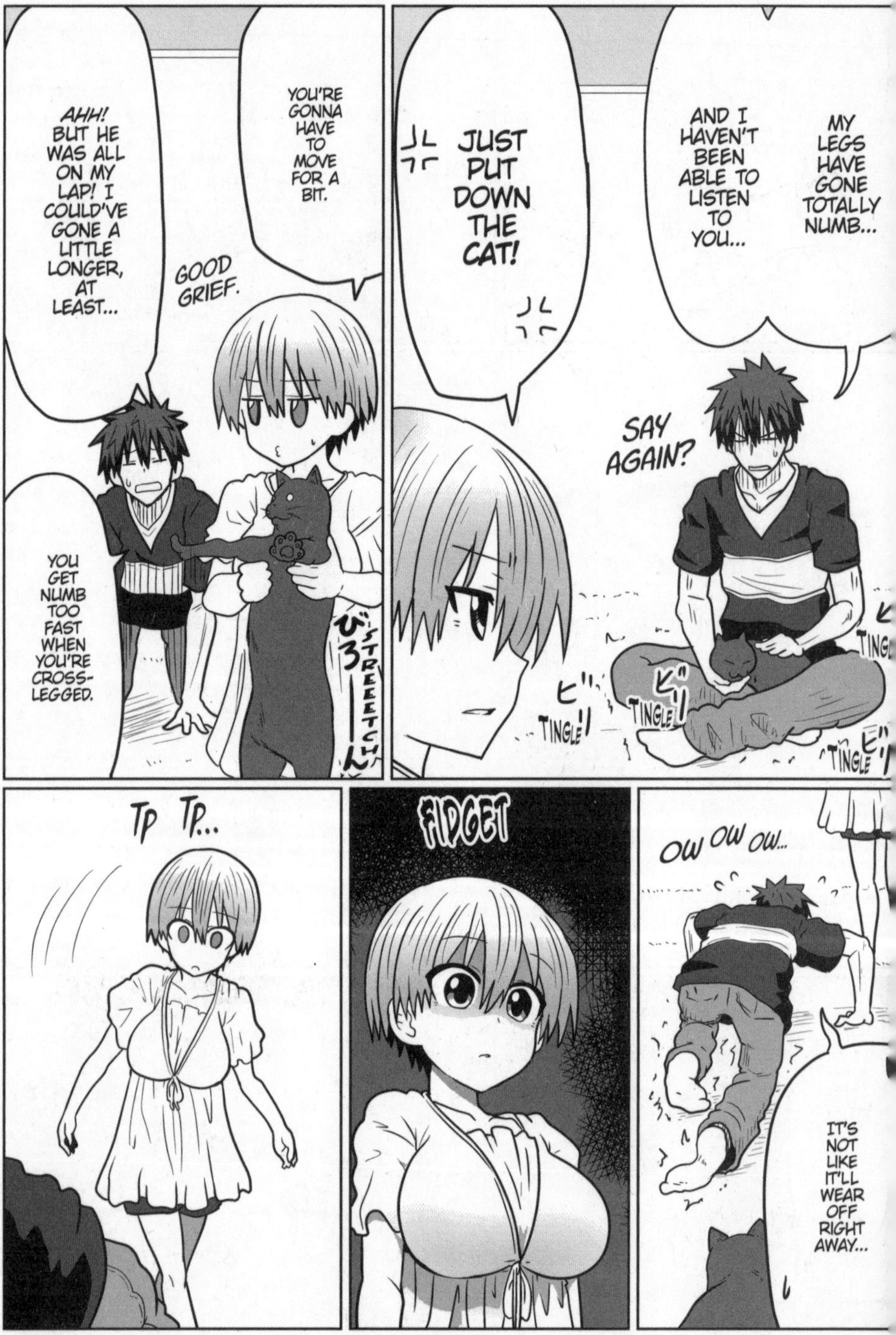
MY LEGS HAVE GONE TOTALLY NUMB...
AND I HAVEN'T BEEN ABLE TO LISTEN TO YOU...
SAY AGAIN?
TINGLE
TINGLE
TINGLE
TINGLE
JUST PUT DOWN THE CAT!
YOU'RE GONNA HAVE TO MOVE FOR A BIT.
AHH! BUT HE WAS ALL ON MY LAP! I COULD'VE GONE A LITTLE LONGER, AT LEAST...
GOOD GRIEF.
STREEEETCH
YOU GET NUMB TOO FAST WHEN YOU'RE CROSS-LEGGED.
OW OW OW...
IT'S NOT LIKE IT'LL WEAR OFF RIGHT AWAY...
FIDGET
TP TP...

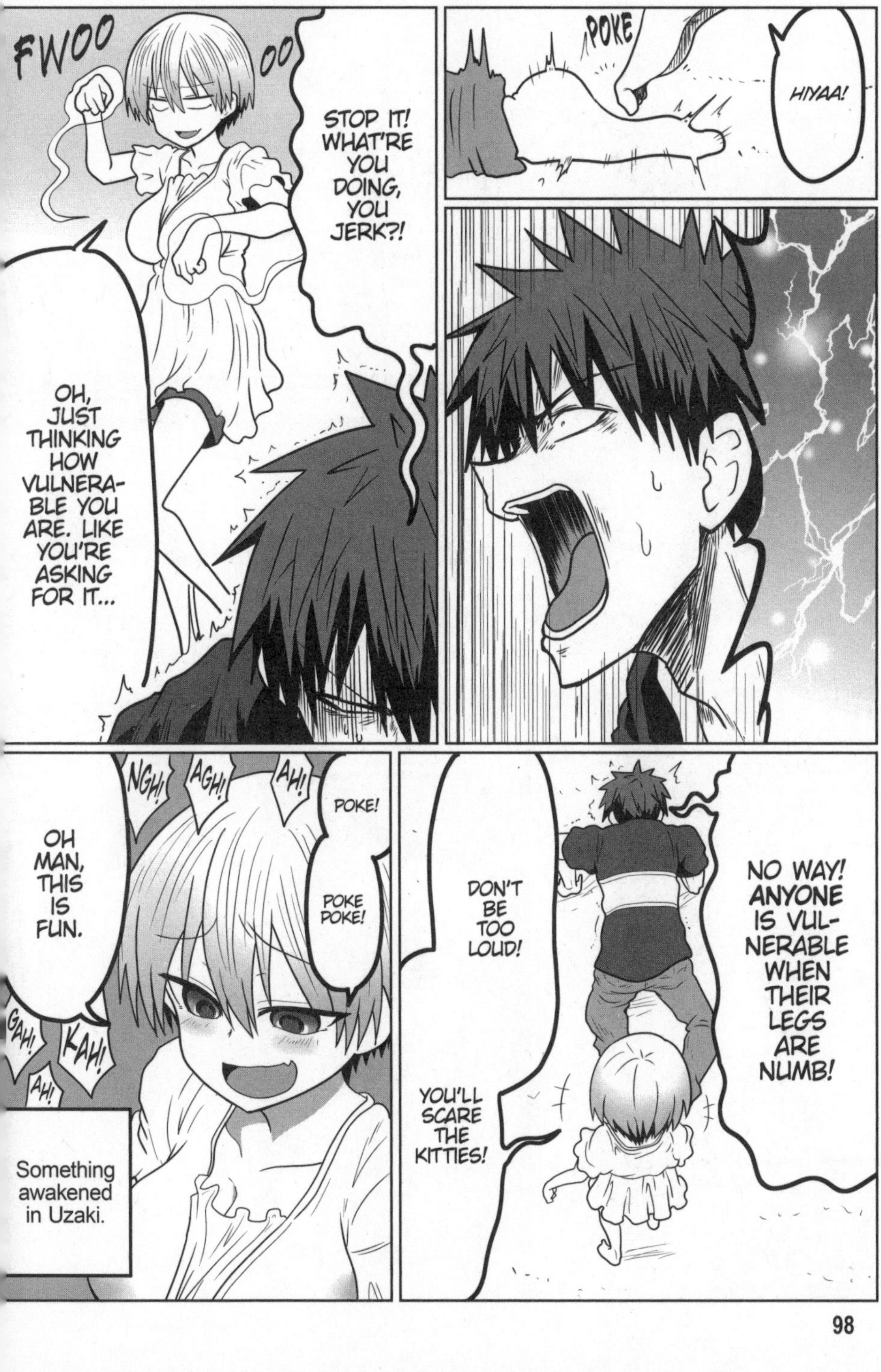
HIYAA!
POKE
FWOOOO
STOP IT! WHAT'RE YOU DOING, YOU JERK?!
OH, JUST THINKING HOW VULNERA-BLE YOU ARE. LIKE YOU'RE ASKING FOR IT...
NO WAY! ANYONE IS VUL-NERABLE WHEN THEIR LEGS ARE NUMB!
DON'T BE TOO LOUD!
YOU'LL SCARE THE KITTIES!
AH!
AGH!
NGH!
POKE!
POKE POKE!
OH MAN, THIS IS FUN.
GAH!
KAH!
AH!
Something awakened in Uzaki.

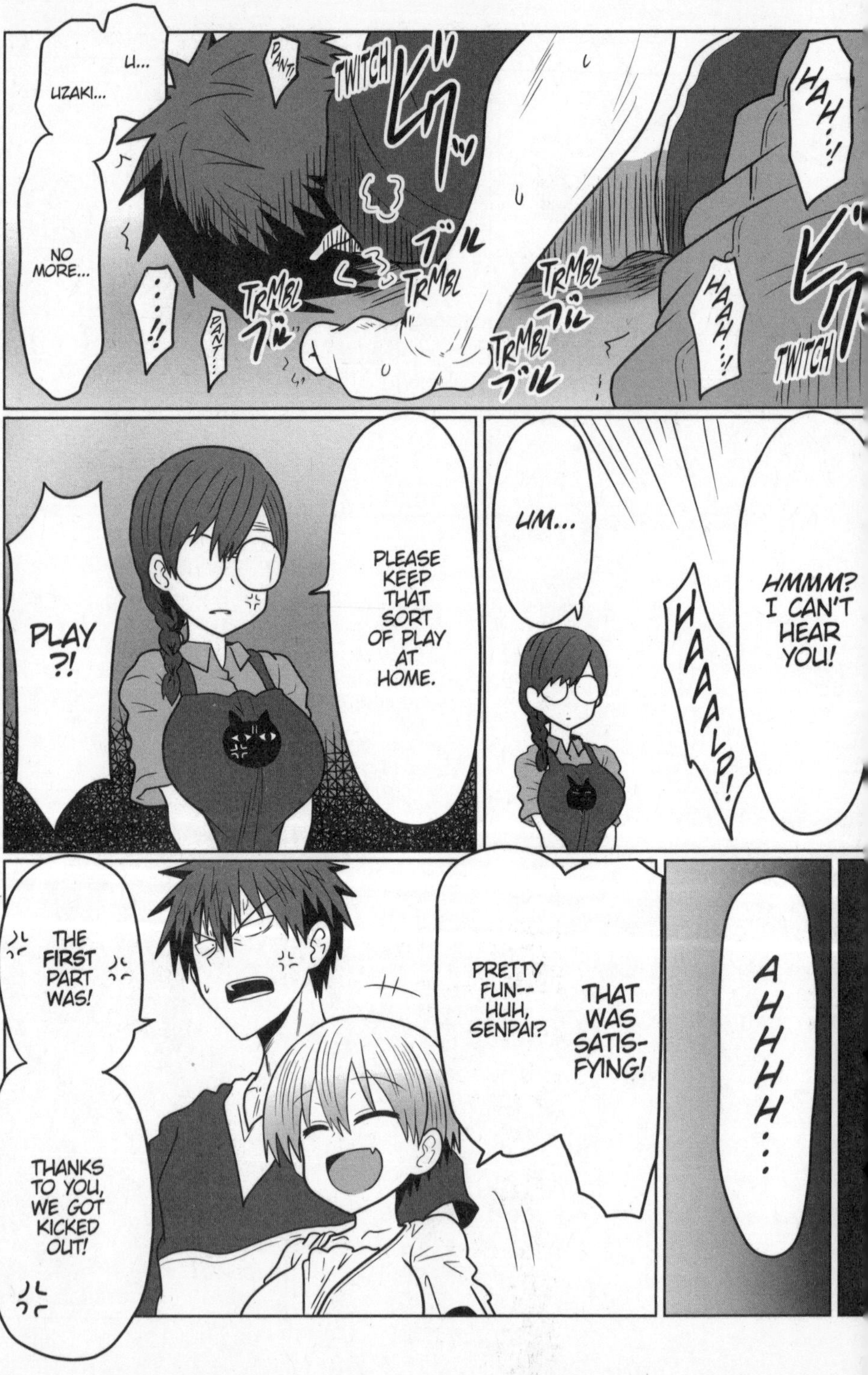
HAH...!
HAAH...!
TWITCH
TWITCH
TRMBL
TRMBL
TRMBL
TRMBL
PANT!
U...
UZAKI...
NO MORE...
...!!
PANT...
HMMM? I CAN'T HEAR YOU!
HAAAALP!
UM...
PLEASE KEEP THAT SORT OF PLAY AT HOME.
PLAY?!
AHHHH...
THAT WAS SATIS-FYING!
PRETTY FUN-- HUH, SENPAI?
THE FIRST PART WAS!
THANKS TO YOU, WE GOT KICKED OUT!

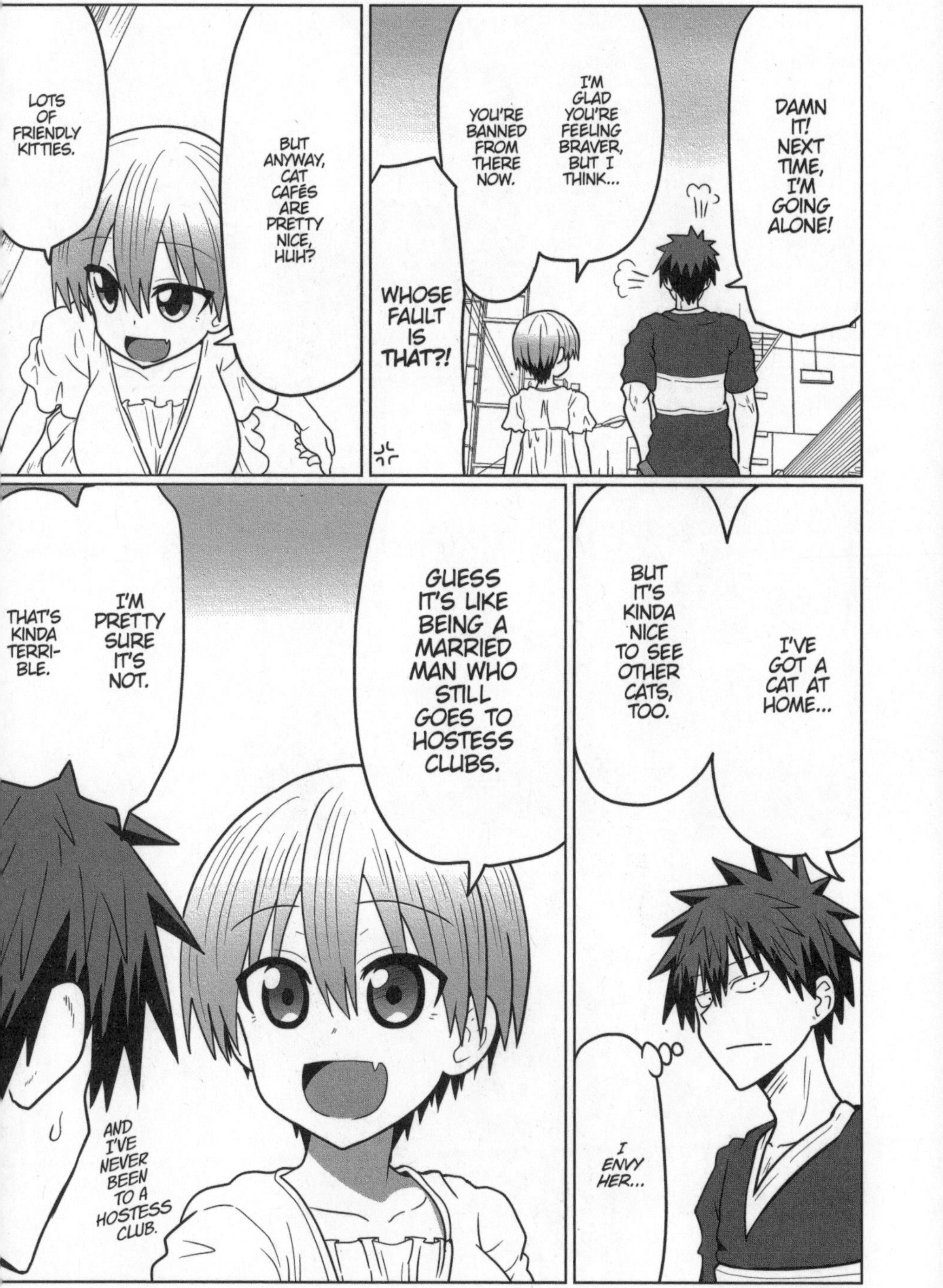
DAMN IT! NEXT TIME, I'M GOING ALONE!
I'M GLAD YOU'RE FEELING BRAVER, BUT I THINK...
YOU'RE BANNED FROM THERE NOW.
WHOSE FAULT IS THAT?!
BUT ANYWAY, CAT CAFÉS ARE PRETTY NICE, HUH?
LOTS OF FRIENDLY KITTIES.
I'VE GOT A CAT AT HOME...
BUT IT'S KINDA NICE TO SEE OTHER CATS, TOO.
I ENVY HER...
GUESS IT'S LIKE BEING A MARRIED MAN WHO STILL GOES TO HOSTESS CLUBS.
I'M PRETTY SURE IT'S NOT.
THAT'S KINDA TERRIBLE.
AND I'VE NEVER BEEN TO A HOSTESS CLUB.

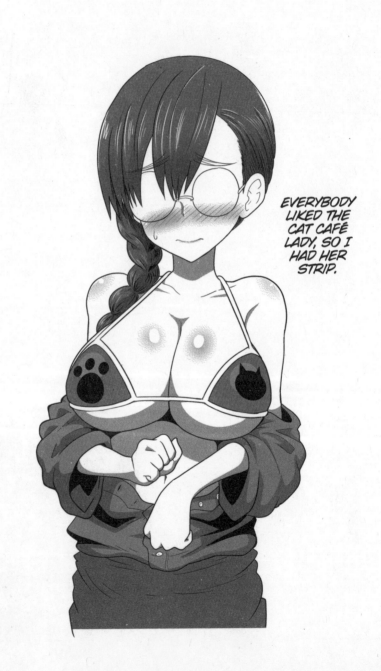

EVERYBODY LIKED THE CAT CAFÉ LADY, SO I HAD HER STRIP.

Uzaki-chan ☆ Wants to Hang Out!

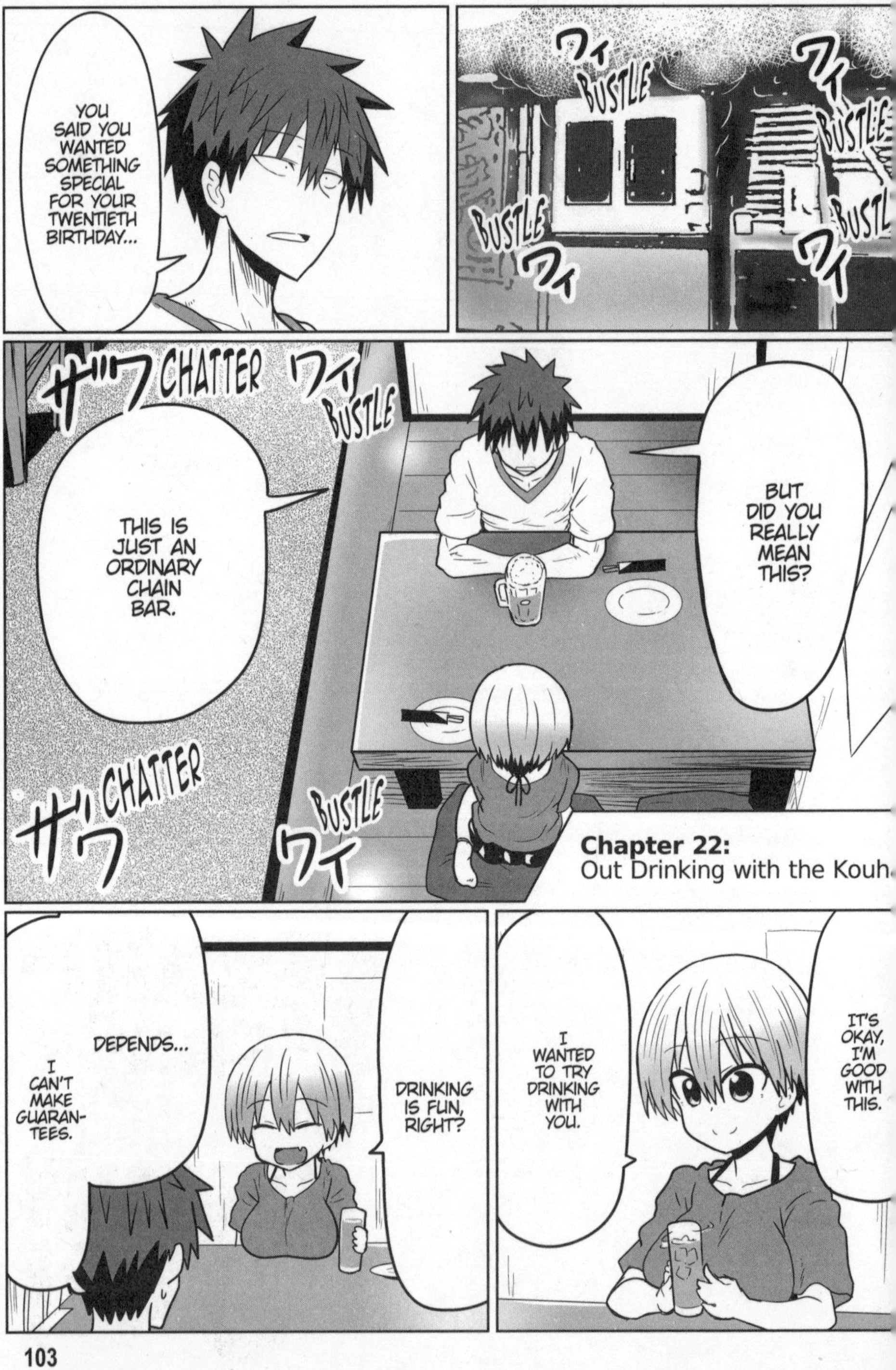
ワィ
BUSTLE
ワィ
BUSTLE
BUSTLE
ワィ
BUSTLE
ワィ
YOU SAID YOU WANTED SOMETHING SPECIAL FOR YOUR TWENTIETH BIRTHDAY...
BUT DID YOU REALLY MEAN THIS?
ワィ BUSTLE
ザワ CHATTER
THIS IS JUST AN ORDINARY CHAIN BAR.
ワィ BUSTLE
ザワ CHATTER
Chapter 22:
Out Drinking with the Kouh
IT'S OKAY, I'M GOOD WITH THIS.
I WANTED TO TRY DRINKING WITH YOU.
DRINKING IS FUN, RIGHT?
DEPENDS...
I CAN'T MAKE GUARAN-TEES.

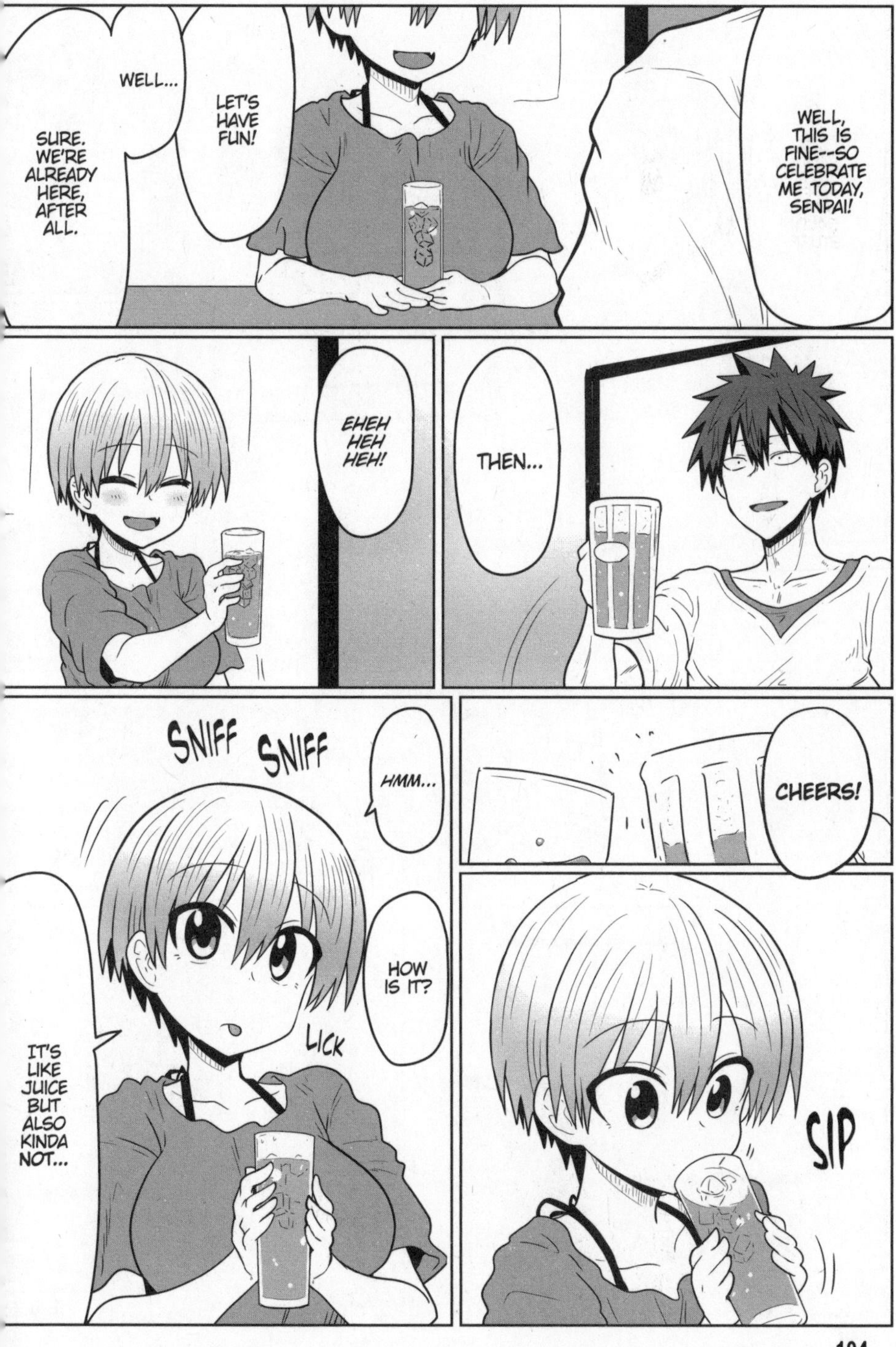
WELL, THIS IS FINE--SO CELEBRATE ME TODAY, SENPAI!
LET'S HAVE FUN!
WELL...
SURE. WE'RE ALREADY HERE, AFTER ALL.
THEN...
EHEH HEH HEH!
CHEERS!
SIP
HMM...
SNIFF SNIFF
HOW IS IT?
LICK
IT'S LIKE JUICE BUT ALSO KINDA NOT...

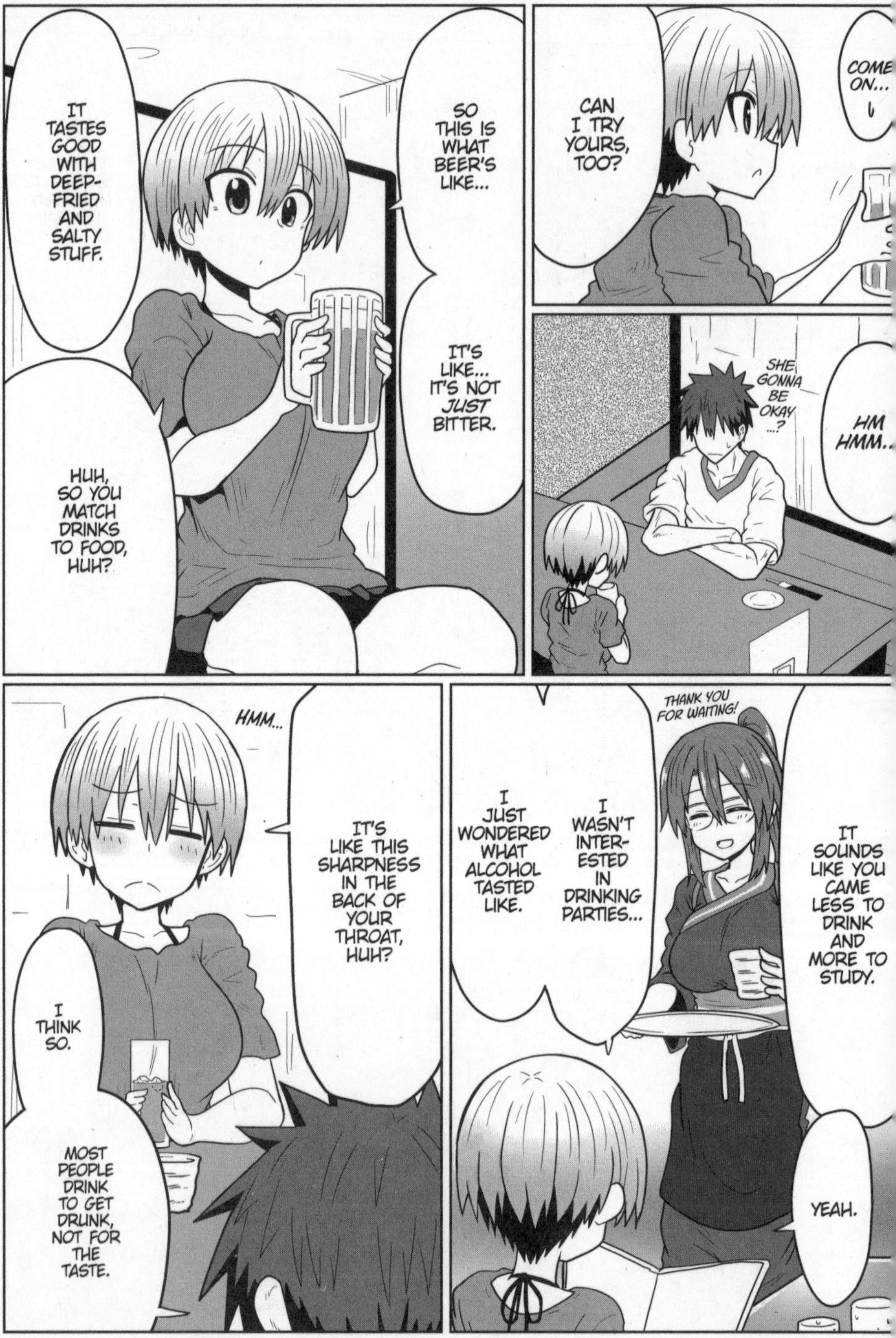
COME ON...
CAN I TRY YOURS, TOO?
HM HMM...
SHE GONNA BE OKAY ...?
SO THIS IS WHAT BEER'S LIKE...
IT'S LIKE... IT'S NOT *JUST* BITTER.
IT TASTES GOOD WITH DEEP-FRIED AND SALTY STUFF.
HUH, SO YOU MATCH DRINKS TO FOOD, HUH?
IT SOUNDS LIKE YOU CAME LESS TO DRINK AND MORE TO STUDY.
THANK YOU FOR WAITING!
I WASN'T INTER-ESTED IN DRINKING PARTIES...
I JUST WONDERED WHAT ALCOHOL TASTED LIKE.
YEAH.
IT'S LIKE THIS SHARPNESS IN THE BACK OF YOUR THROAT, HUH?
HMM...
I THINK SO.
MOST PEOPLE DRINK TO GET DRUNK, NOT FOR THE TASTE.

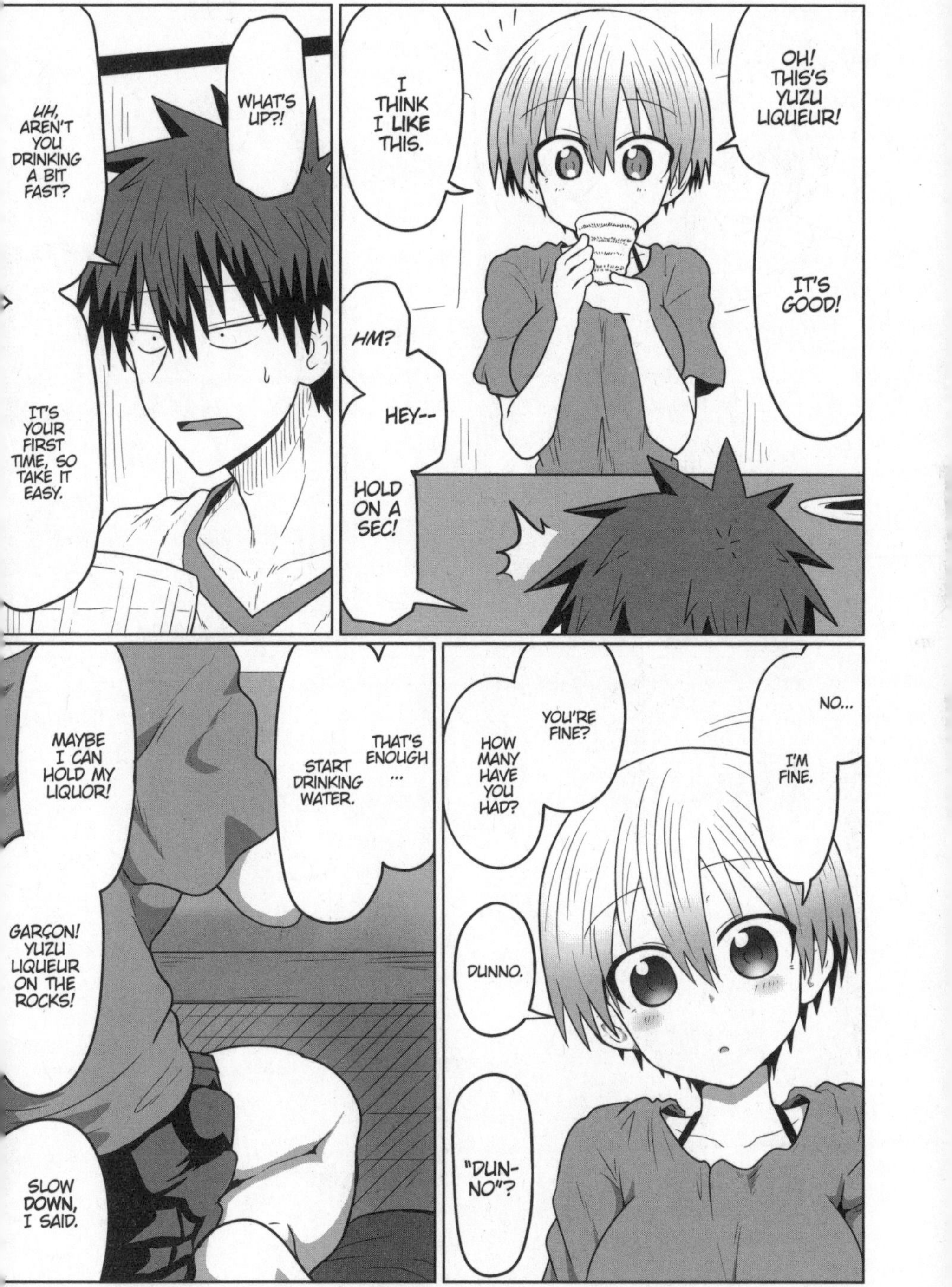
OH! THIS'S YUZU LIQUEUR!
IT'S GOOD!
I THINK I LIKE THIS.
HM?
HEY--
HOLD ON A SEC!
WHAT'S UP?!
UH, AREN'T YOU DRINKING A BIT FAST?
IT'S YOUR FIRST TIME, SO TAKE IT EASY.
NO...
I'M FINE.
YOU'RE FINE?
HOW MANY HAVE YOU HAD?
DUNNO.
"DUN-NO"?
THAT'S ENOUGH ...
START DRINKING WATER.
MAYBE I CAN HOLD MY LIQUOR!
GARÇON! YUZU LIQUEUR ON THE ROCKS!
SLOW DOWN, I SAID.

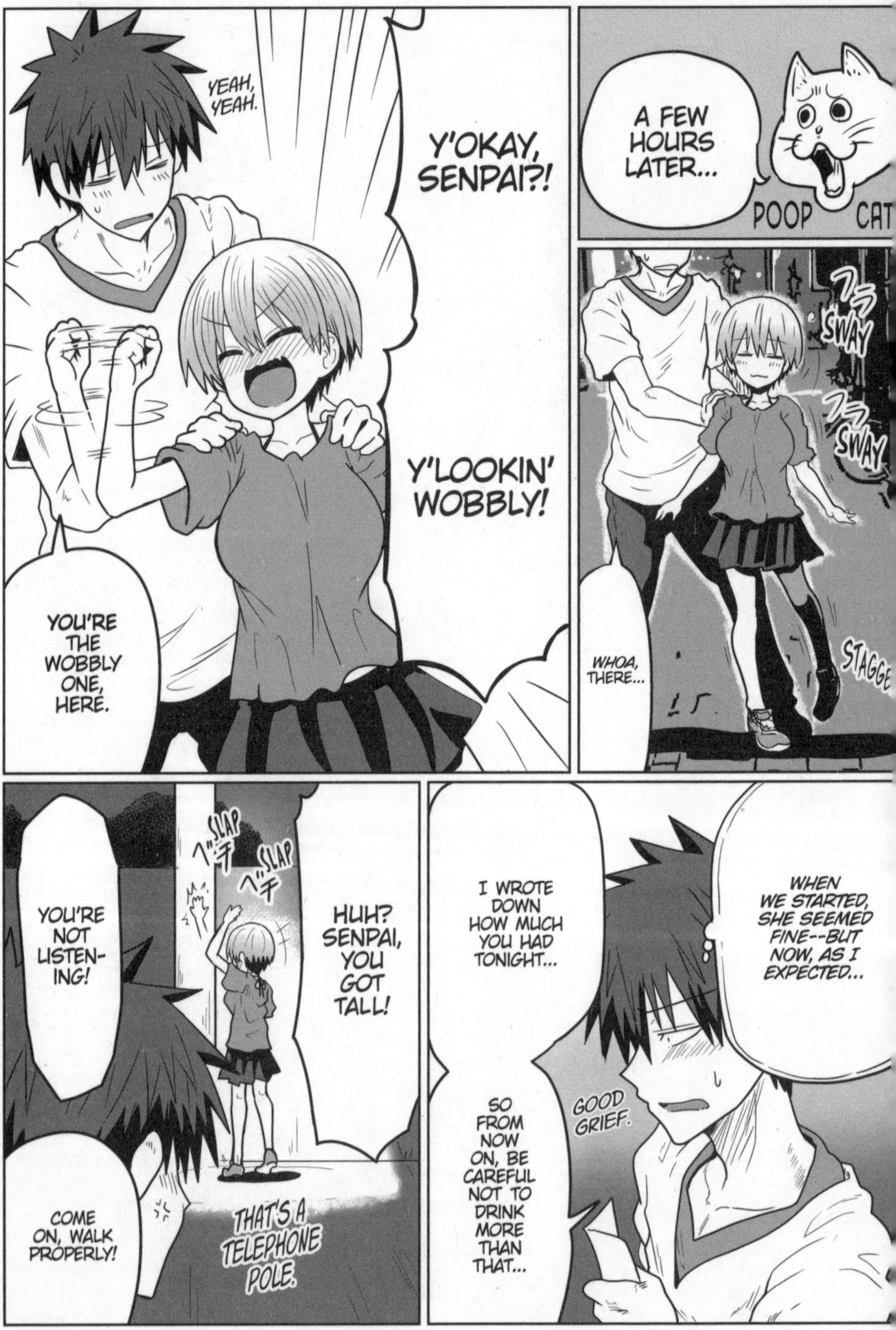
A FEW HOURS LATER...
POOP CAT
フラ SWAY
フラ SWAY
WHOA, THERE...
STAGGE
Y'OKAY, SENPAI?!
Y'LOOKIN' WOBBLY!
YEAH, YEAH.
YOU'RE THE WOBBLY ONE, HERE.
WHEN WE STARTED, SHE SEEMED FINE--BUT NOW, AS I EXPECTED...
I WROTE DOWN HOW MUCH YOU HAD TONIGHT...
GOOD GRIEF.
SO FROM NOW ON, BE CAREFUL NOT TO DRINK MORE THAN THAT...
ペチ SLAP
ペチ SLAP
HUH? SENPAI, YOU GOT TALL!
YOU'RE NOT LISTEN-ING!
THAT'S A TELEPHONE POLE.
COME ON, WALK PROPERLY!

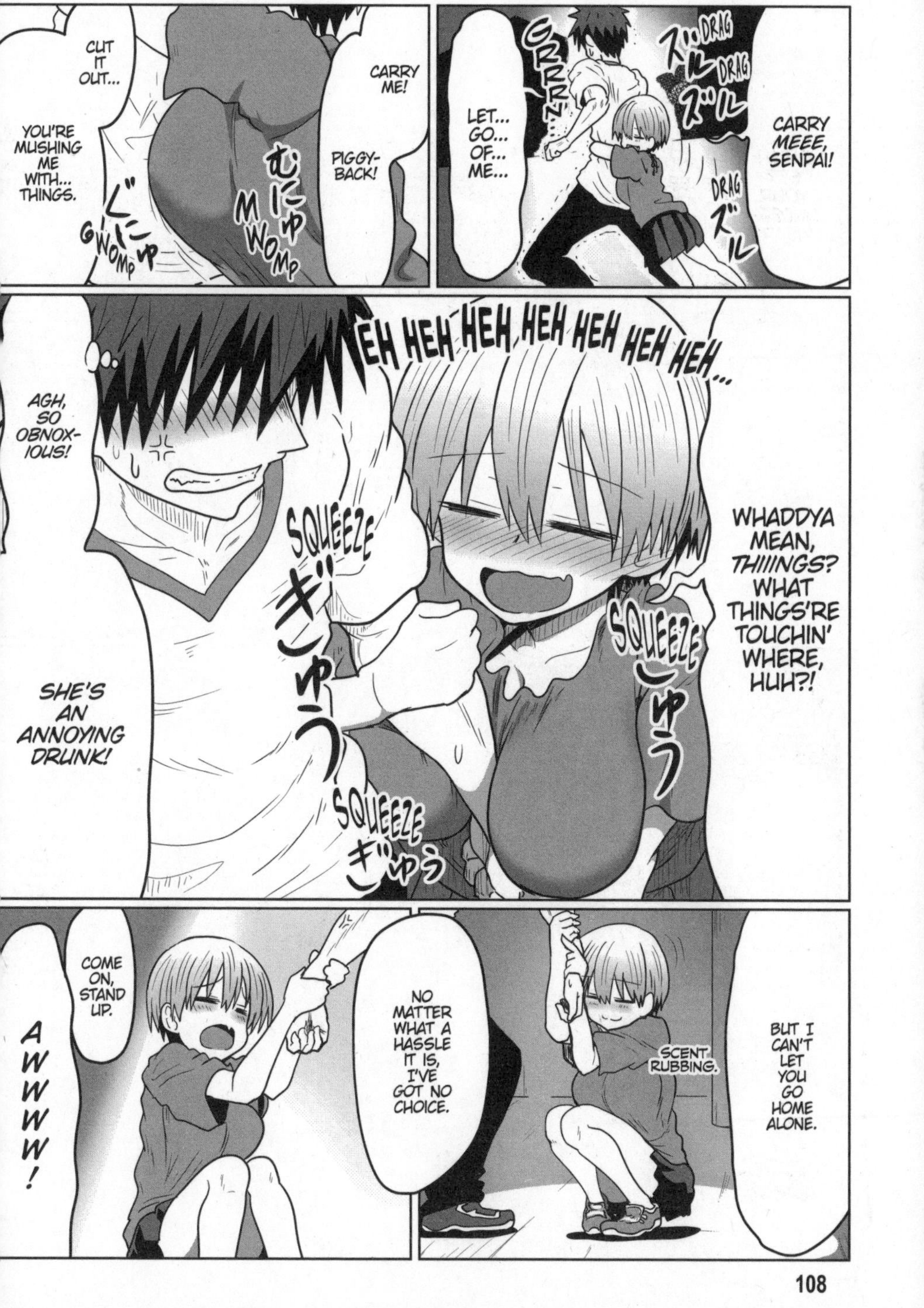
CARRY MEEE, SENPAI!
ズル DRAG
ズル DRAG
ズル DRAG
GRRRN
LET... GO... OF... ME...
CARRY ME!
PIGGY-BACK!
むにゅ MWOMP
CUT IT OUT...
YOU'RE MUSHING ME WITH... THINGS.
ぐにゅ GWOMP
EH HEH HEH HEH HEH HEH HEH...
WHADDYA MEAN, *THIIINGS*? WHAT THINGS'RE TOUCHIN' WHERE, HUH?!
SQUEEZE じゅう
SQUEEZE ぎゅう
SQUEEZE ぎゅう
AGH, SO OBNOX-IOUS!
SHE'S AN ANNOYING DRUNK!
BUT I CAN'T LET YOU GO HOME ALONE.
SCENT RUBBING.
NO MATTER WHAT A HASSLE IT IS, I'VE GOT NO CHOICE.
COME ON, STAND UP.
AWWWWW!

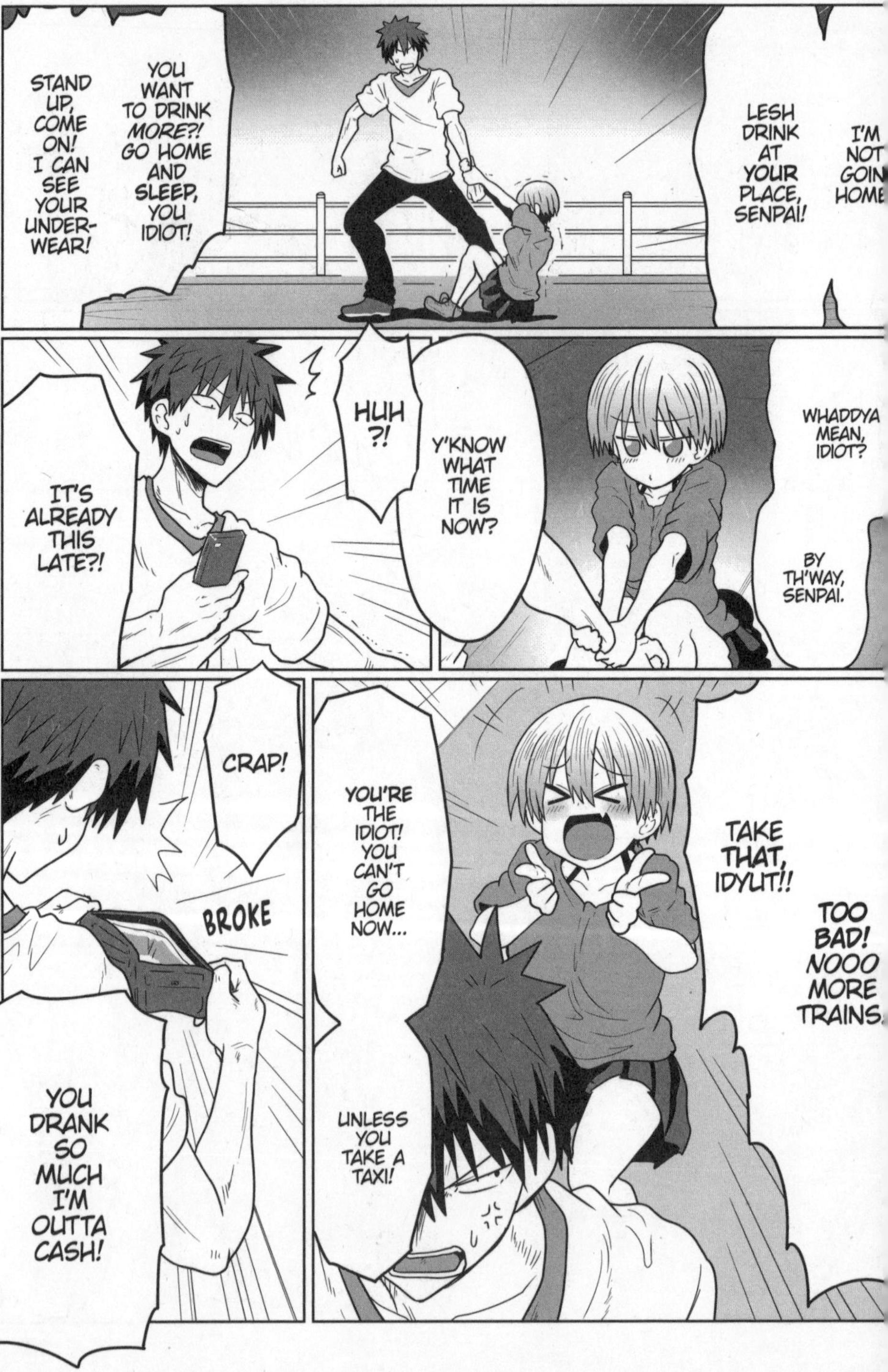
I'M NOT GOIN HOME
LESH DRINK AT YOUR PLACE, SENPAI!
YOU WANT TO DRINK MORE?! GO HOME AND SLEEP, YOU IDIOT!
STAND UP, COME ON! I CAN SEE YOUR UNDER-WEAR!
WHADDYA MEAN, IDIOT?
BY TH'WAY, SENPAI.
Y'KNOW WHAT TIME IT IS NOW?
HUH?!
IT'S ALREADY THIS LATE?!
TOO BAD! NOOO MORE TRAINS.
TAKE THAT, IDYUT!!
YOU'RE THE IDIOT! YOU CAN'T GO HOME NOW...
UNLESS YOU TAKE A TAXI!
CRAP!
BROKE
YOU DRANK SO MUCH I'M OUTTA CASH!

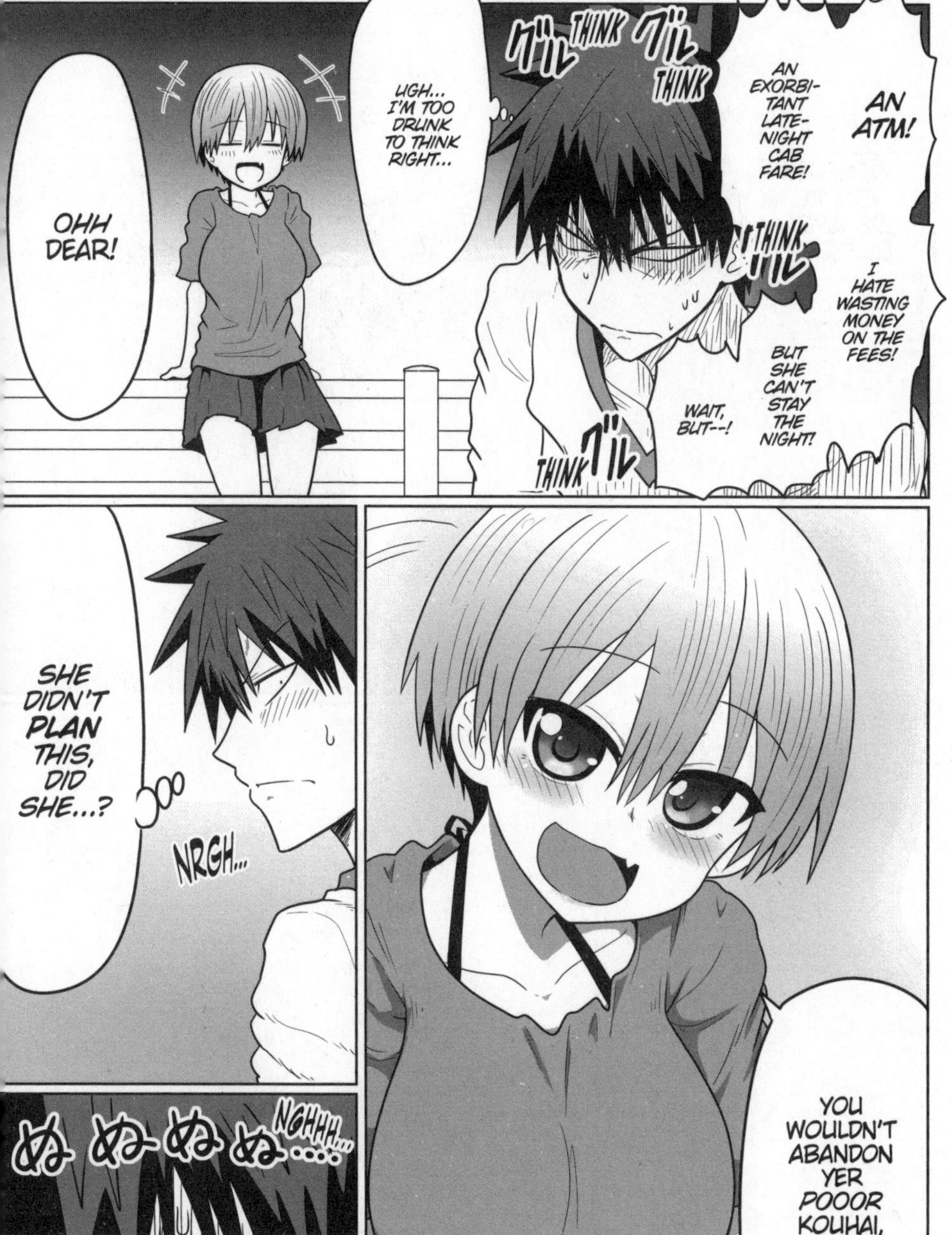
AN ATM!
AN EXORBITANT LATE-NIGHT CAB FARE!
グル THINK グル THINK
I HATE WASTING MONEY ON THE FEES!
THINK グル
BUT SHE CAN'T STAY THE NIGHT!
WAIT, BUT--!
THINK グル
UGH... I'M TOO DRUNK TO THINK RIGHT...
OHH DEAR!
YOU WOULDN'T ABANDON YER POOOR KOUHAI, WUDJA?
SHE DIDN'T PLAN THIS, DID SHE...?
NRGH...
ぬぬぬぬ... NGHHH...

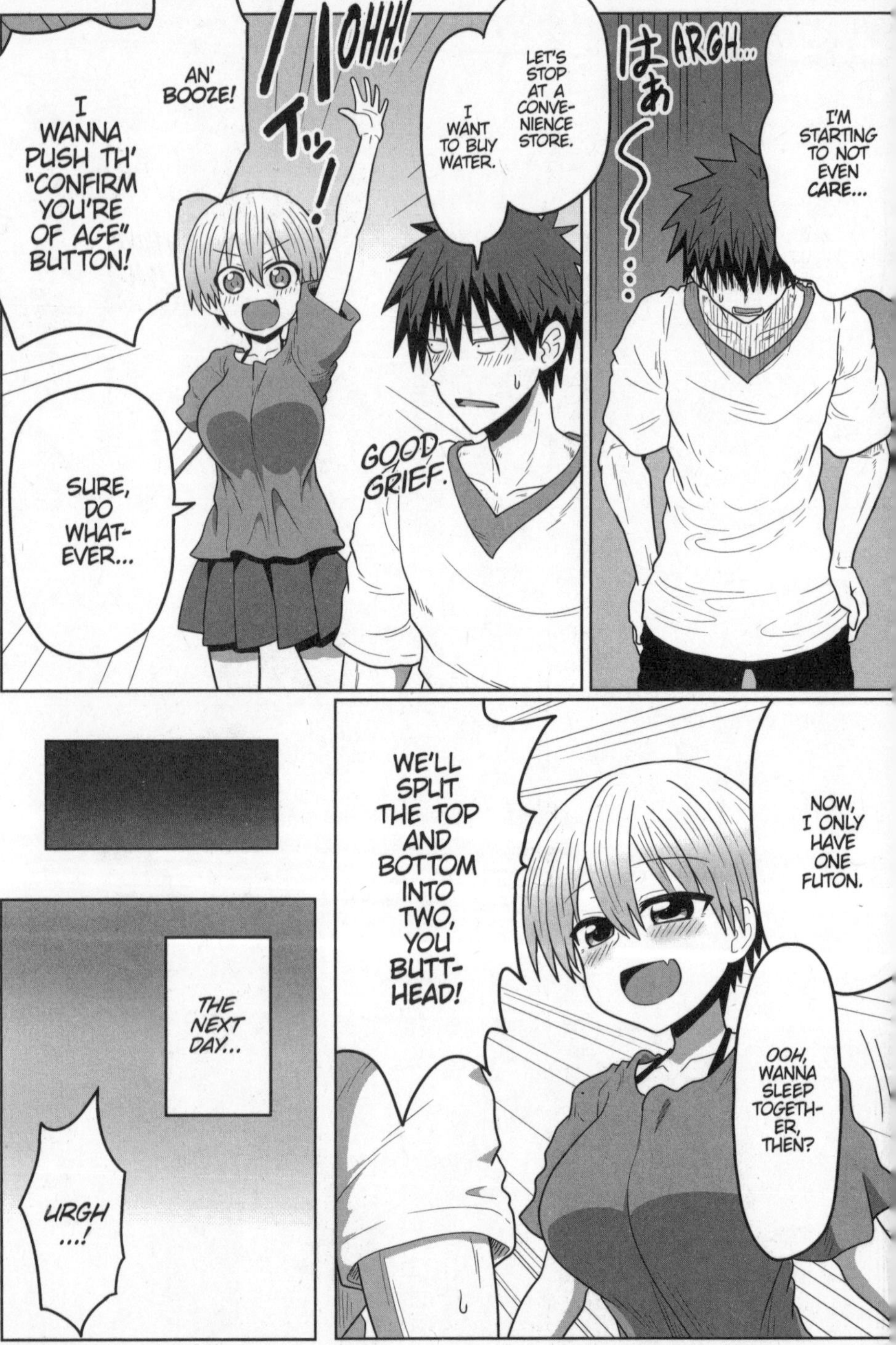
はぁ〜〜…
ARGH...
I'M STARTING TO NOT EVEN CARE...
LET'S STOP AT A CONVENIENCE STORE. I WANT TO BUY WATER.
イッ!
OHH!
AN' BOOZE!
I WANNA PUSH TH' "CONFIRM YOU'RE OF AGE" BUTTON!
GOOD GRIEF.
SURE, DO WHATEVER...
NOW, I ONLY HAVE ONE FUTON.
OOH, WANNA SLEEP TOGETHER, THEN?
WE'LL SPLIT THE TOP AND BOTTOM INTO TWO, YOU BUTT-HEAD!
THE NEXT DAY...
URGH...!

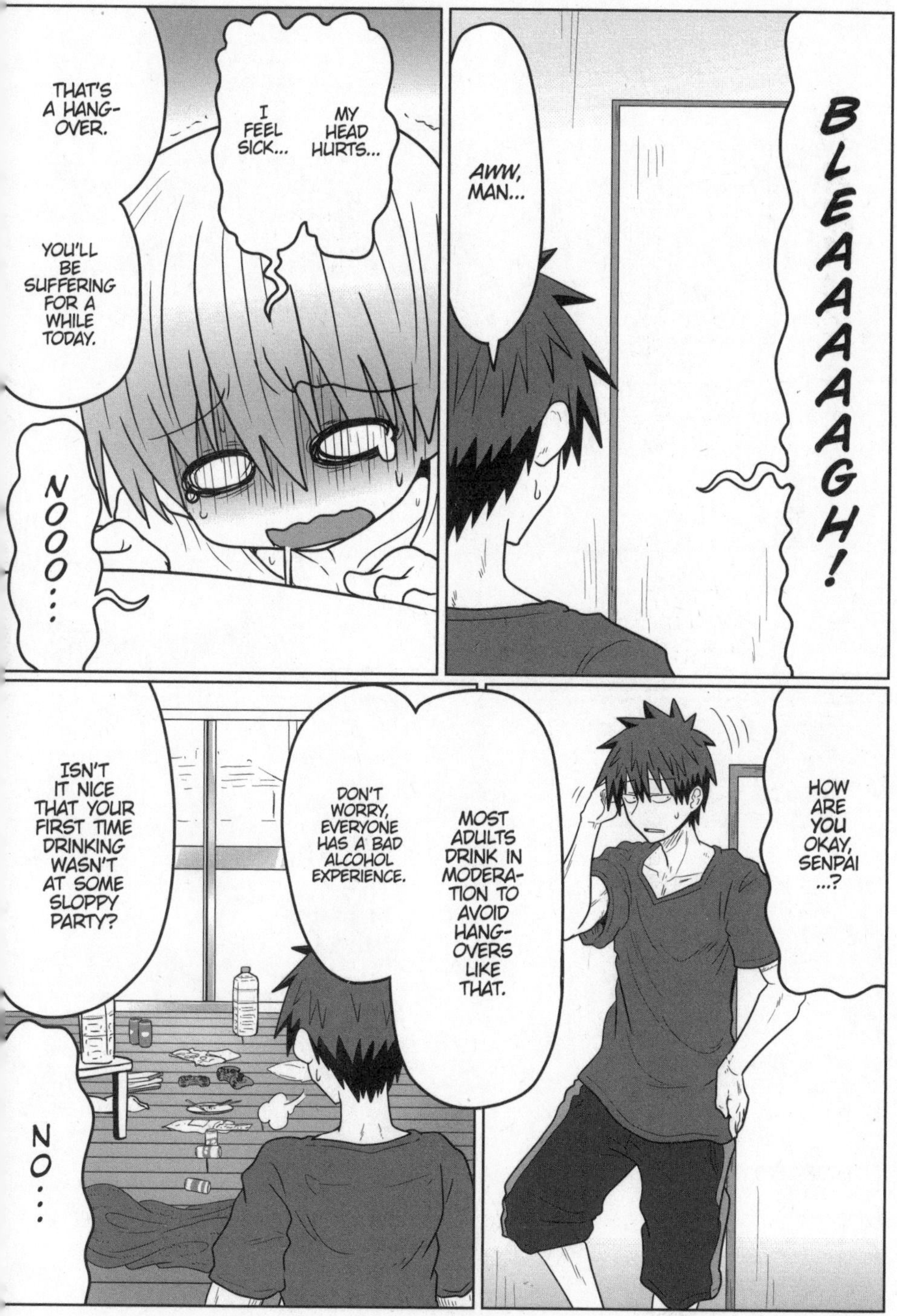
BLEAAAAAGH!
AWW, MAN...
MY HEAD HURTS...
I FEEL SICK...
THAT'S A HANG-OVER.
YOU'LL BE SUFFERING FOR A WHILE TODAY.
NOOO...
HOW ARE YOU OKAY, SENPAI ...?
MOST ADULTS DRINK IN MODERA-TION TO AVOID HANG-OVERS LIKE THAT.
DON'T WORRY, EVERYONE HAS A BAD ALCOHOL EXPERIENCE.
ISN'T IT NICE THAT YOUR FIRST TIME DRINKING WASN'T AT SOME SLOPPY PARTY?
NO...

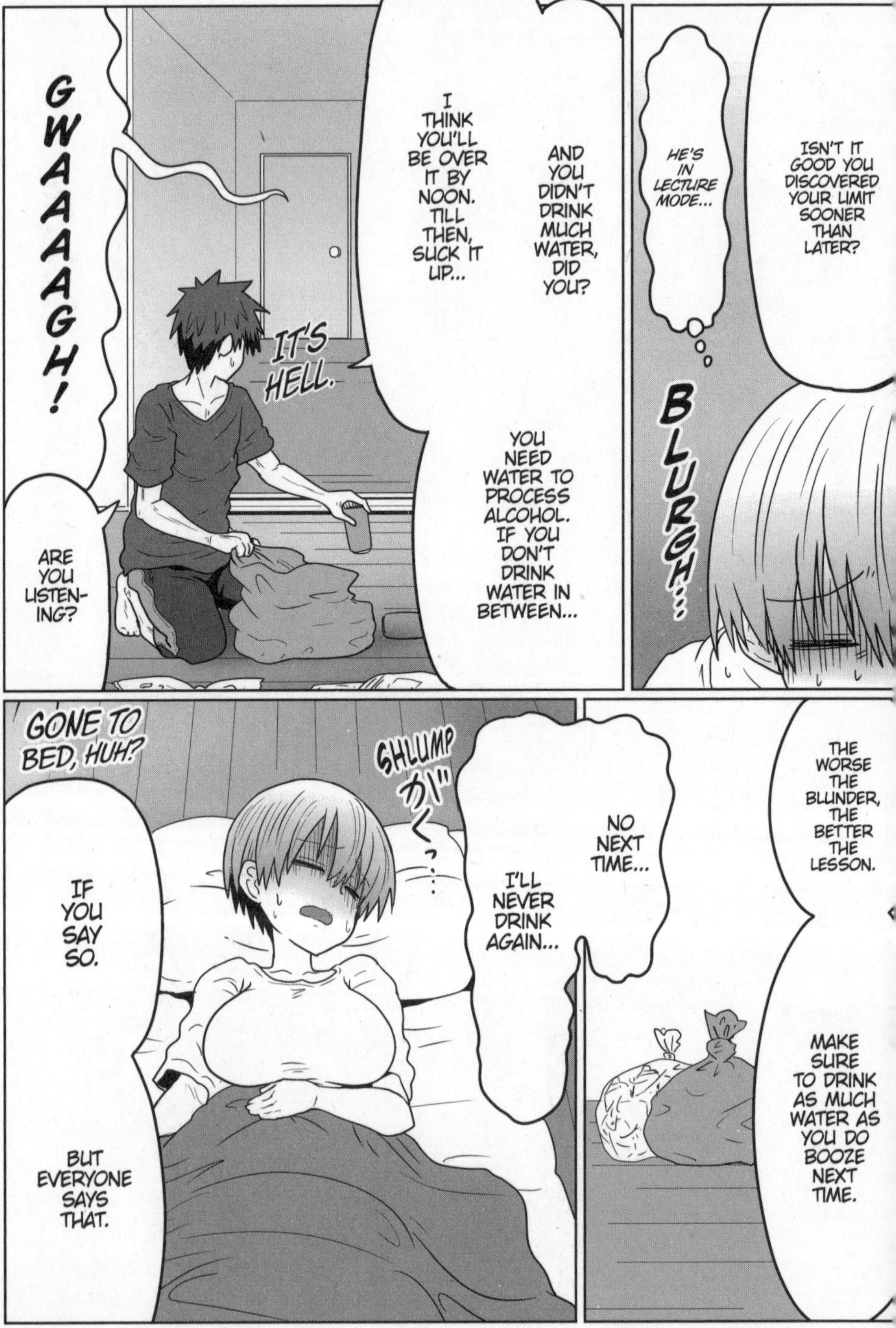

ISN'T IT GOOD YOU DISCOVERED YOUR LIMIT SOONER THAN LATER?
HE'S IN LECTURE MODE...
BLURGH...
I THINK YOU'LL BE OVER IT BY NOON. TILL THEN, SUCK IT UP...
AND YOU DIDN'T DRINK MUCH WATER, DID YOU?
YOU NEED WATER TO PROCESS ALCOHOL. IF YOU DON'T DRINK WATER IN BETWEEN...
IT'S HELL.
GWAAAAAGH!
ARE YOU LISTENING?
THE WORSE THE BLUNDER, THE BETTER THE LESSON.
MAKE SURE TO DRINK AS MUCH WATER AS YOU DO BOOZE NEXT TIME.
NO NEXT TIME...
I'LL NEVER DRINK AGAIN...
SHLUMP
がくっ…
GONE TO BED, HUH?
IF YOU SAY SO.
BUT EVERYONE SAYS THAT.

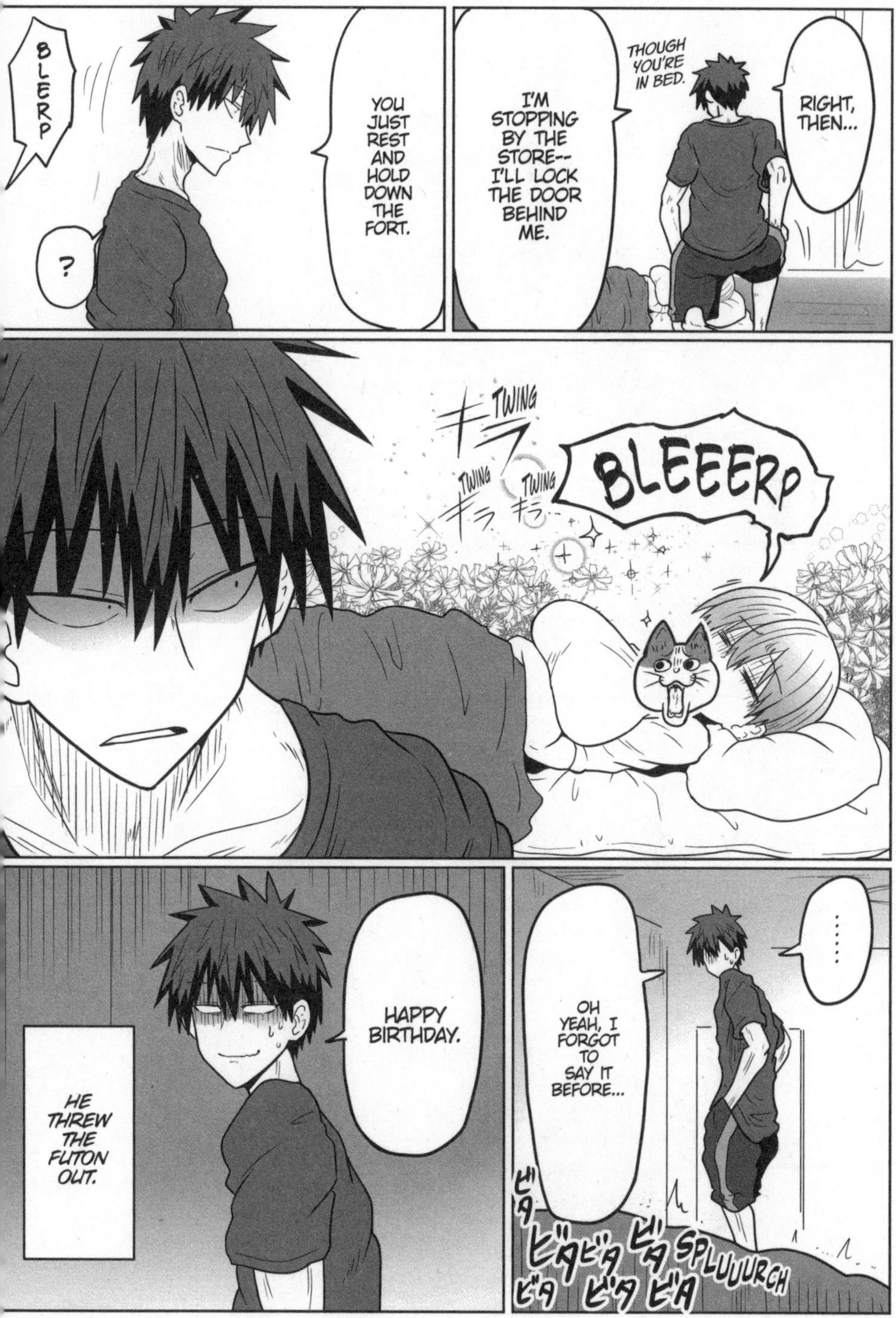
RIGHT, THEN...
THOUGH YOU'RE IN BED.
I'M STOPPING BY THE STORE-- I'LL LOCK THE DOOR BEHIND ME.
YOU JUST REST AND HOLD DOWN THE FORT.
BLERP
?
TWING
BLEEERP
TWING
TWING
......
OH YEAH, I FORGOT TO SAY IT BEFORE...
SPLUUURCH
HAPPY BIRTHDAY.
HE THREW THE FUTON OUT.

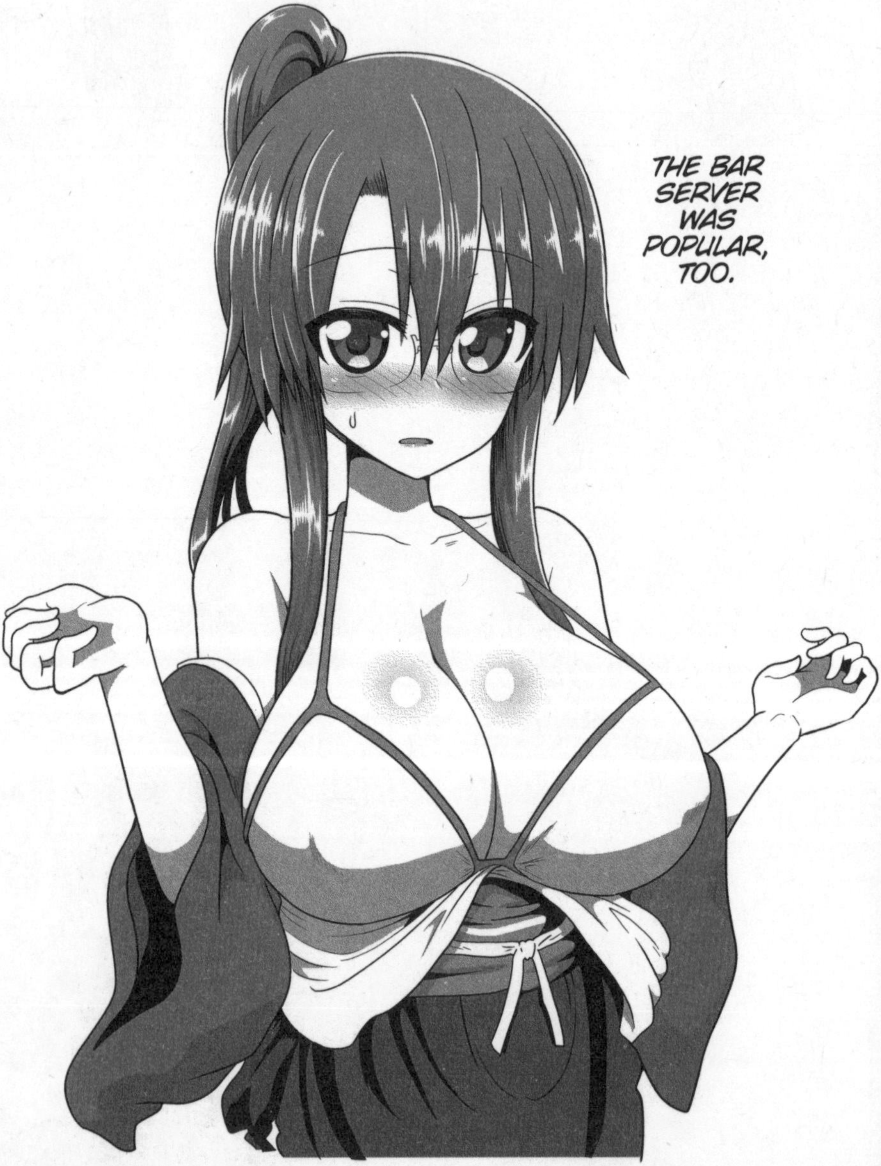
THE BAR SERVER WAS POPULAR, TOO.

Uzaki-
chan☆
Wants
to Hang
Out!

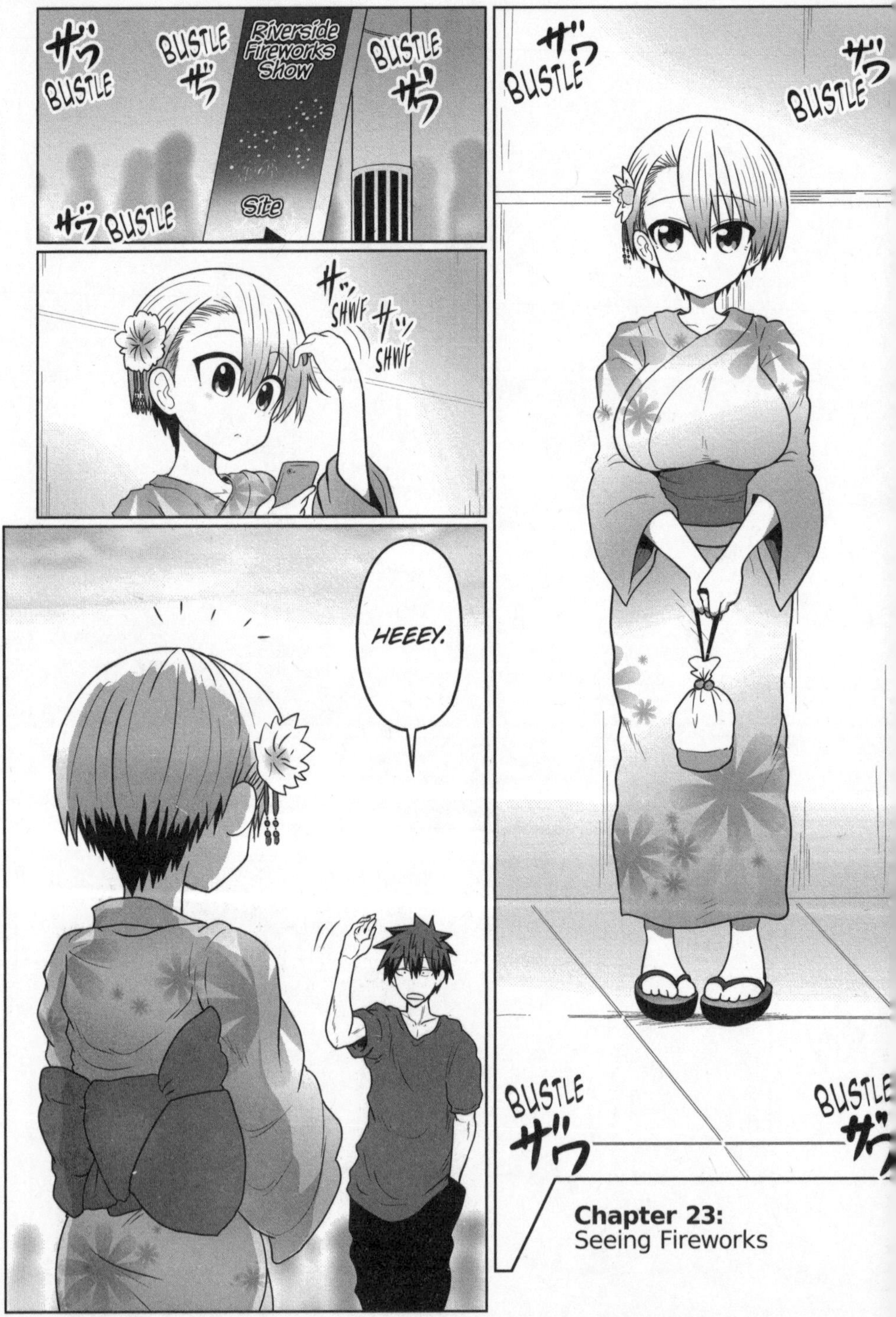
ザワ BUSTLE
ザワ BUSTLE
BUSTLE ザワ
BUSTLE ザワ
ザワ BUSTLE
BUSTLE ザワ
Riverside Fireworks Show
BUSTLE ザワ
ザワ BUSTLE
Site
ザッ SHWF
ザッ SHWF
HEEEY.

**Chapter 23:**
Seeing Fireworks

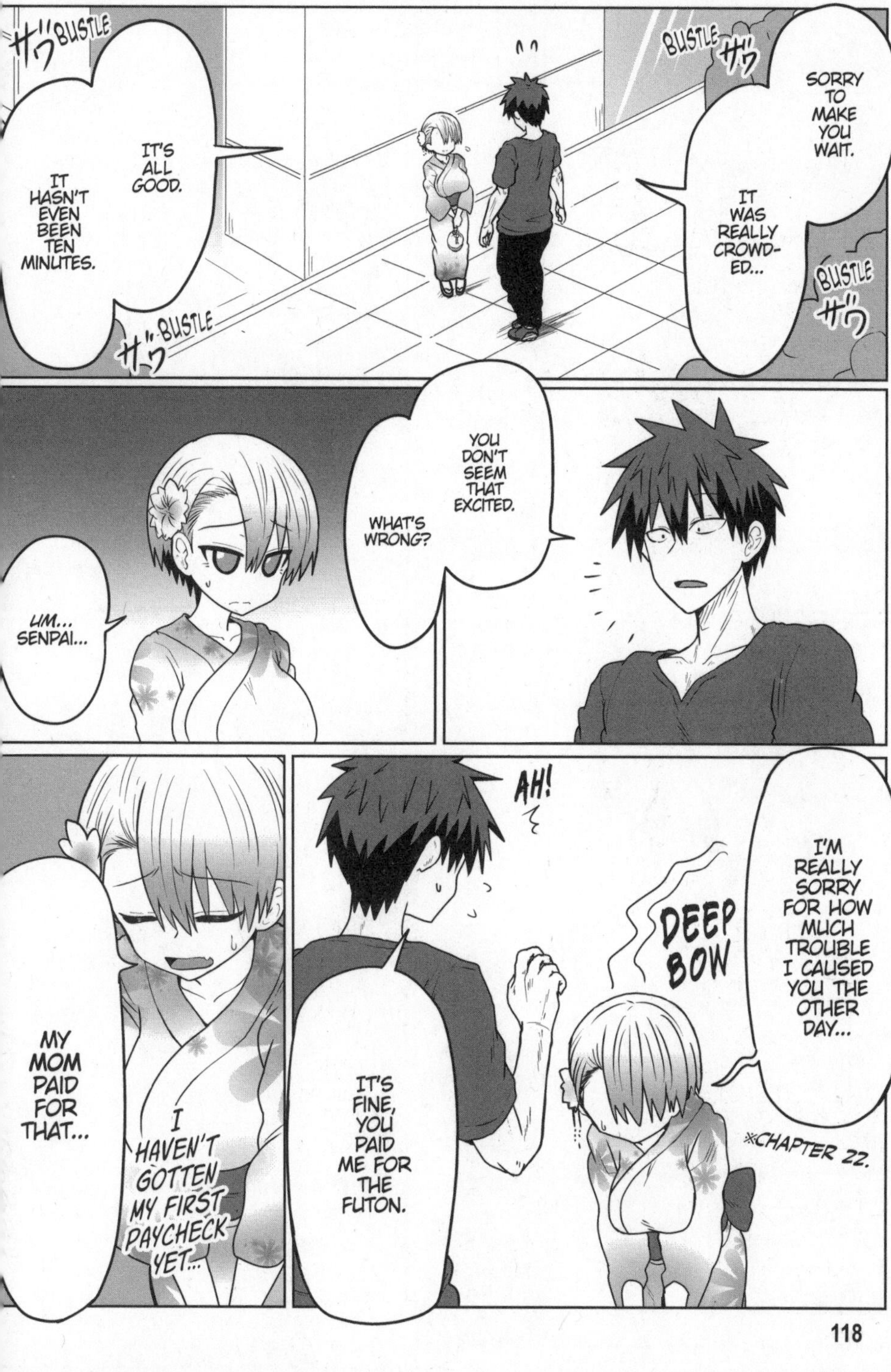
BUSTLE ザワ
SORRY TO MAKE YOU WAIT.
IT WAS REALLY CROWDED...
BUSTLE ザワ
BUSTLE ザワ
IT'S ALL GOOD.
IT HASN'T EVEN BEEN TEN MINUTES.
BUSTLE ザワ
YOU DON'T SEEM THAT EXCITED.
WHAT'S WRONG?
UM... SENPAI...
I'M REALLY SORRY FOR HOW MUCH TROUBLE I CAUSED YOU THE OTHER DAY...
DEEP BOW
※CHAPTER 22.
AH!
IT'S FINE, YOU PAID ME FOR THE FUTON.
MY MOM PAID FOR THAT...
I HAVEN'T GOTTEN MY FIRST PAYCHECK YET...

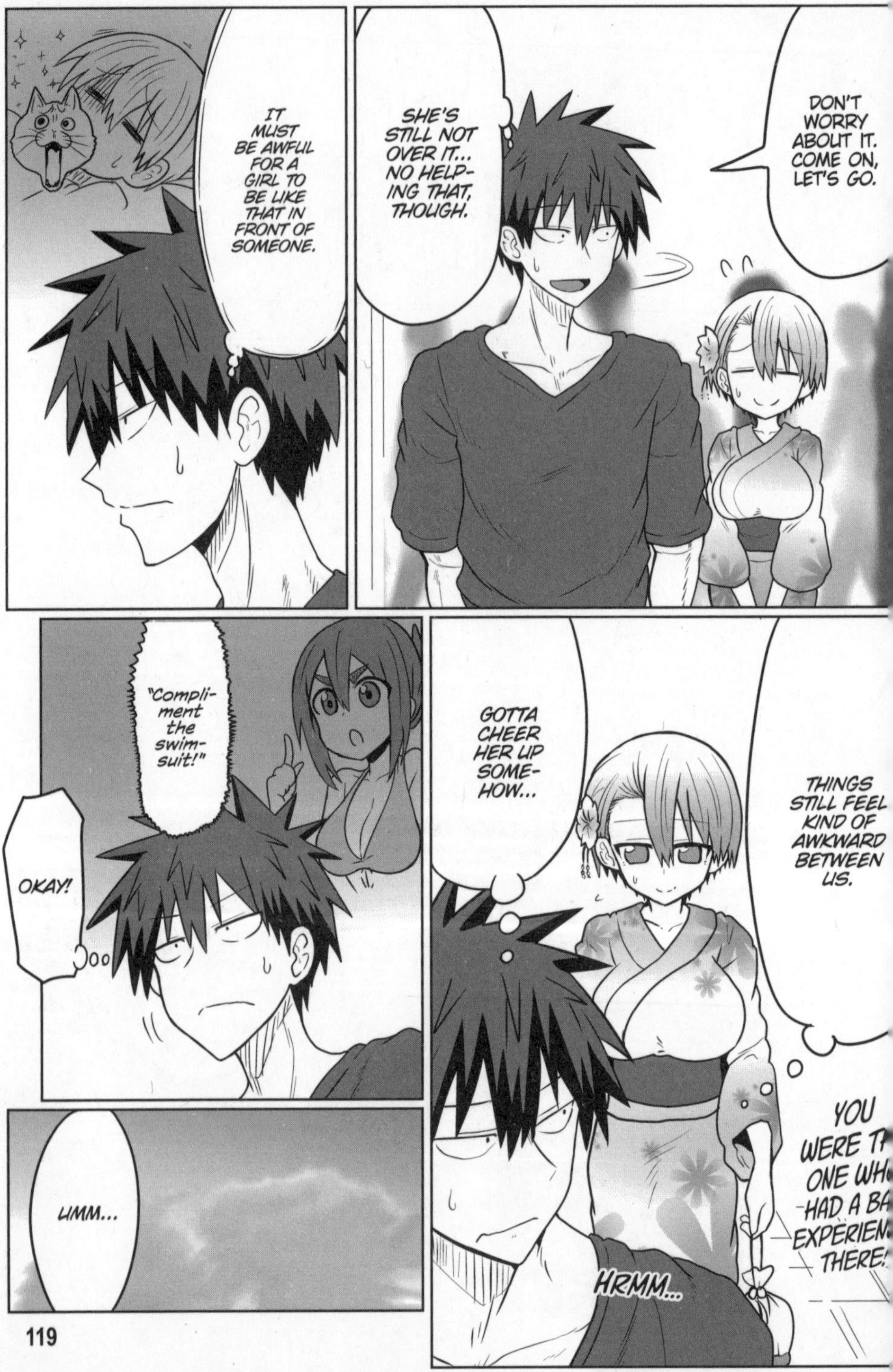
DON'T WORRY ABOUT IT. COME ON, LET'S GO.
SHE'S STILL NOT OVER IT... NO HELPING THAT, THOUGH.
IT MUST BE AWFUL FOR A GIRL TO BE LIKE THAT IN FRONT OF SOMEONE.
THINGS STILL FEEL KIND OF AWKWARD BETWEEN US.
GOTTA CHEER HER UP SOMEHOW...
YOU WERE TH ONE WH HAD A BA EXPERIEN THERE!
HRMM...
"Compliment the swimsuit!"
OKAY!
UMM...

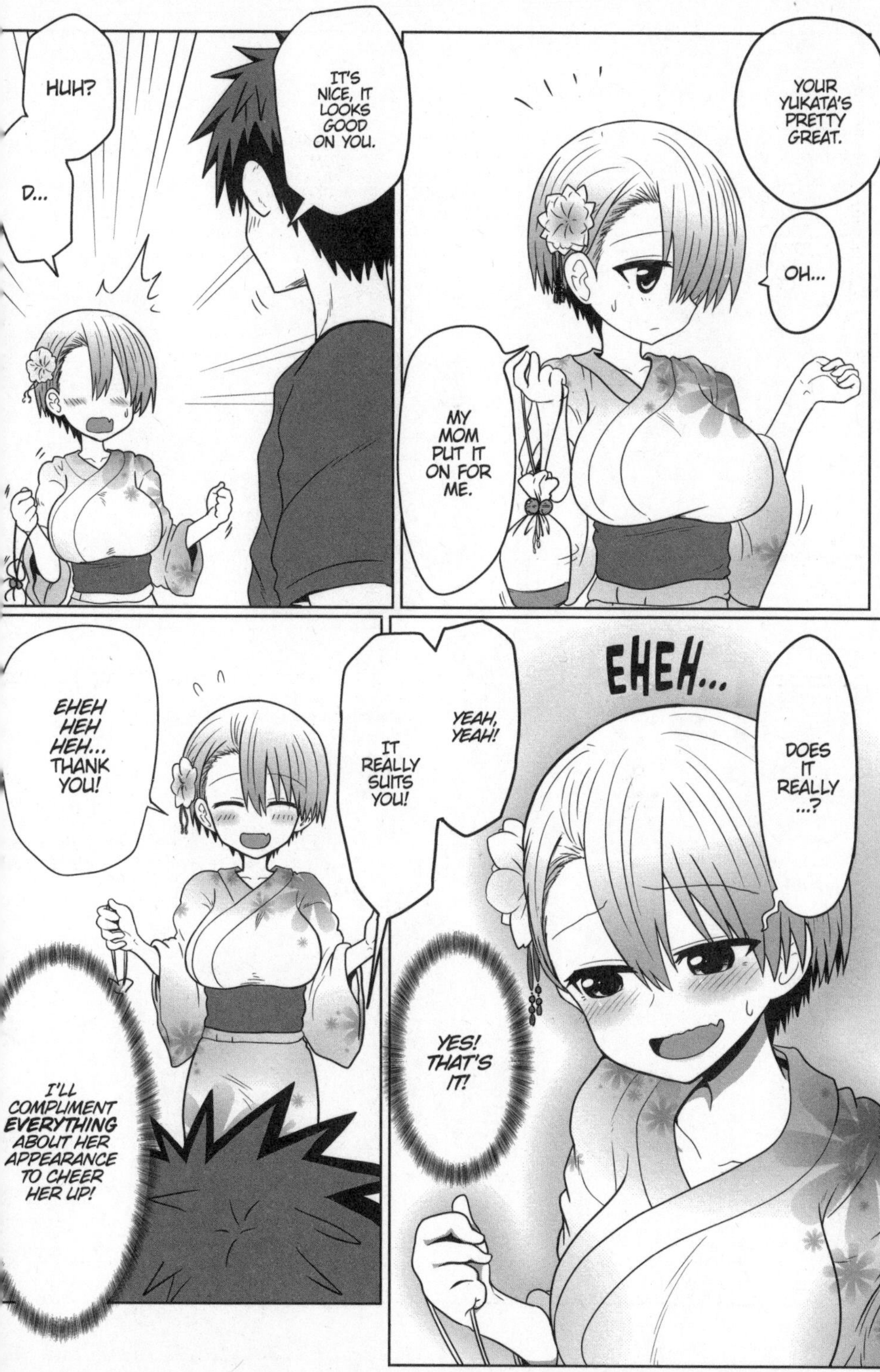
YOUR YUKATA'S PRETTY GREAT.
OH...
MY MOM PUT IT ON FOR ME.
IT'S NICE, IT LOOKS GOOD ON YOU.
HUH?
D...
EHEH...
DOES IT REALLY ...?
YES! THAT'S IT!
YEAH, YEAH!
IT REALLY SUITS YOU!
EHEH HEH HEH... THANK YOU!
I'LL COMPLIMENT **EVERYTHING** ABOUT HER APPEARANCE TO CHEER HER UP!

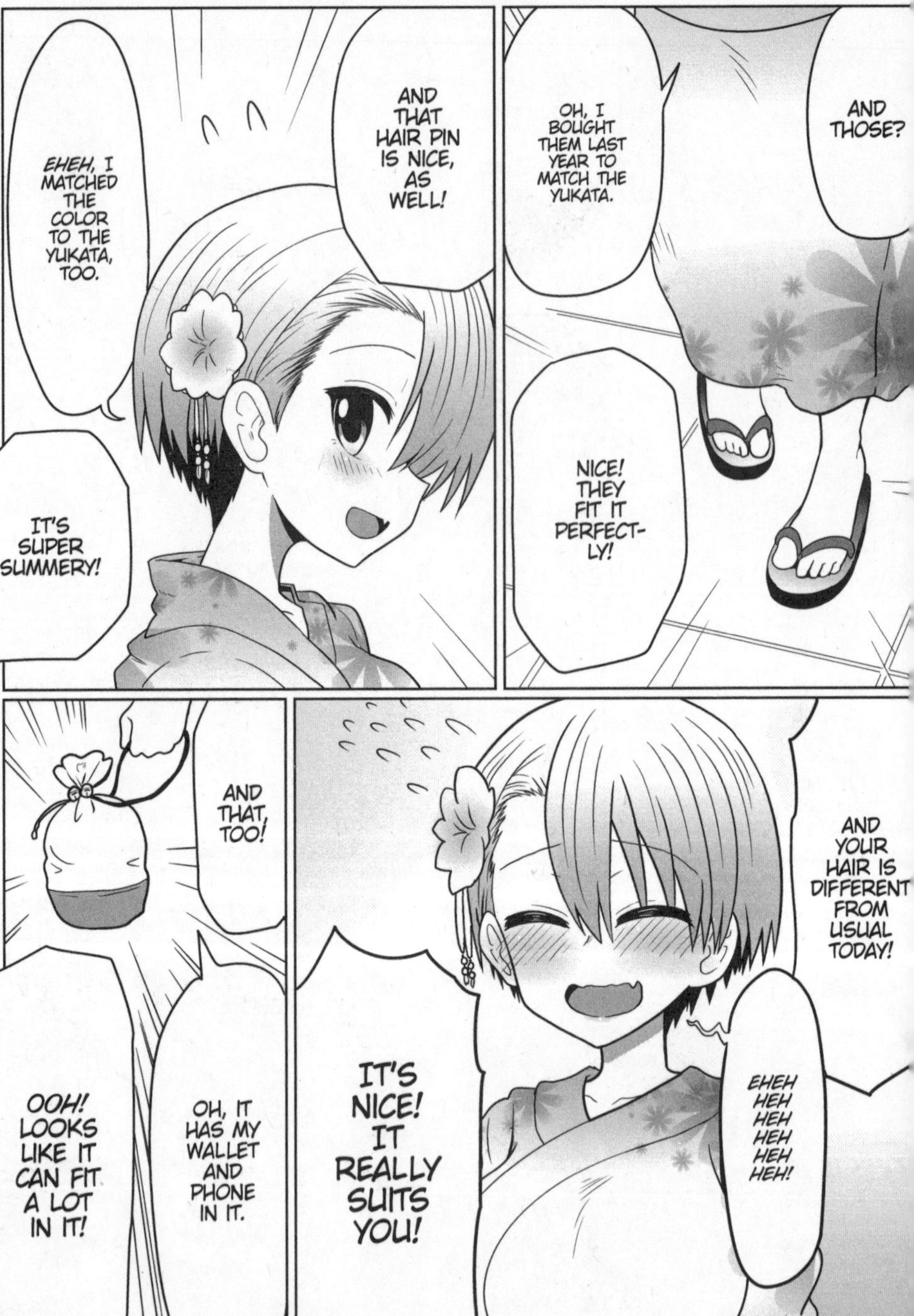
AND THOSE?
OH, I BOUGHT THEM LAST YEAR TO MATCH THE YUKATA.
NICE! THEY FIT IT PERFECT-LY!
AND THAT HAIR PIN IS NICE, AS WELL!
*EHEH*, I MATCHED THE COLOR TO THE YUKATA, TOO.
IT'S SUPER SUMMERY!
AND YOUR HAIR IS DIFFERENT FROM USUAL TODAY!
*EHEH HEH HEH HEH HEH HEH!*
IT'S NICE! IT REALLY SUITS YOU!
AND THAT, TOO!
OH, IT HAS MY WALLET AND PHONE IN IT.
OOH! LOOKS LIKE IT CAN FIT A LOT IN IT!

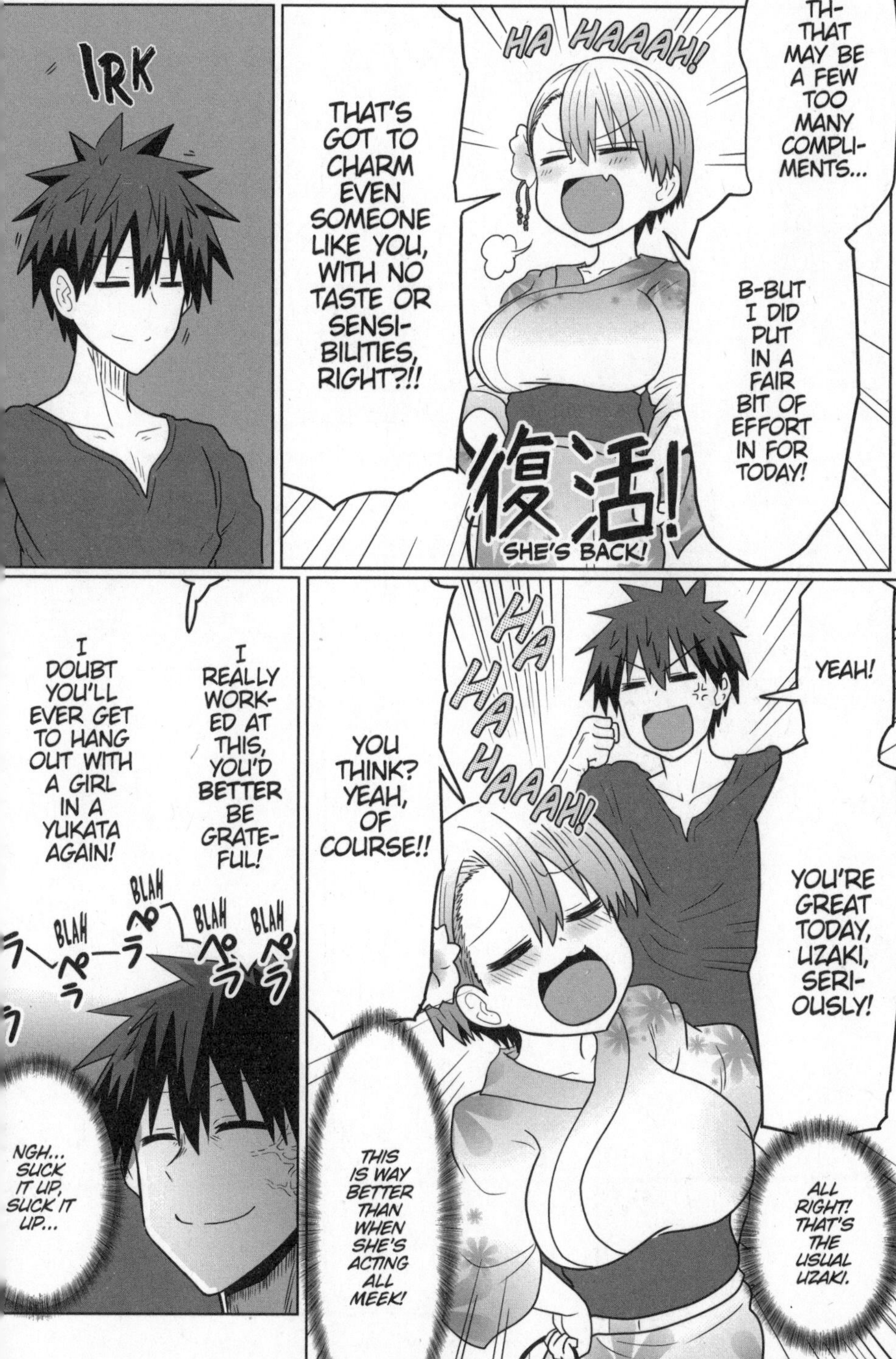
TH-THAT MAY BE A FEW TOO MANY COMPLIMENTS...
B-BUT I DID PUT IN A FAIR BIT OF EFFORT IN FOR TODAY!
HA HAAAH!
THAT'S GOT TO CHARM EVEN SOMEONE LIKE YOU, WITH NO TASTE OR SENSIBILITIES, RIGHT?!!
復活!
SHE'S BACK!
IRK
YEAH!
YOU'RE GREAT TODAY, UZAKI, SERIOUSLY!
HA HA HA HAAAAH!
YOU THINK? YEAH, OF COURSE!!
ALL RIGHT! THAT'S THE USUAL UZAKI.
THIS IS WAY BETTER THAN WHEN SHE'S ACTING ALL MEEK!
I REALLY WORKED AT THIS, YOU'D BETTER BE GRATEFUL!
I DOUBT YOU'LL EVER GET TO HANG OUT WITH A GIRL IN A YUKATA AGAIN!
ペラ BLAH
ペラ BLAH
ペラ BLAH
ペラ BLAH
NGH... SUCK IT UP, SUCK IT UP...

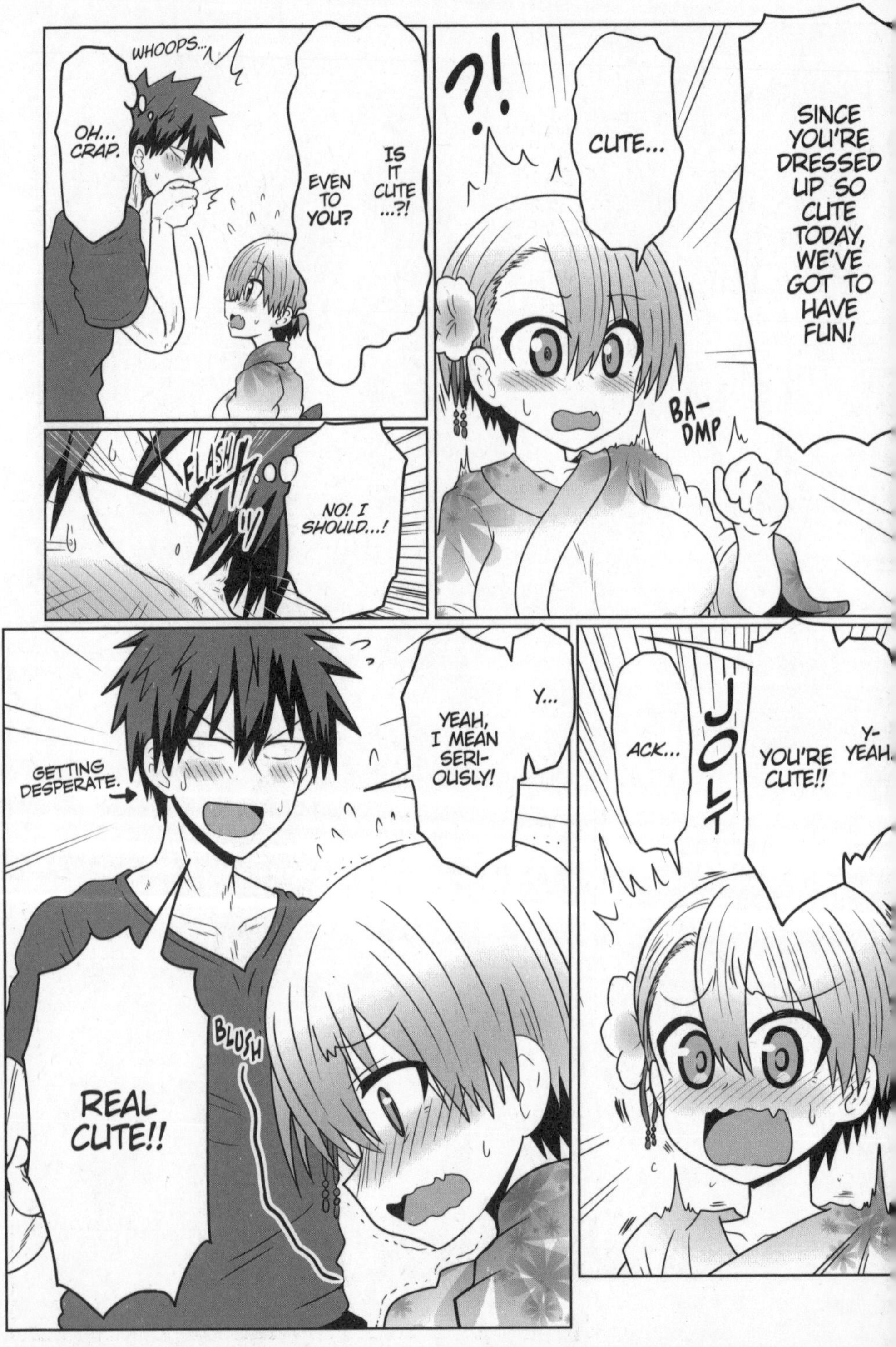
SINCE YOU'RE DRESSED UP SO CUTE TODAY, WE'VE GOT TO HAVE FUN!
CUTE...
?!
BA-DMP
IS IT CUTE ...?!
EVEN TO YOU?
WHOOPS...
OH... CRAP.
FLASH
NO! I SHOULD...!
Y- YEAH.
YOU'RE CUTE!!
JOLT
ACK...
Y...
YEAH, I MEAN SERIOUSLY!
GETTING DESPERATE.
BLUSH
REAL CUTE!!

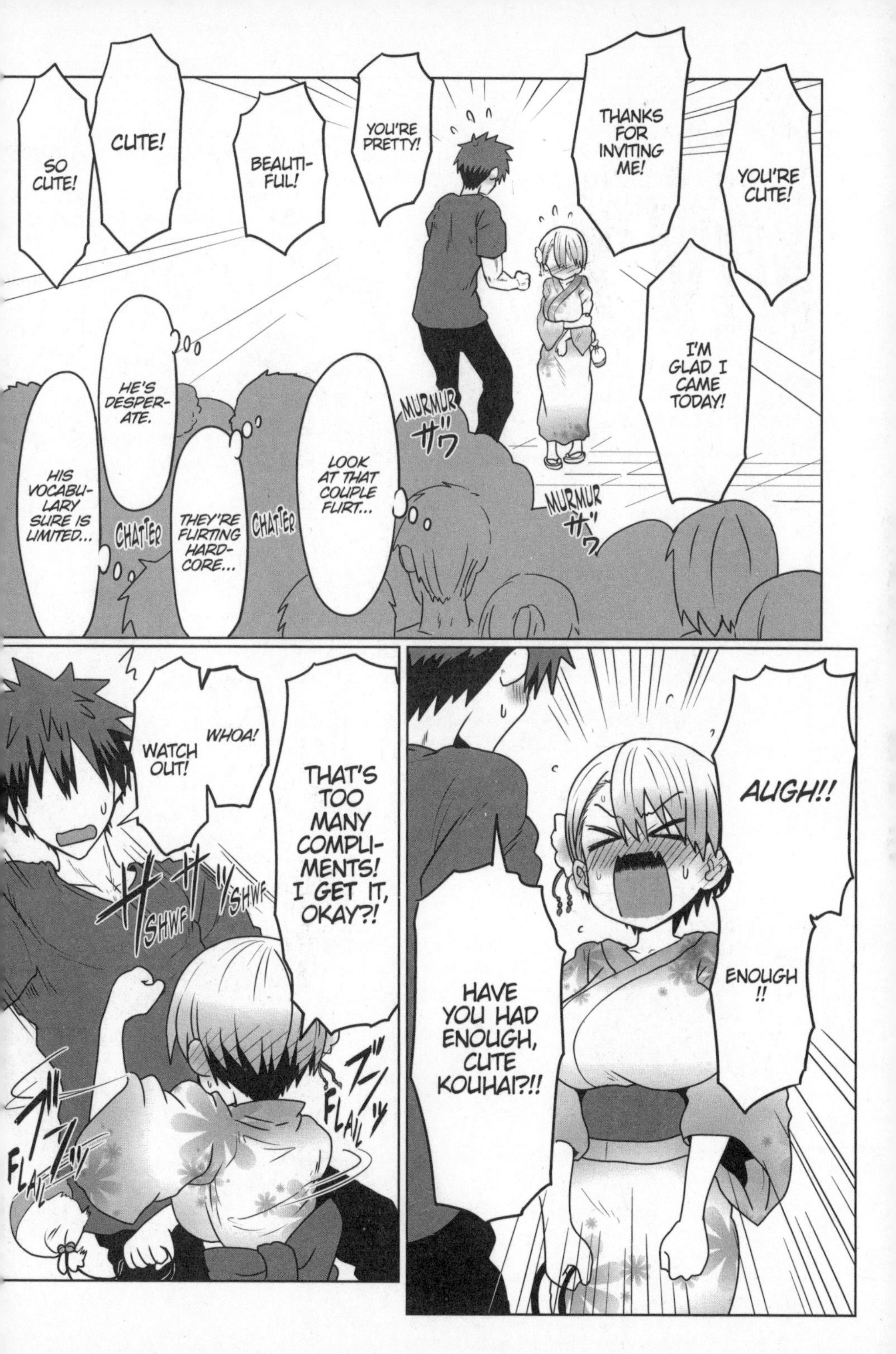
YOU'RE CUTE!
THANKS FOR INVITING ME!
I'M GLAD I CAME TODAY!
YOU'RE PRETTY!
BEAUTI-FUL!
CUTE!
SO CUTE!
MURMUR ザワ
LOOK AT THAT COUPLE FLIRT...
HE'S DESPERATE.
CHATTER
THEY'RE FLIRTING HARD-CORE...
CHATTER
HIS VOCABU-LARY SURE IS LIMITED...
MURMUR ザワ
AUGH!!
ENOUGH !!
HAVE YOU HAD ENOUGH, CUTE KOUHAI?!!
THAT'S TOO MANY COMPLI-MENTS! I GET IT, OKAY?!
WHOA!
WATCH OUT!
SHWF
SHWF
FLAIL
FLAIL

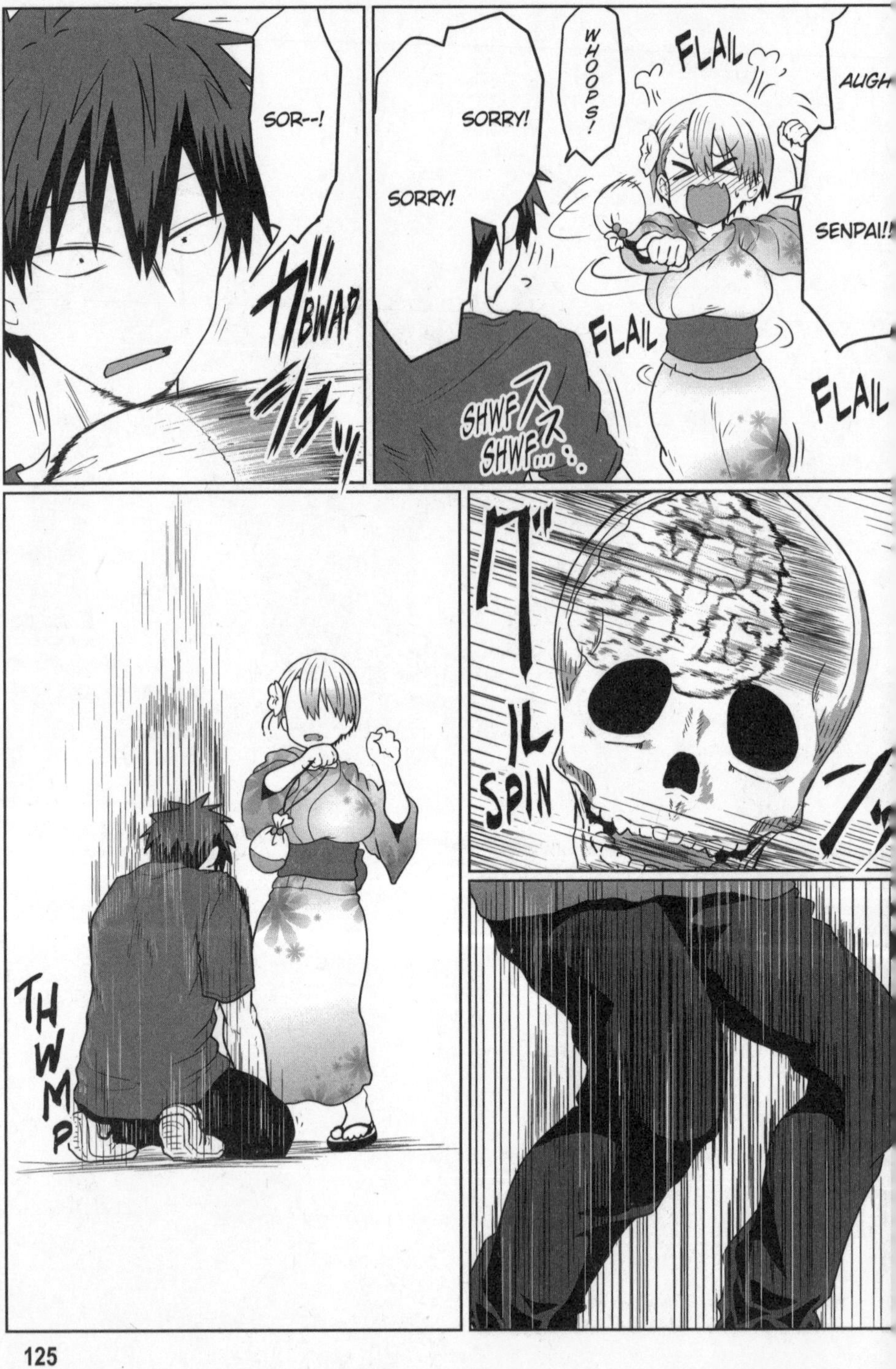

AUGH
SENPAI!!
FLAIL
WHOOPS!
FLAIL
SORRY!
SORRY!
FLAIL
SHWF SHWF...
SOR--!
BWAP
SPIN
THWMP

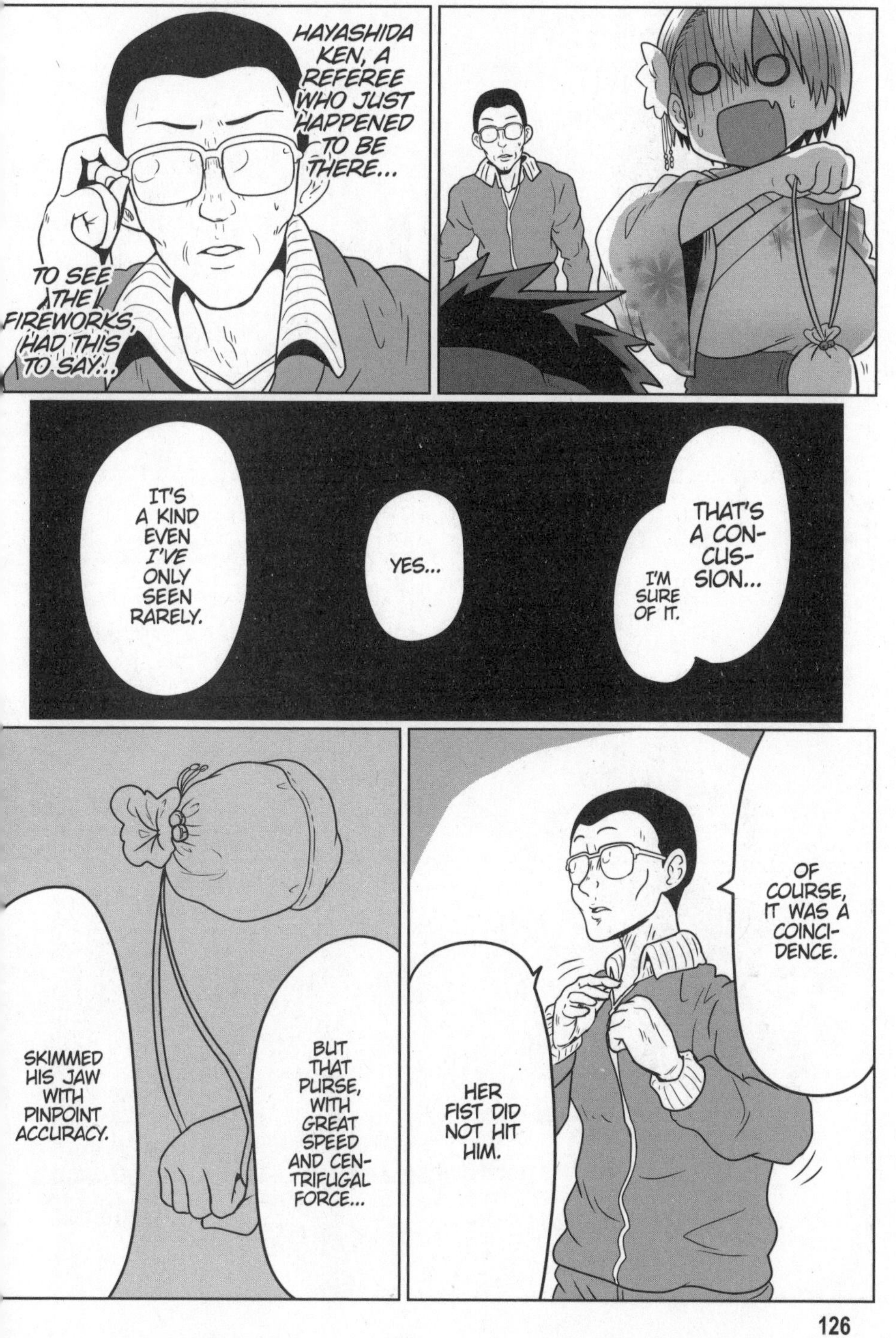
HAYASHIDA KEN, A REFEREE WHO JUST HAPPENED TO BE THERE...
TO SEE THE FIREWORKS, HAD THIS TO SAY...
THAT'S A CON-CUS-SION...
I'M SURE OF IT.
YES...
IT'S A KIND EVEN I'VE ONLY SEEN RARELY.
OF COURSE, IT WAS A COINCI-DENCE.
HER FIST DID NOT HIT HIM.
BUT THAT PURSE, WITH GREAT SPEED AND CEN-TRIFUGAL FORCE...
SKIMMED HIS JAW WITH PINPOINT ACCURACY.

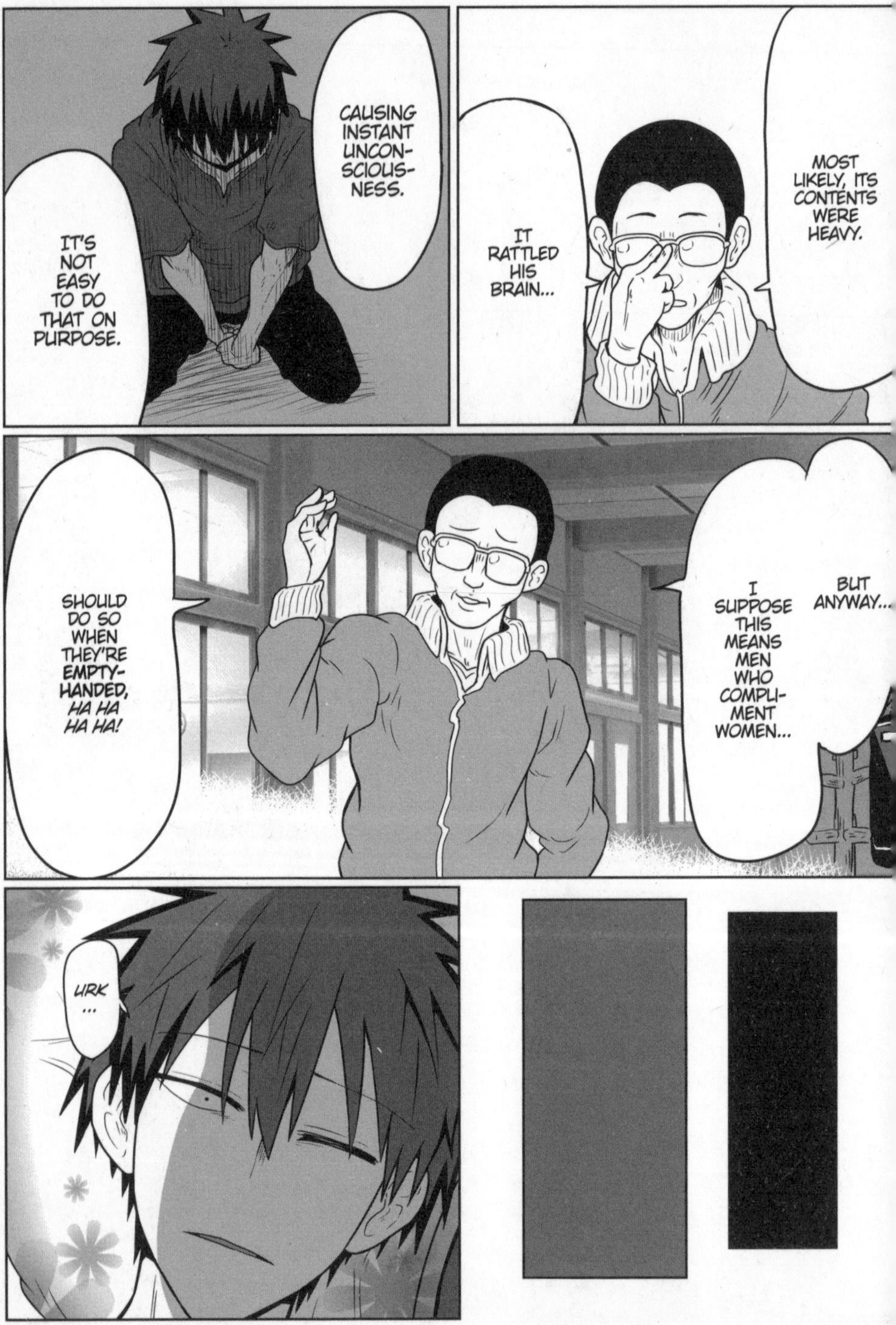
MOST LIKELY, ITS CONTENTS WERE HEAVY.
IT RATTLED HIS BRAIN...
CAUSING INSTANT UNCONSCIOUS-NESS.
IT'S NOT EASY TO DO THAT ON PURPOSE.
BUT ANYWAY...
I SUPPOSE THIS MEANS MEN WHO COMPLI-MENT WOMEN...
SHOULD DO SO WHEN THEY'RE EMPTY-HANDED, *HA HA HA HA!*
*URK* ...

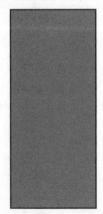

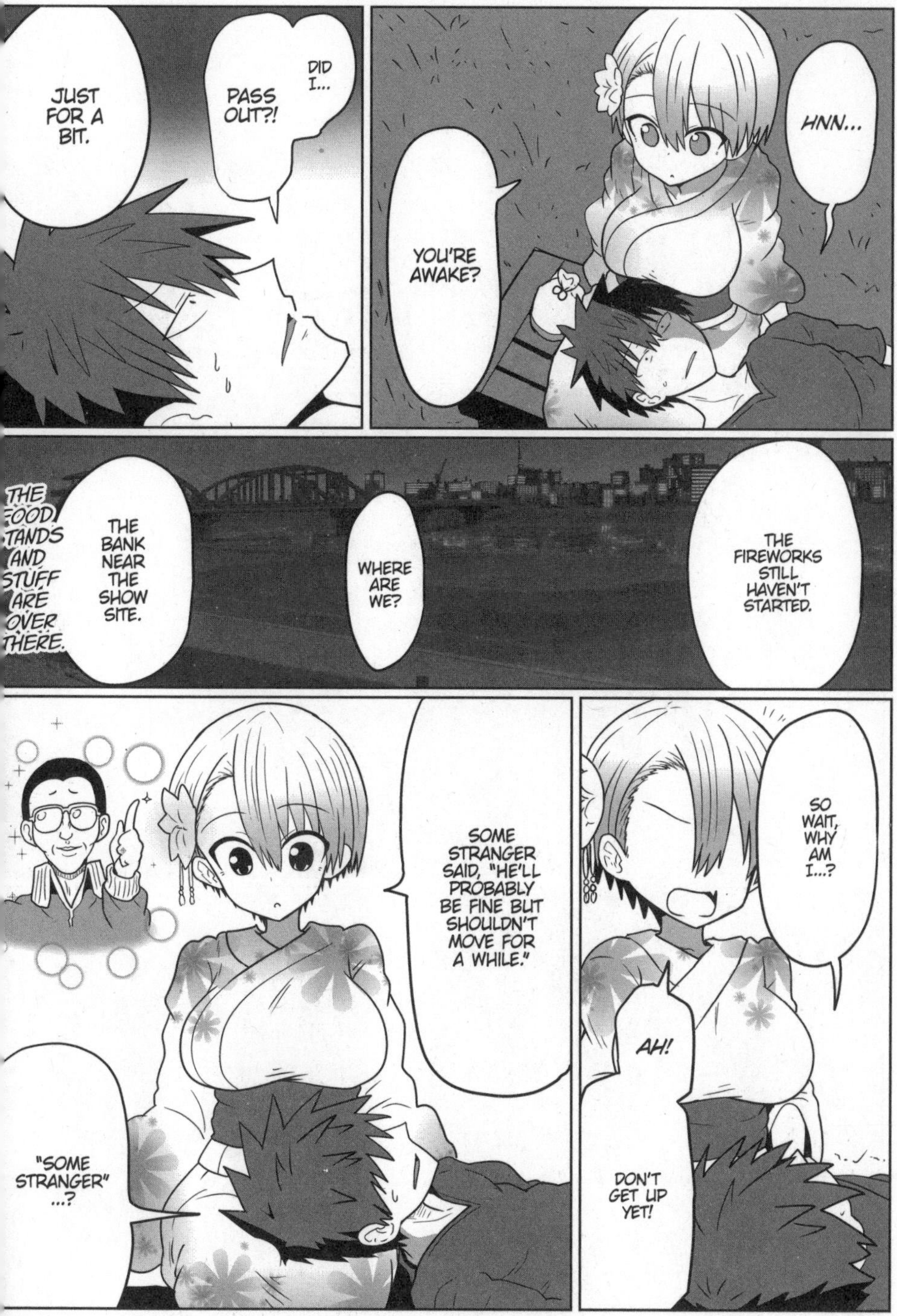
HNN...
YOU'RE AWAKE?
DID I...
PASS OUT?!
JUST FOR A BIT.
THE FIREWORKS STILL HAVEN'T STARTED.
WHERE ARE WE?
THE BANK NEAR THE SHOW SITE.
THE FOOD STANDS AND STUFF ARE OVER THERE.
SO WAIT, WHY AM I...?
AH!
DON'T GET UP YET!
SOME STRANGER SAID, "HE'LL PROBABLY BE FINE BUT SHOULDN'T MOVE FOR A WHILE."
"SOME STRANGER"...?

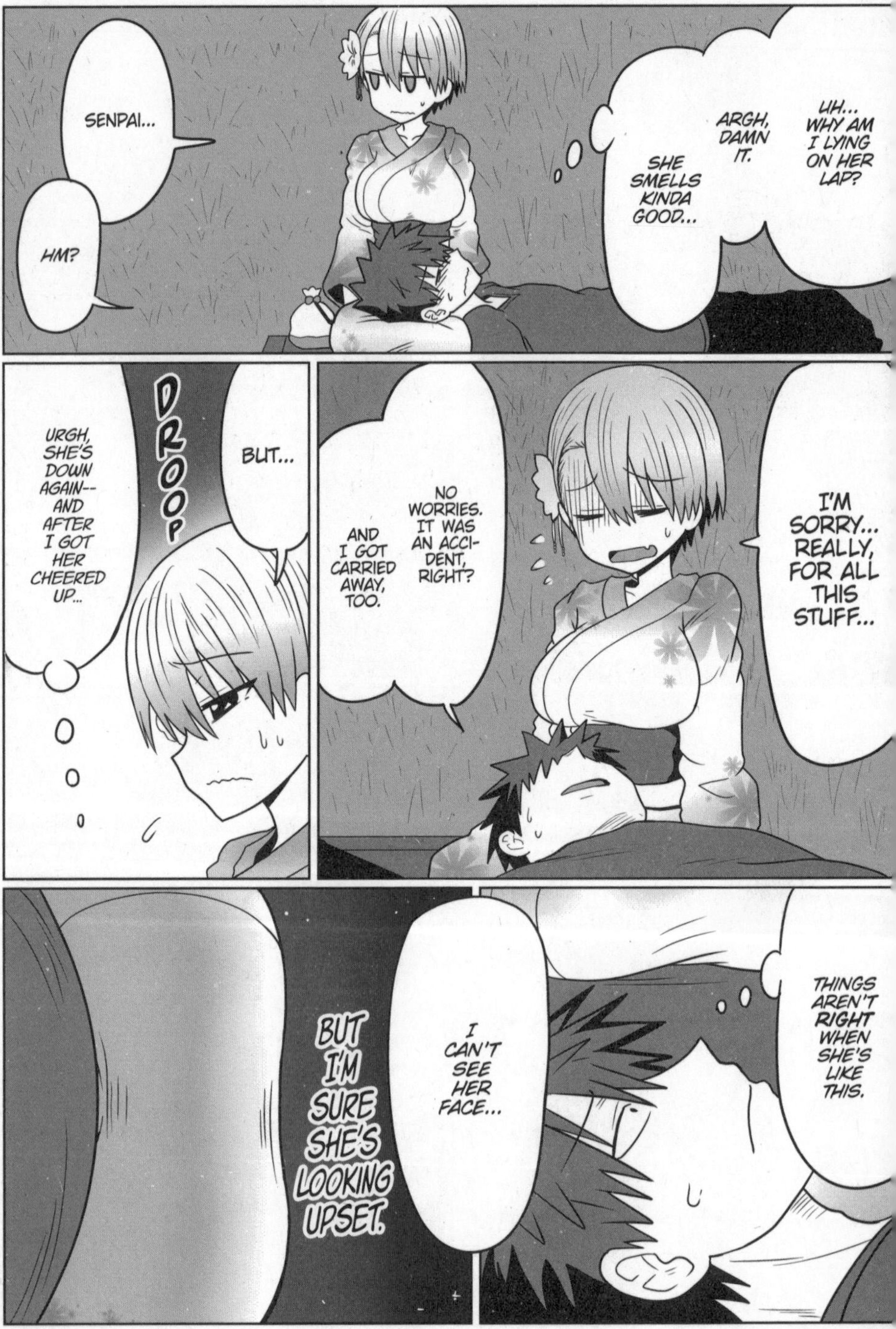
UH... WHY AM I LYING ON HER LAP?
ARGH, DAMN IT.
SHE SMELLS KINDA GOOD...
SENPAI...
HM?
I'M SORRY... REALLY, FOR ALL THIS STUFF...
NO WORRIES. IT WAS AN ACCI-DENT, RIGHT?
AND I GOT CARRIED AWAY, TOO.
BUT...
DROOP
URGH, SHE'S DOWN AGAIN-- AND AFTER I GOT HER CHEERED UP...
THINGS AREN'T RIGHT WHEN SHE'S LIKE THIS.
I CAN'T SEE HER FACE...
BUT I'M SURE SHE'S LOOKING UPSET.

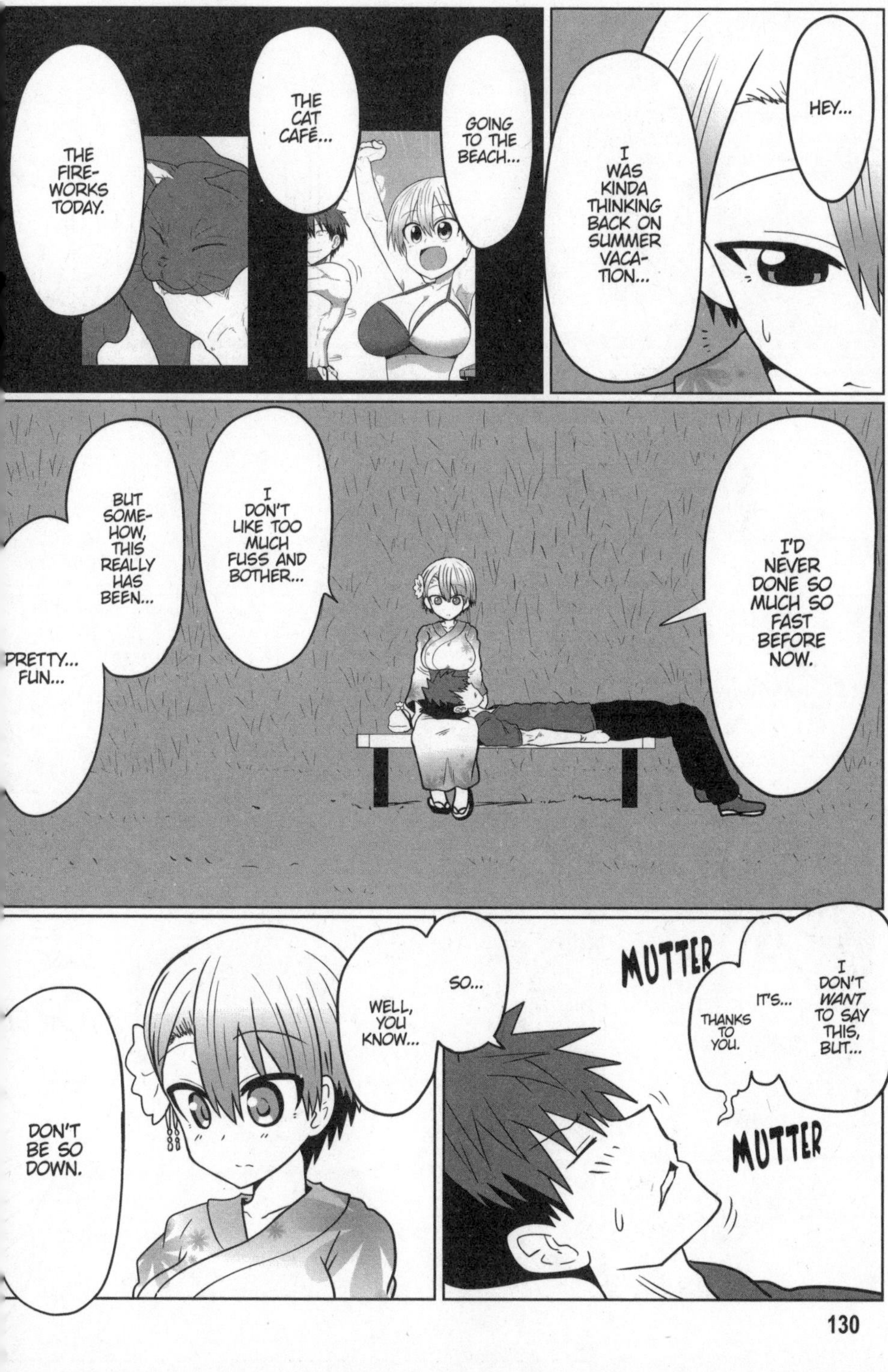
HEY...
I WAS KINDA THINKING BACK ON SUMMER VACA-TION...
GOING TO THE BEACH...
THE CAT CAFÉ...
THE FIRE-WORKS TODAY.
I'D NEVER DONE SO MUCH SO FAST BEFORE NOW.
I DON'T LIKE TOO MUCH FUSS AND BOTHER...
BUT SOME-HOW, THIS REALLY HAS BEEN...
PRETTY... FUN...
MUTTER
I DON'T *WANT* TO SAY THIS, BUT...
IT'S...
THANKS TO YOU.
MUTTER
SO...
WELL, YOU KNOW...
DON'T BE SO DOWN.

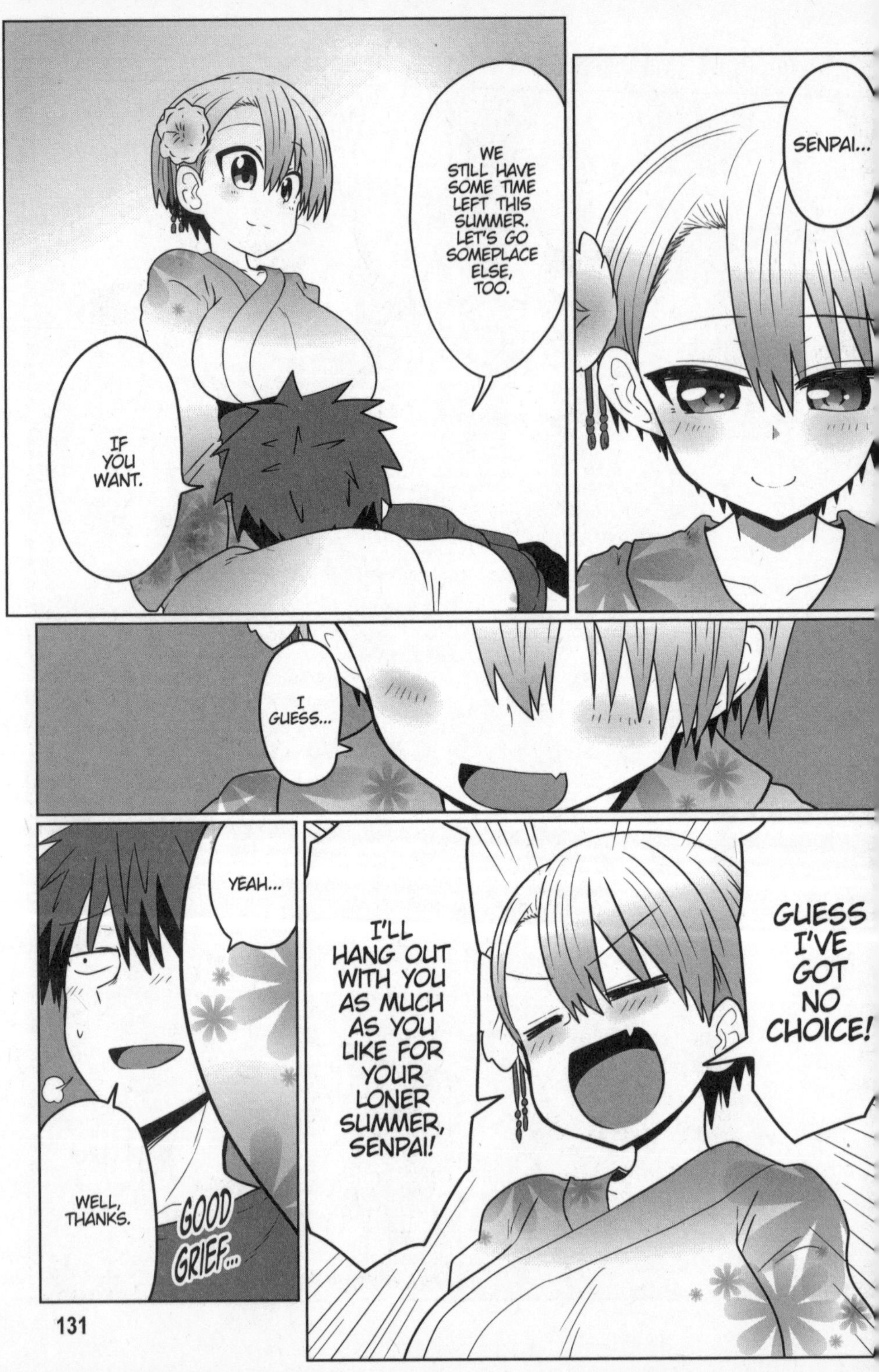
SENPAI...
WE STILL HAVE SOME TIME LEFT THIS SUMMER. LET'S GO SOMEPLACE ELSE, TOO.
IF YOU WANT.
I GUESS...
GUESS I'VE GOT NO CHOICE!
I'LL HANG OUT WITH YOU AS MUCH AS YOU LIKE FOR YOUR LONER SUMMER, SENPAI!
YEAH...
WELL, THANKS.
GOOD GRIEF...

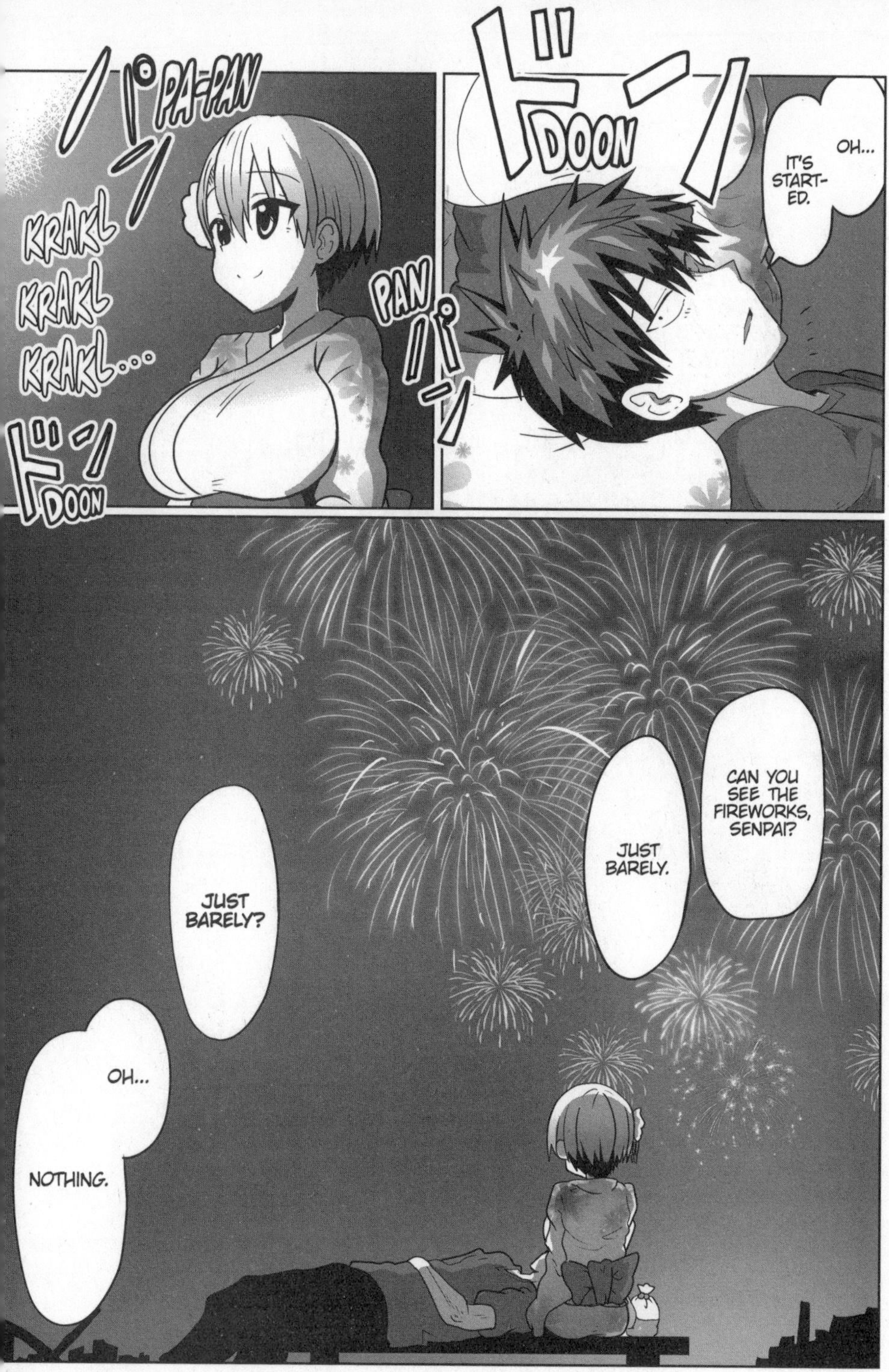
ドーン
DOON
OH... IT'S START-ED.
パーン
PAN
パパン
PA-PAN
KRAKL KRAKL KRAKL...
ドーン
DOON
CAN YOU SEE THE FIREWORKS, SENPAI?
JUST BARELY.
JUST BARELY?
OH... NOTHING.

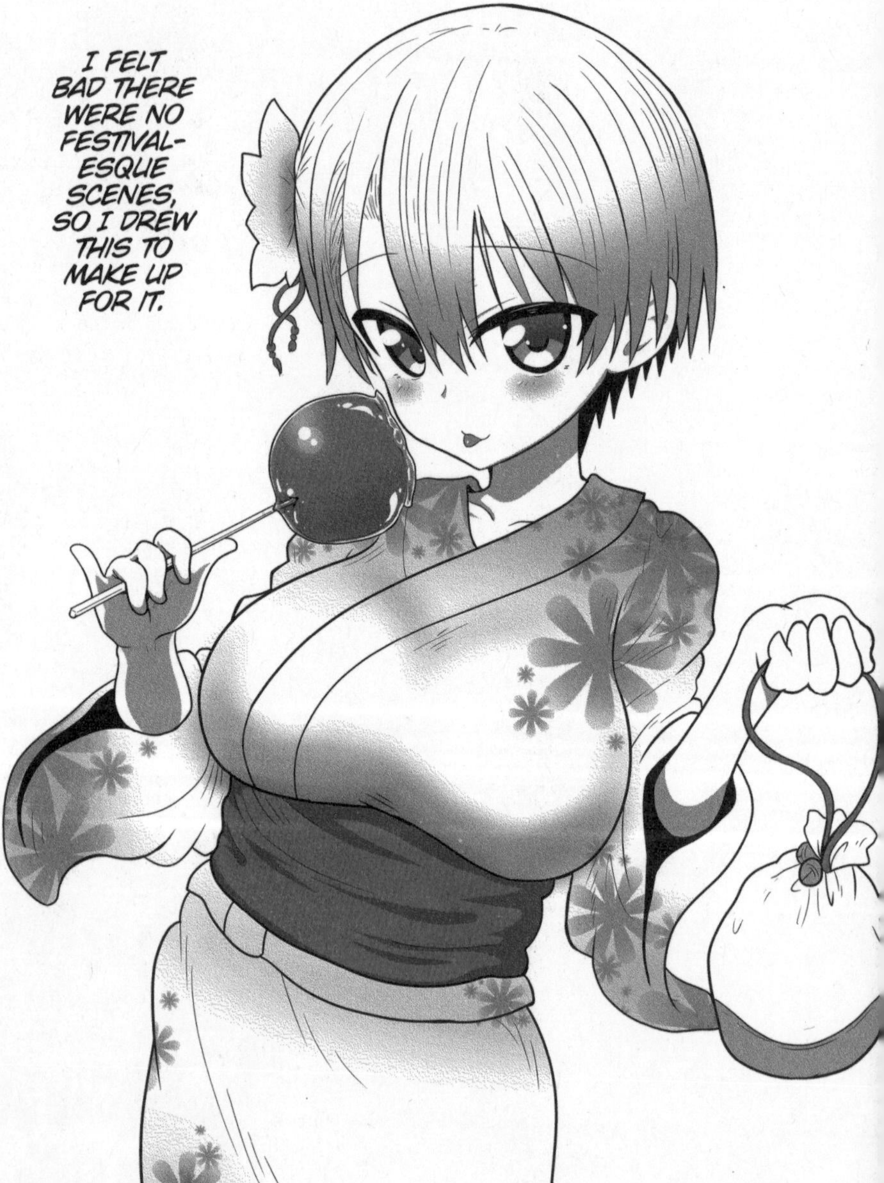
I FELT BAD THERE WERE NO FESTIVAL-ESQUE SCENES, SO I DREW THIS TO MAKE UP FOR IT.

Uzaki-chan☆Wants to Hang Out!

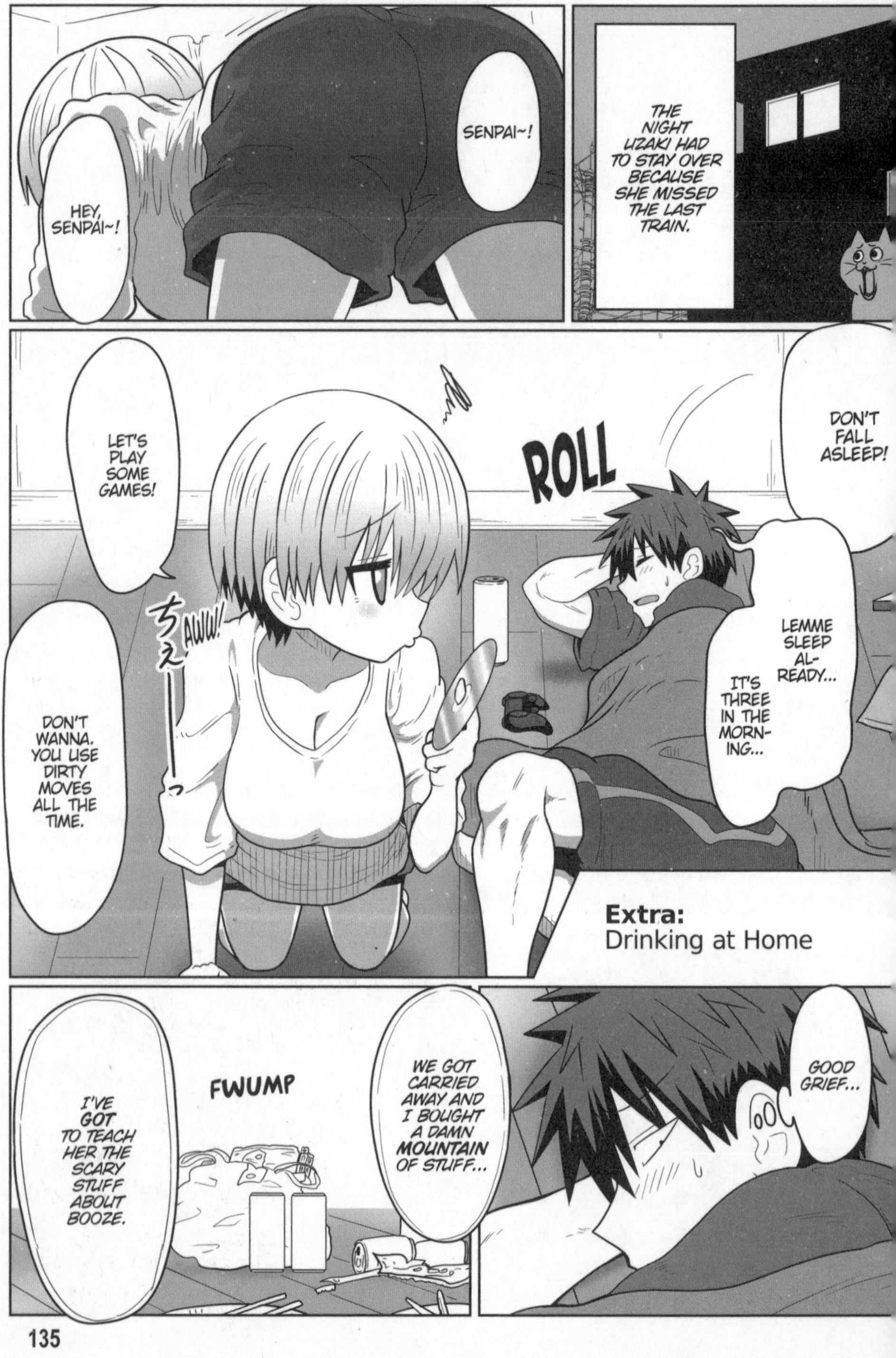
THE NIGHT UZAKI HAD TO STAY OVER BECAUSE SHE MISSED THE LAST TRAIN.
SENPAI~!
HEY, SENPAI~!
DON'T FALL ASLEEP!
ROLL
LEMME SLEEP AL-READY...
IT'S THREE IN THE MORN-ING...
LET'S PLAY SOME GAMES!
ちぇーっ AWW!
DON'T WANNA. YOU USE DIRTY MOVES ALL THE TIME.
Extra: Drinking at Home
GOOD GRIEF...
WE GOT CARRIED AWAY AND I BOUGHT A DAMN MOUNTAIN OF STUFF...
FWUMP
I'VE GOT TO TEACH HER THE SCARY STUFF ABOUT BOOZE.

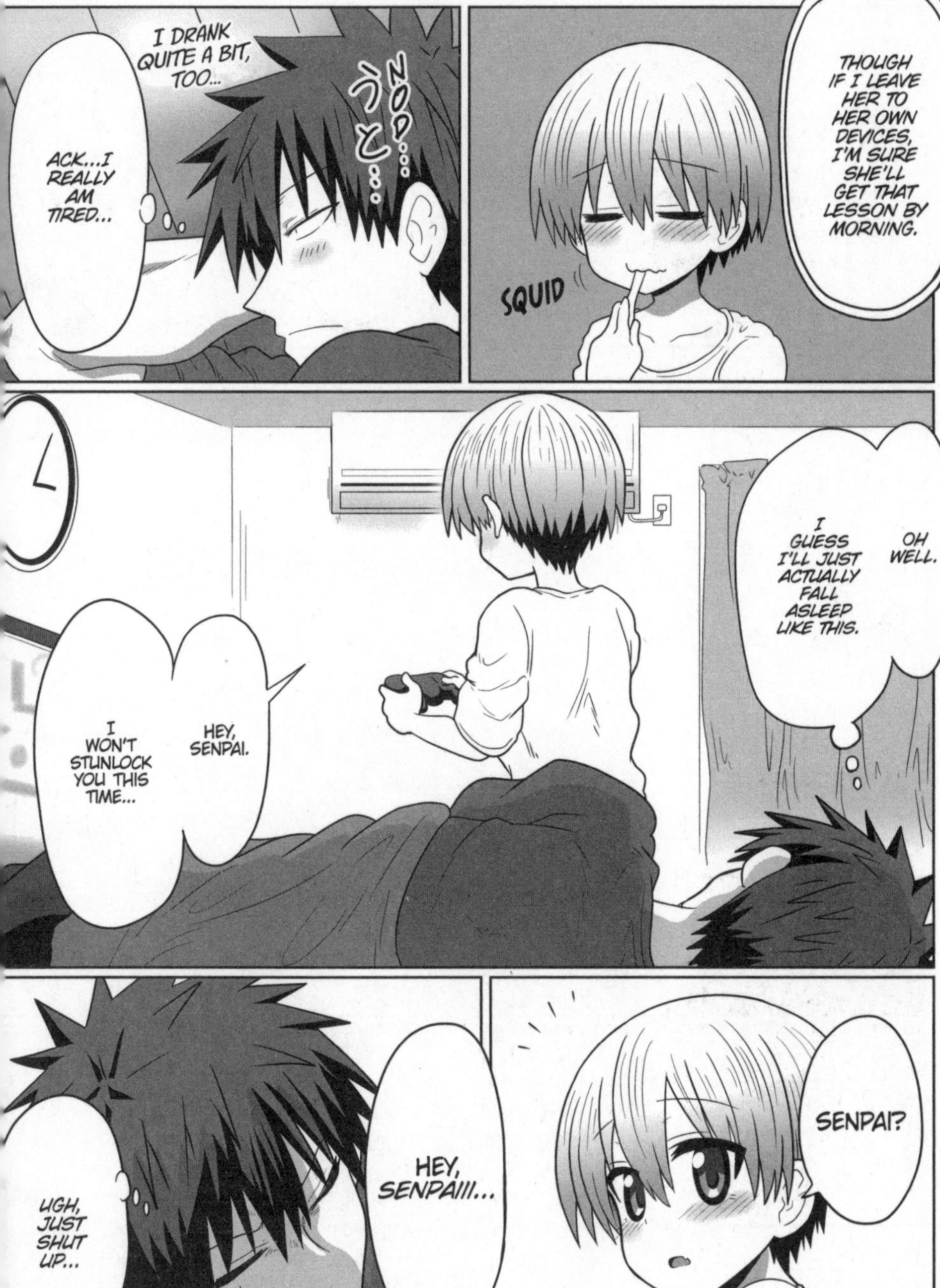
THOUGH IF I LEAVE HER TO HER OWN DEVICES, I'M SURE SHE'LL GET THAT LESSON BY MORNING.
SQUID
I DRANK QUITE A BIT, TOO...
NOD... うと...
ACK...I REALLY AM TIRED...
OH WELL.
I GUESS I'LL JUST ACTUALLY FALL ASLEEP LIKE THIS.
HEY, SENPAI.
I WON'T STUNLOCK YOU THIS TIME...
SENPAI?
HEY, SENPAIII...
UGH, JUST SHUT UP...

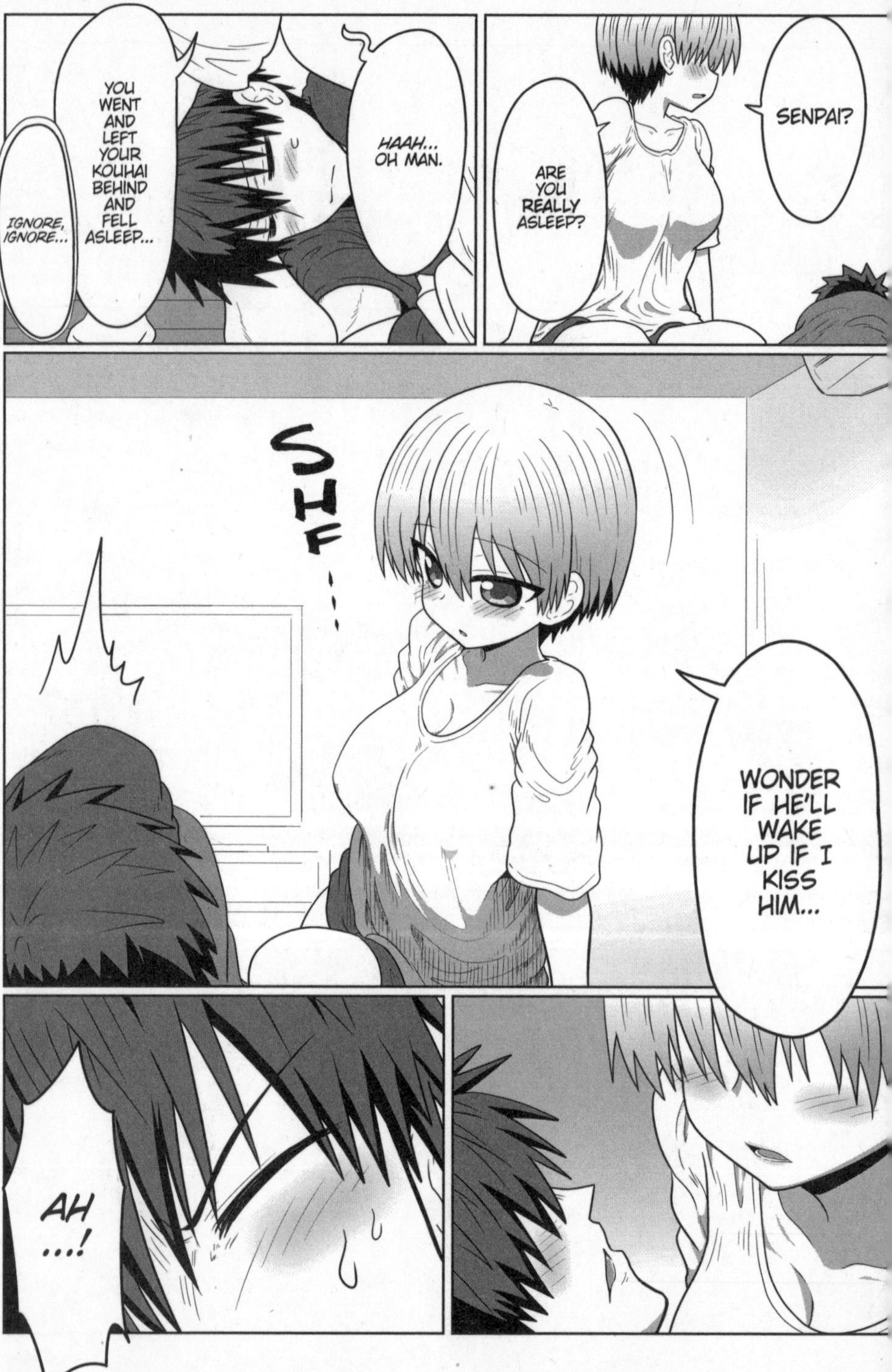
SENPAI?
ARE YOU REALLY ASLEEP?
HAAH... OH MAN.
YOU WENT AND LEFT YOUR KOUHAI BEHIND AND FELL ASLEEP...
IGNORE, IGNORE...
WONDER IF HE'LL WAKE UP IF I KISS HIM...
SHF...
AH ...!

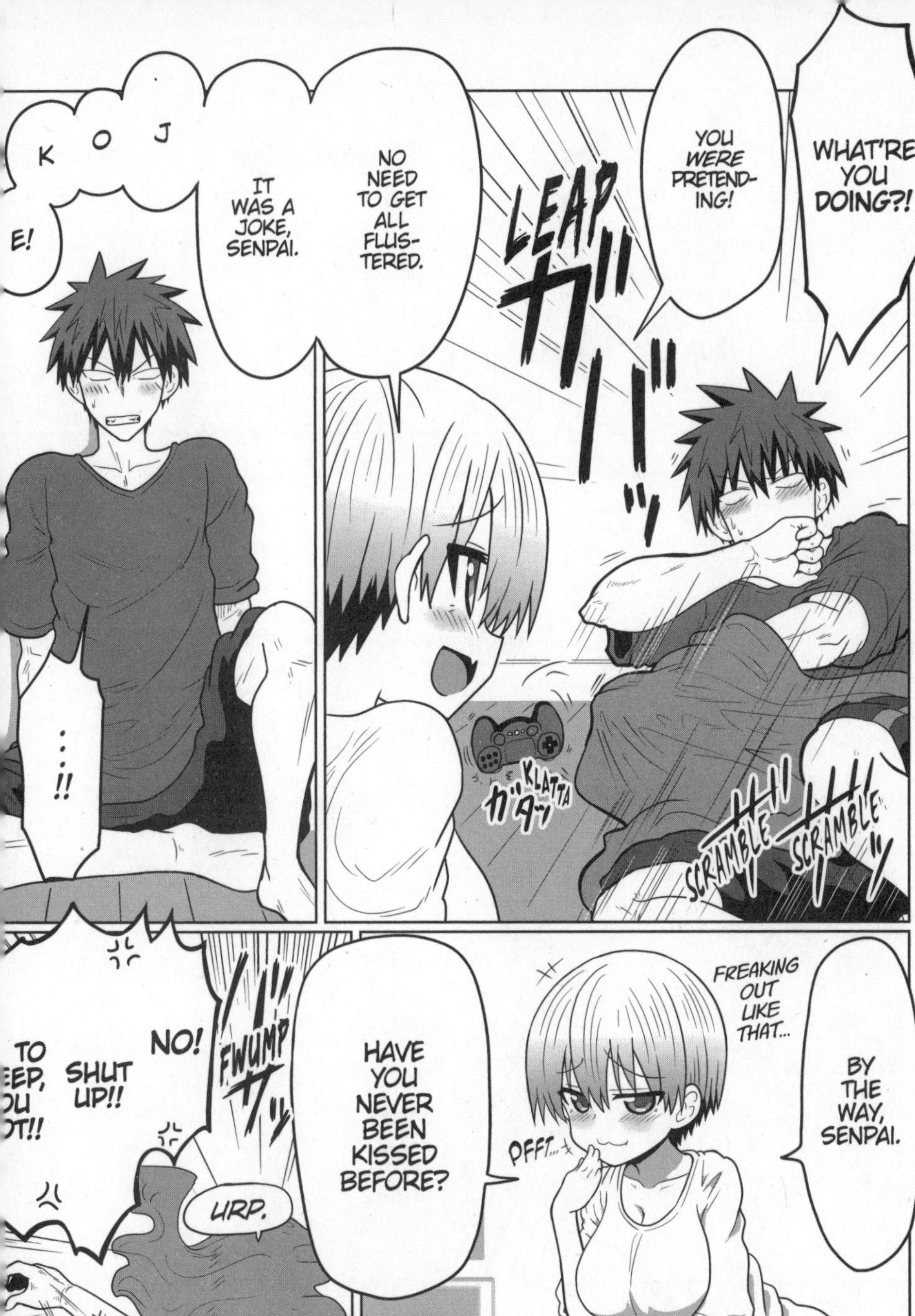
WHAT'RE YOU DOING?!
YOU WERE PRETEND-ING!
LEAP
SCRAMBLE
SCRAMBLE
NO NEED TO GET ALL FLUS-TERED.
KLATTA
IT WAS A JOKE, SENPAI.
K O J
E!
...!!
BY THE WAY, SENPAI.
FREAKING OUT LIKE THAT...
PFFT...
HAVE YOU NEVER BEEN KISSED BEFORE?
FWUMP
NO!
SHUT UP!!
TO EEP, OU OT!!
URP.

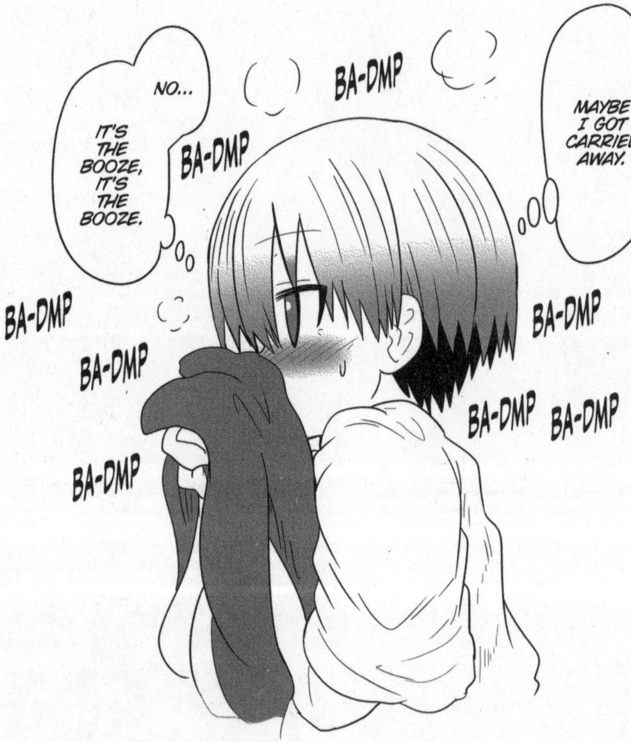
MAYBE I GOT CARRIED AWAY.
BA-DMP
NO...
IT'S THE BOOZE, IT'S THE BOOZE.
BA-DMP
BA-DMP
BA-DMP
BA-DMP
BA-DMP
BA-DMP
BA-DMP

Uzaki-chan Wants to Hang Out!

This manga is from an event on Niconico Manga that was held when Volume 1 was released. We asked readers what they wanted sandwiched between Uzaki-chan's boobs.

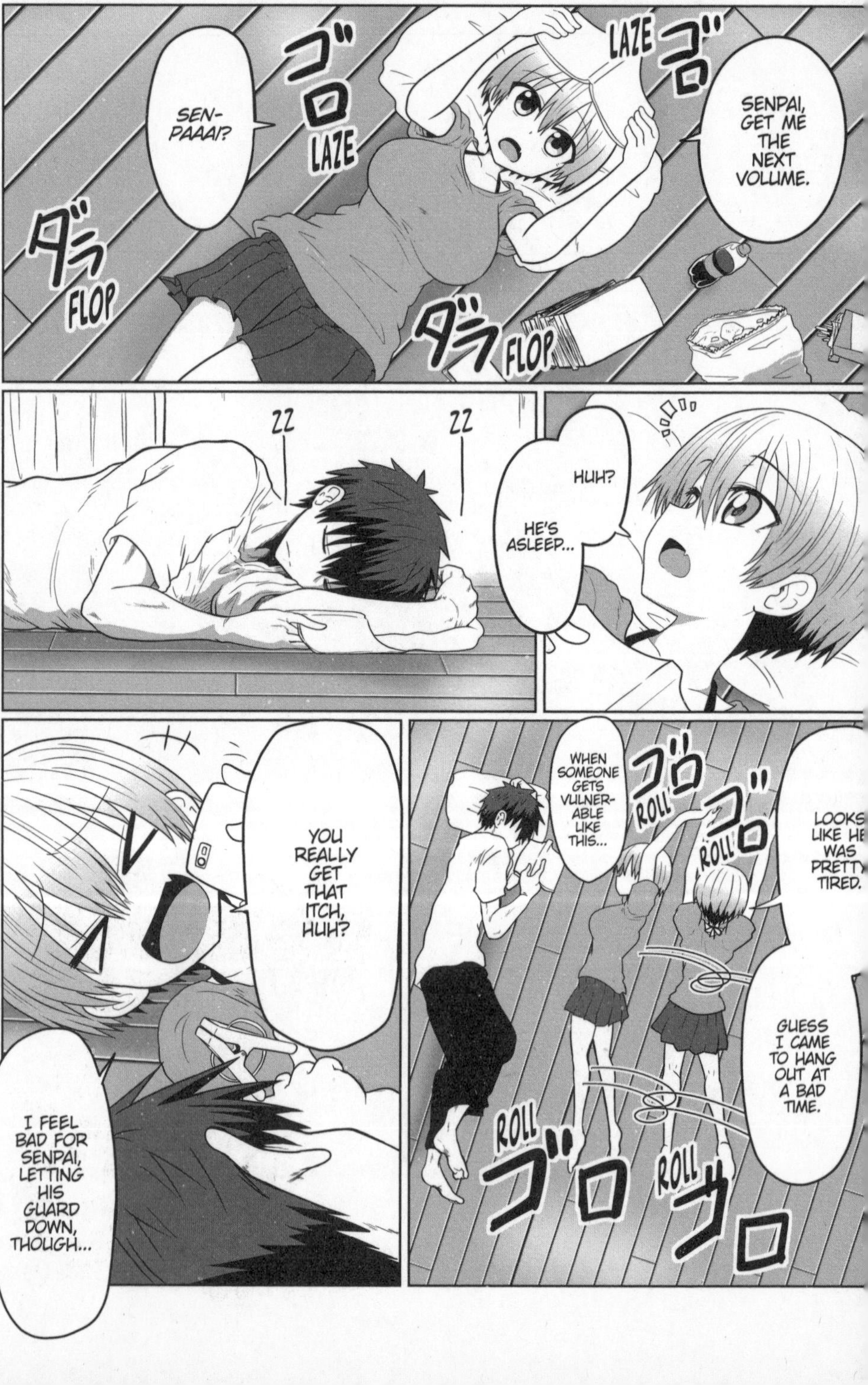
ゴロ LAZE
SENPAI, GET ME THE NEXT VOLUME.
ゴロ LAZE
SEN-PAAAI?
ダラ FLOP
ダラ FLOP
HUH?
HE'S ASLEEP...
ZZ
ZZ
LOOKS LIKE HE WAS PRETTY TIRED.
GUESS I CAME TO HANG OUT AT A BAD TIME.
ゴロ ROLL
ゴロ ROLL
WHEN SOMEONE GETS VULNERABLE LIKE THIS...
ゴロ ROLL
ゴロ ROLL
YOU REALLY GET THAT ITCH, HUH?
I FEEL BAD FOR SENPAI, LETTING HIS GUARD DOWN, THOUGH...

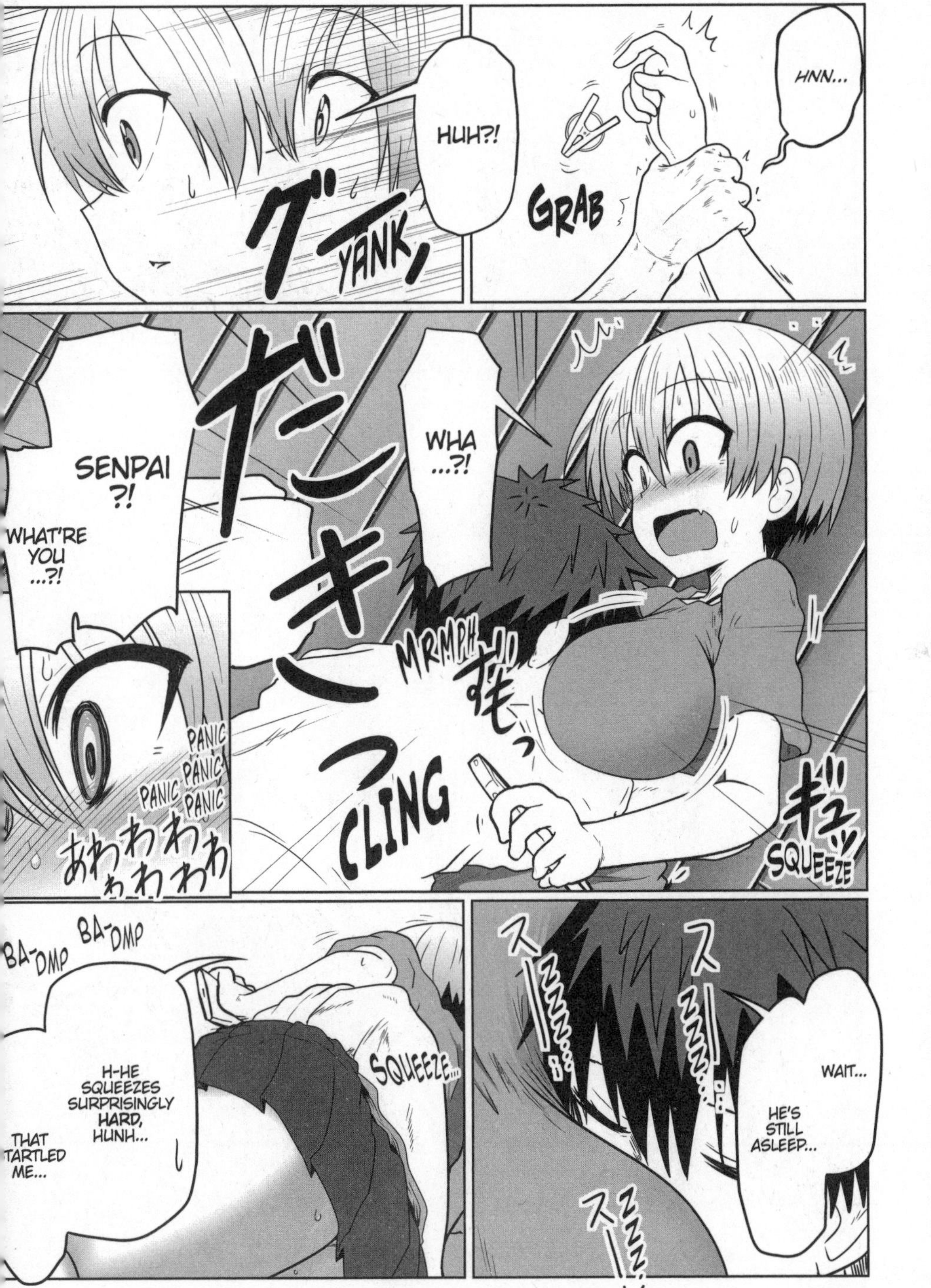
HNN...
GRAB
HUH?!
YANK
WHA...?!
SQUEEZE
MRMPH
CLING
SENPAI ?!
WHAT'RE YOU ...?!
PANIC PANIC PANIC PANIC
あわわわわわわ
WAIT...
HE'S STILL ASLEEP...
ZZZ...
SQUEEZE...
BA-DMP BA-DMP
H-HE SQUEEZES SURPRISINGLY HARD, HUNH...
THAT TARTLED ME...

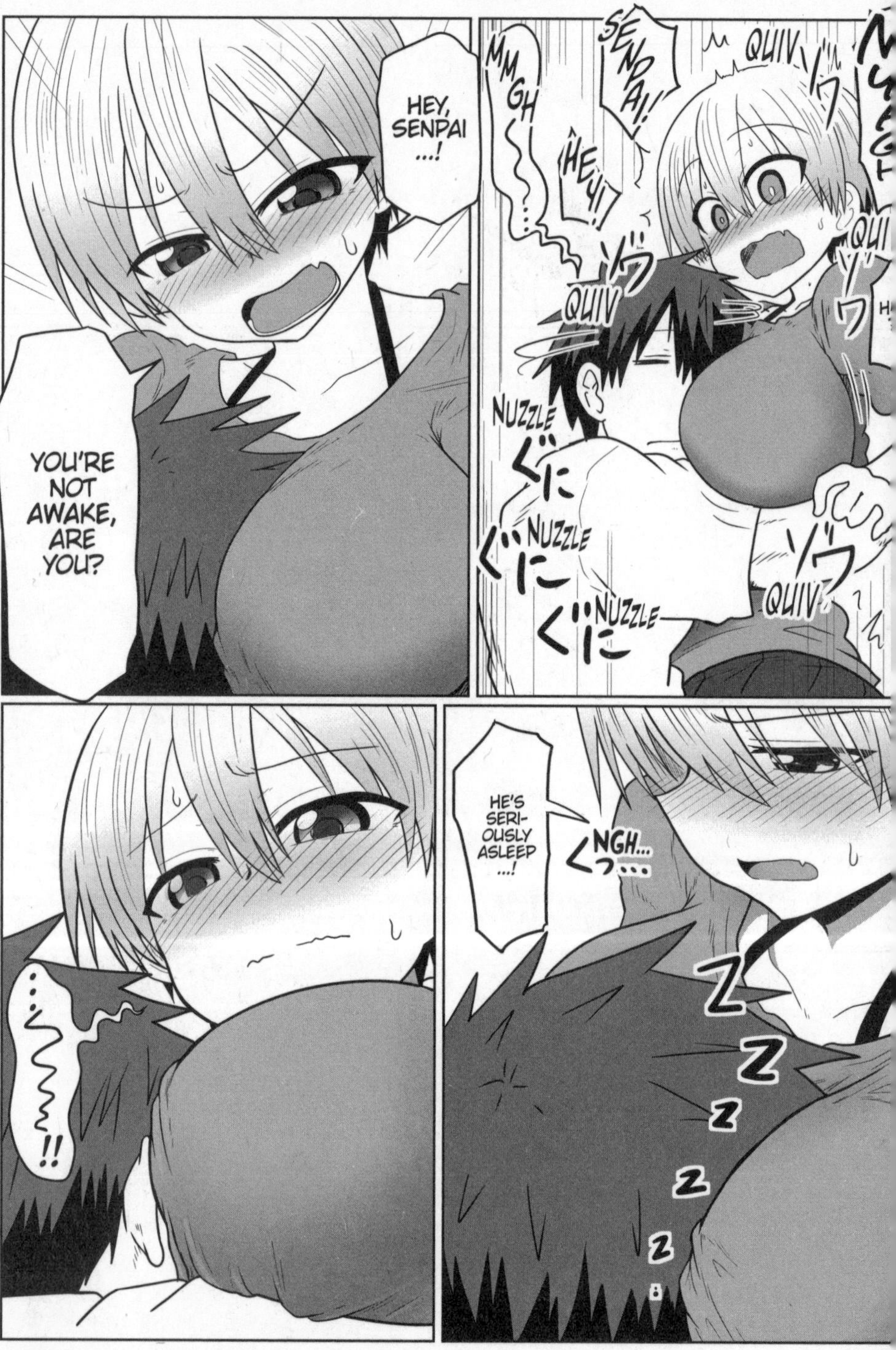

SENPAI!
MMGH...
HEY!!
QUIV ゾワ
QUIV ゾワ
QUIV ゾワ
NUZZLE ぐに
NUZZLE ぐに
NUZZLE ぐに
QUIV ゾワ
HEY, SENPAI...!
YOU'RE NOT AWAKE, ARE YOU?
HE'S SERIOUSLY ASLEEP...!
NGH... くっ...
Z Z Z Z Z ...
...く~~!!

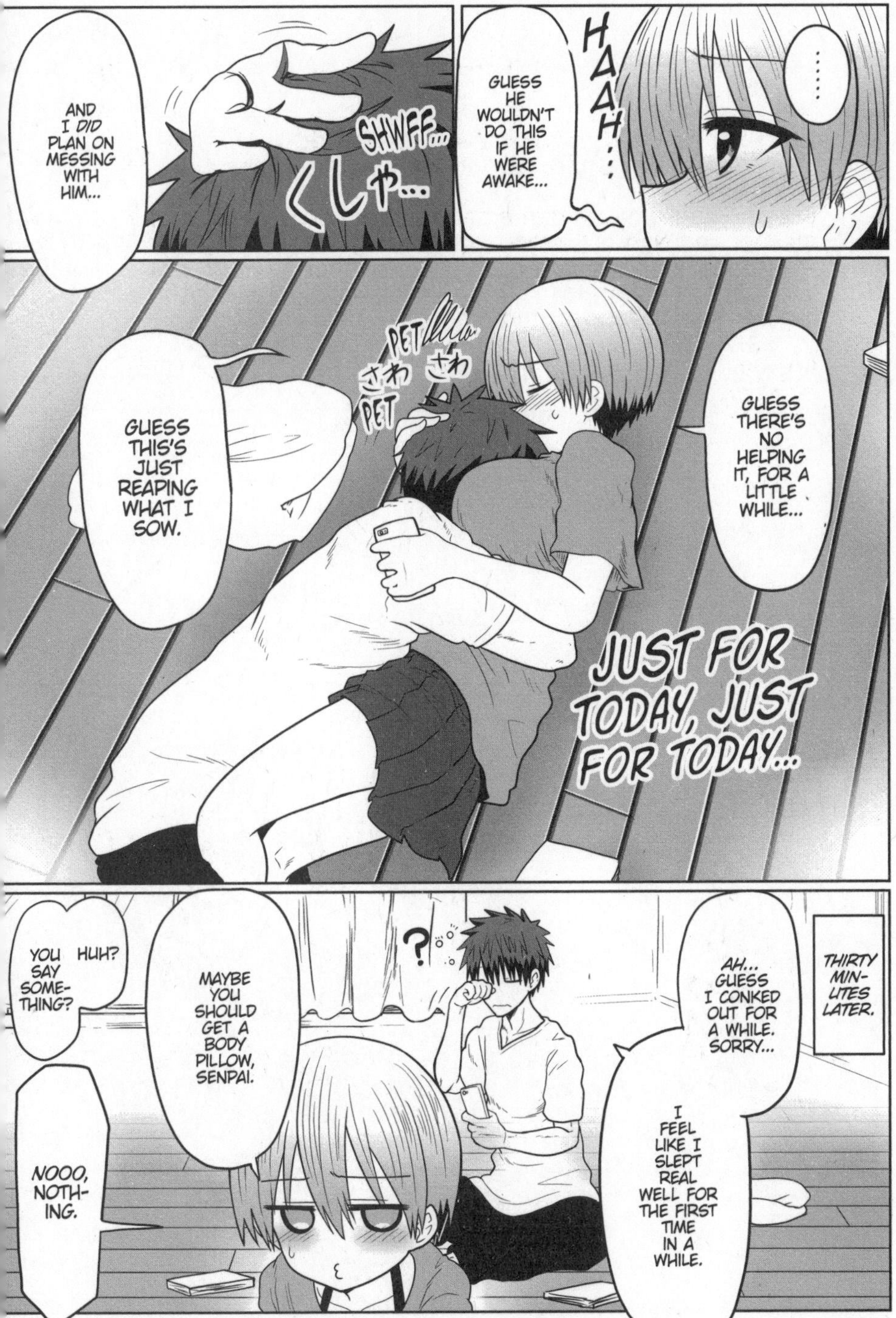
......
HAAAH...
GUESS HE WOULDN'T DO THIS IF HE WERE AWAKE...
SHWFF...
くしゃ...
AND I *DID* PLAN ON MESSING WITH HIM...
GUESS THERE'S NO HELPING IT, FOR A LITTLE WHILE...
PET さわ さわ PET
GUESS THIS'S JUST REAPING WHAT I SOW.
JUST FOR TODAY, JUST FOR TODAY...
THIRTY MINUTES LATER.
AH... GUESS I CONKED OUT FOR A WHILE. SORRY...
I FEEL LIKE I SLEPT REAL WELL FOR THE FIRST TIME IN A WHILE.
?
MAYBE YOU SHOULD GET A BODY PILLOW, SENPAI.
HUH? YOU SAY SOMETHING?
NOOO, NOTHING.

To be continued...

Thanks to all of you, we've made it to Volume 2.
Thank you for your constant support!

I'm asked to write comments so often at the end of the
year that I really can't think of anything else to say.

But oh yeah--I had a game commentary-style video made
for me, and Naomi Oozora-san (playing Uzaki) and Kenji
Akabane-san (playing Senpai) reprised their roles. It was
such an honor, I'm absolutely blown away. It was a lot of
fun to make the video, too--so please take a look at it!

Anyway, I'm going to continue to do my best as I continue
into Volume 3!

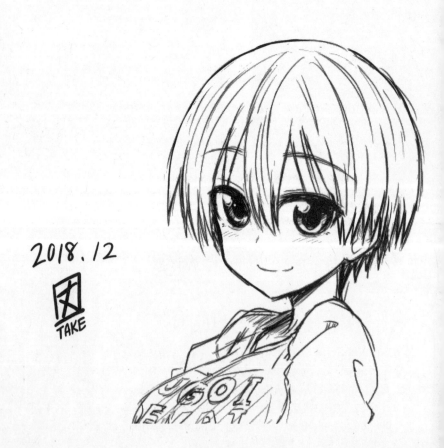

2018. 12

TAKE

# SEVEN SEAS ENTERTAINMENT PRESENTS

# Uzaki-chan Wants to Hang Out!

VOLUME 2

story and art by TAKE

TRANSLATION
**Jennifer Ward**

ADAPTATION
**T Campbell**

LETTERING
**Ludwig Sacramento**

COVER DESIGN
**KC Fabellon**

PROOFREADER
**Kurestin Armada**

EDITOR
**Jenn Grunigen**

PREPRESS TECHNICIAN
**Rhiannon Rasmussen-Silverstein**

PRODUCTION MANAGER
**Lissa Pattillo**

MANAGING EDITOR
**Julie Davis**

EDITOR-IN-CHIEF
**Adam Arnold**

PUBLISHER
**Jason DeAngelis**

Seven Seas press and purchase enquiries can be sent to Marketing Manager
Lianne Sentar at press@gomanga.com. Information regarding the distribution
and purchase of digital editions is available from Digital Manager CK Russell
at digital@gomanga.com.

Seven Seas and the Seven Seas logo are trademarks of
Seven Seas Entertainment. All rights reserved.

ISBN: 978-1-64505-193-0

Printed in Canada

First Printing: January 2020

10 9 8 7 6 5 4 3 2 1

FOLLOW US ONLINE: www.sevenseasentertainment.com

# READING DIRECTIONS

This book reads from *right to left*, Japanese style.
If this is your first time reading manga, you start
reading from the top right panel on each page and
take it from there. If you get lost, just follow the
numbered diagram here. It may seem backwards at
first, but you'll get the hang of it! Have fun!!

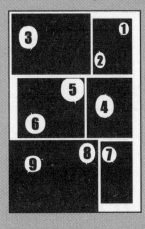